The story goes...

NICO TER LINDEN was born in 1936 and studied theology in the Netherlands and the United States. After working as a prison chaplain in Alkmaar and a hospital chaplain in Nijmegen, in 1977 he became minister of the Westerkerk in Amsterdam, where he remained until 1995. His biblical sermons brought him fame, and he became a newspaper columnist and a television broadcaster as well as writing many books. In 1995 he retired to devote himself to full-time writing and began on *The story goes...*, which became a bestseller on publication in the Netherlands in 1997. More than 150,000 copies of the first volume, on the stories of the Torah, have been sold, and 80,000 of the second volume, on the Gospels of Matthew and Mark, which appeared in 1998. Both are available in English.

Three more volumes are planned and will appear in English versions. Volume 3, on the 'Former and Latter Prophets', the historical and prophetic books of the Old Testament, is due in 1999; volumes on the 'Writings', including Job, Proverbs and the Psalms, and on the works attributed to Luke (the Gospels and Acts) and John (the Gospel and the Book of Revelation) will appear by 2002.

Nico ter Linden

The

story

goes...

2

MARK'S STORY

AND MATTHEW'S STORY

SCM PRESS

Translated by John Bowden from the Dutch *Het verhaal gaat... 2. Het verhaal van Marcus an het Verhaal van Mattheüs*, published 1998 by Uitgeverij Balans, Amsterdam, seventh impression 1999.

0 334 02765 9

This edition first published 1999 by
SCM Press
9–17 St Albans Place London N1 0NX

SCM Press is a division of SCM–Canterbury Press Ltd

Typeset by Regent Typesetting, London
Printed in Great Britain by
Biddles Ltd, Guildford and King's Lynn

CONTENTS

PREFACE

This book, the second part of *The story goes...*, differs in many respects from the first part. In the first part I told the great stories from the first five books of the Old Testament, about Israel's patriarchs and matriarchs and about Moses, figures of flesh and blood with whom you could gradually identify.

The stories from the New Testament in this book are very different: little anecdotes, fragments from Jesus' life and teaching, brief encounters with a colourful crowd of passers-by, most of whom remain nameless. And along with that there are sayings, parables, fragments of preaching, both from Jesus and from the early church. There is less to tell and more to explain.

First I shall tell you the stories from the earliest Gospel, that of Mark. I shall follow that up with the Gospel of Matthew, leaving out the passages which Matthew took from Mark.* Rather than simply bring out the well-known stories, I have tried to do justice to the whole work of both evangelists, also including the less accessible passages.

I do not in any way pretend that my interpretation of these Gospels is *the* interpretation; I have no monopoly of truth. Of course you are all free to interpret these stories for yourself. And that's what you have to do, if you want to make them your own.

The asterisks in the text refer to the sources of quotations at the end of the book.

MARK'S STORY

1

A BEGINNING THAT ISN'T
A BEGINNING

MARK 1.1-8

Beginning of the Gospel of Jesus Messiah, Son of God.

The story goes that Jesus is the Messiah – the Son of God. It's Mark's story – at least, that's what this evangelist is called in the tradition. It isn't certain that that was his name, nor do we have any idea where he lived. Probably this Gospel isn't even the work of one author, but rather a text produced by a community of believers who handed down its contents and worked on them over a number of generations. As a result the text bears the traces both of its Jewish background and of an alienation from it. However, although the work will thus have been written by several 'Mark's, for the sake of simplicity I shall continue to speak of one Mark in the singular.

Presumably the story was set down in writing in its present form shortly after AD 70, the year in which Jerusalem and the temple were destroyed. Who was Mark writing for? Obviously for those who want to know about the way that Jesus took and who want to follow him on that way, even when it becomes a way of suffering. In fact, Mark could well have told his story specifically for the persecuted Christian community in Rome.

It's a *story,* not a biography. We don't hear from Mark about the life of the historical Jesus. But he isn't inventing the story; he's drawing on Jesus' life. He shapes into a story the faith which the words and actions of Jesus aroused in him, playing with the words and images of the tradition of faith in which he stood. As a writer, he allows himself a great deal of freedom here. So as readers we never know whether any of Jesus' words really come from Jesus, or from Mark, or from both. We never know whether an action performed by Jesus is really something he did, a story which Mark is using to illustrate his faith, or both. But it's always preaching. Mark sees Jesus as the Messiah, as Son of God. Those who want to understand this secret language, who want to know how the evangelist arrived at that faith, must read his Gospel.

Mark called his story *good news*, and when he wrote it Jesus had already been dead and buried for some forty years. More precisely, by then Jesus had been dead for forty years. He was probably never buried; he was crucified, and those who were crucified weren't given a grave. Mark probably gave Jesus a grave in his story because he wanted to make him rise from it. That makes it possible for him to bear witness to his belief that the Father in heaven had pity on this royal child, even beyond death. In this way he can also bear witness to his belief that all those who follow Jesus on his way will follow him to the kingdom of heaven. Mark isn't telling the story of a dead person; he's telling the story of a living person. That's the principle behind his Gospel, the beginning of his story.

But it isn't the beginning of the whole story.

The whole story began with God, who created the heavens and the earth and called his people of Israel to life in order to bear witness to him on the earth. It began with Abraham, Isaac and Jacob, and with Jacob's twelve sons. It began with the prophet Moses, who led the Israelites out of Egyptian slavery and for forty years looked with them for a way through the wilderness to the promised land. It began with Isaiah, who centuries later reported a second exodus: again a journey through the wilderness, but now from exile in Babylon to the promised land. It began with Elijah with his camel-hair coat, with a leather girdle around his waist, the man of God who ate locusts and wild honey, and who wandered through the wilderness for forty days and forty nights to meet God on his holy mountain. It began with the prophet Malachi, who dreamed in pious fantasy that one day Elijah would return to herald the dawn of the kingdom of God, the coming of the anointed, the Messiah, the Christ.*

Mark believes that Jesus is this anointed one, but before he can begin to tell that good news Elijah must return to appear on stage: the messenger, the one who prepares the way, the prophet of the end time. And who can this be but John the Baptist, the servant of God with whom Jesus felt such a strong bond, the prophet of repentance who went before him in life and also in death? Mark picks up his pen and writes about John, who, like Elijah, wears a camel-hair coat and eats locusts and wild honey. Then his readers will know right from the beginning of the story how things stand: the kingdom of God has come near.

So that kingdom doesn't just come out of the blue: for centuries, the

Torah and the Prophets have already been full of it. That's why the Torah and the Prophets are echoed three times in the one short sentence that Mark uses to characterize John the Baptist: *'Behold, I send my messenger before you, who shall prepare your way. The voice of one crying in the wilderness: Prepare a way for the Lord, make his paths straight.'** In other words, if you want to know where the Messiah comes from, turn to the Old Testament. That's where it all began.

John the Baptist baptized in the wilderness, preaching a baptism of repentance for the forgiveness of sins.

The wilderness is the place where an angel once went before the people, first out of Egypt, then out of exile, on the way to the promised land. In the wilderness you can reflect and repent, give up your old life and opt for a new way. In the river that separates the wilderness from the promised land you can be cleansed from your sins, and arise reborn. It's a place where you can encounter God.

That baptism probably wasn't John's own invention. Israel already had proselyte baptism, a ritual in which believers from the peoples, the Gentiles, were accepted into the people of God. Israel too was already familiar with the ritual bath of purification after a period of uncleanness. You could say that John extends the uncleanness that needs to be washed away. He sees his baptism as a ritual for all children of God, both Gentiles and Jews, so that they can confess that from now on they want to begin to think and live in a different way.

And all Judaea and all the inhabitants of Jerusalem came out to confess their sins and to be baptized by John in the Jordan.

All Judaea, *all* the inhabitants of Jerusalem, Mark? Do the temple authorities also long for a new beginning? Do they, too, see John as a man of God? If so, how will they see Jesus?

'The one who comes after me is stronger than I am,' John exclaimed. *'I am not worthy to stoop down and untie his sandals. I baptize you with water. He will immerse you in the Holy Spirit, the Spirit of God.'*

For that is the faith in which Mark writes: the one to whom John the Baptist bears witness was brim full of God. *Son of God,* you might say. The very image of his Father.

2

THE HEAVENS OPEN

MARK 1.9-13

A wicked and ruthless person can be called the son of a devil, while a good and holy person can be seen as a son of God.

In Israel the king was called Son of God, for he was the one who above all was called to represent the Eternal One on earth and to be a model for his people in his kingly life. Moreover when he was anointed king, the words of an old royal psalm always rang out:* '*You are my son, today I have begotten you.*' He's an ordinary mortal, a man of flesh and blood, yet he's been called to be God's Son on earth.

In Jesus, Mark saw a figure who was more royal than any king before him. To illustrate that, he makes John the Baptist, the herald who prepares the way for Jesus, proclaim: 'Someone is coming who is mightier than I.'

In those days Jesus came from Nazareth in Galilee and was baptized by John in the Jordan.

What John is doing is new, and Jesus goes along with it. He leaves his familiar Nazareth and goes to the Jordan. Like the men and women of Judaea and Jerusalem, he too is in search of a new beginning. John's right: what you were must be done away with; only total repentance and dedication to God can bring salvation. Jesus goes down into the water, sheds what he was, receives baptism and rises again from the water reborn, a new person.

Later, tradition was now and then to distort Jesus, so that he became a sinless and therefore bloodless creature. For Mark, the earliest evangelist, he is still a man of flesh and blood.

And when he came up out of the water, immediately he saw the heavens torn open and the Spirit descending upon him like a dove. And a voice rang out from heaven, 'You are my Son, my beloved; in you I am well pleased.'

This was an experience of God, a voice, a vision. Just like Israel's prophets before him, Jesus sees something, hears something, and so it begins. Words from an old royal psalm and words of the great Isaiah* descend on him from on high and, just as in the beginning, a bird hovers over the water, a dove, a sign of new life, of peace and reconciliation. Filled with the scriptures, filled with God, Jesus hears the call of the Eternal One. From now on he will be one who has been called, a child in whom God is well pleased. He has found God, found himself and his work, and he has experienced it all as a gift.

'O God, tear open the heavens; let us get a glimpse of you.' This old prayer from Isaiah*, repeated century by century after him, seems to be heard here. The heavens are torn open, a voice rings out, the Spirit descends like a dove.

This is how Mark makes Jesus' inspiration visible and audible. It's an experience of unspeakable joy, a vision that will accompany him all his life, his short life: nothing and no one will be able to separate him from God's love.

And the Spirit immediately drove him into the wilderness, and he was in the wilderness forty days, constantly tempted by the devil.

What now, Mark? We've just heard heaven singing psalms, and now all hell breaks loose. Jesus is suddenly alone. John has gone, the people have gone, the voice is silent, the bird has flown, the devil and his minions loom, wild animals creep closer. What is this?

And why is it the Spirit that drives Jesus into the wilderness? Is it because a calling always has to be put through the mill?

Jesus is alone in the wilderness for forty days, just as Moses was alone for forty days on God's holy mountain, and Elijah spent forty days and forty nights searching for the Eternal One. Is Jesus following in their footsteps, going through what they went through? And how does he make out? Having just seen the heavens open, will he be able to withstand the gates of hell, now that the devil has raised his voice and in a flash wants to rob him of God's will?

Mark senses that Jesus would never have been able to heal people's torn spirits and anxieties had he not first tamed these evil spirits in his own soul.

And he was with the wild beasts; and the angels ministered to him.

The storm has subsided again. There he stands, like Adam in the garden of Eden, with the lion at his feet like a lamb. It's a scene out of paradise.

This royal son has clearly defeated the powers of evil in the wilderness. And the ministering angels – one of the rabbis' old fantasies of paradise – fly back and forth with heavenly dishes and chilled wine. He's a man after God's own heart. Son of God.

Incidentally, that's what the ancient Egyptians called their kings: son of God. And they added: 'The one who unites both lands'. By that they meant that the true man, the royal man, has united in himself both 'above' and 'below'. He has given a place to both the realm of the spirit and the realm of the desires. In this harmony with himself he sits on the throne of his life, sovereign and free as the wind.

We also hear something like this in Mark's story. Jesus has curbed his wild beasts. Aggression, assertiveness, sexual drive, possessiveness are all gifts from God and therefore aren't intrinsically evil. They simply have to be reined in. *And he was with the wild beasts.*

Greek mythology has a similar image: a young hero riding on the back of a dolphin like a prince, crossing the unfathomable depths of the sea and the whirlpools of death.

3

FISHERS OF MEN

MARK 1.14-20

After John had been arrested, Jesus went to Galilee.

Wait a minute, Mark, you're going too fast. Has John been arrested? When? By whom? And why? It sounds ominous. Are you preparing us for the fact that soon Jesus, too, will be arrested? Did Jesus already have an anxious feeling that a similar fate awaited him? Is that why he went off to Galilee?

After John had been arrested, Jesus went to Galilee to preach the gospel of God. 'The time is fulfilled, the kingdom of God is at hand. Repent and believe in the gospel of God.'

So the gospel of Jesus is the gospel of God. Jesus doesn't want us to 'give our hearts' to him in a sentimental piety; he wants us to entrust ourselves to God. We mustn't confuse the two. God is the king, and Jesus, like the prophets before him, proclaims God's kingdom. It will happen soon; the time is fulfilled; it's almost here. Jesus believed that, and Mark believed it along with him. High time to give your heart to God. *'Repent and believe in the gospel of God.'*

John the Baptist had already proclaimed that people had to repent. Jesus adds that they have to entrust themselves to God. He clearly has a different image of God. John insists on repentance; otherwise the flood waters will rise, as they did in the days of Noah. Jesus seems more moved by the story of what happened *after* the flood: the story of the dove that returned to the ark in the evening with an olive branch in its beak, a symbol of peace and reconciliation.

'The kingdom of God is at hand.'

But Mark, what does 'kingdom of God' mean? Could you explain it so that ordinary people can understand? After all, Jesus explained it to ordinary people too, didn't he?

And passing along the Sea of Galilee, he saw Simon and Andrew, his brother, casting a net in the sea; for they were fishermen. And Jesus said to them, 'Follow me and I will make you fishers of men.' And immediately they left their nets and followed him.

That's fast! Discipleship at first sight! Doesn't this kind of thing take time?

Of course it does. But once again: Mark isn't a reporter, he's a story-teller, and he puts together his account of Jesus in compact form. His stories are like Oxo cubes. We know nothing about the historical meeting between Jesus, Simon and Andrew, but that's not Mark's concern. Rather, the evangelist wants to summon his readers to discipleship, over the heads of Simon and Andrew, and he does so by telling a story about the calling of the two of them with a hidden meaning.

The action takes place on the shores of the sea: that's already the first double meaning. This isn't only a place on the map, but also a place deep within us. That's exactly where we are, on the frontier between life and death. In the Bible, water stands for both life and death. We live on the seashore, on the frontier between time and eternity, where the everyday and the mysterious touch each other. It's there that Jesus calls Simon and Andrew. They're to be his first disciples.

What in God's name could have prompted those two immediately to leave their nets and follow Jesus?

Probably they did so precisely because of that 'in God's name'. These men must have felt that Jesus really did appear in their lives in God's name. It was evident to them that this man had come 'from the other side'. This carpenter from Nazareth had something of God about him, as if he came from 'across the water'. Should they go with him? The time is fulfilled, the kingdom of God is at hand.

And going on a little farther, Jesus saw James the son of Zebedee and John his brother, who were in their boat mending their nets. And immediately he called them; and they left their father Zebedee in the boat with the hired labourers, and followed him.

Simon and Andrew are called and they leave their nets behind. James and John are called and they leave their father behind. That's almost the way it has to go in a story like this, for the days of the prophet Elijah have returned. Mark wants his story to match the story of Elijah, who calls his disciple Elisha: Elisha is out ploughing the fields when Elijah comes past and puts his prophet's mantle on Elisha's shoulders. Elisha immediately slaughters his cattle, roasts them on a fire made from the wood of his plough, kisses his father and mother goodbye and follows his master.

So too here: Jesus saw Andrew and Simon, he saw James and John, and they followed him. What magnetism he must have radiated! Those fishermen didn't know what had come over them, there on the seashore, but they felt it: this man has something of the Eternal One in him. When you're close to him, you're close to God. Never before in their lives had they felt so strong and so free, and that's why – just like Elisha in days long past – they were able to leave their work and the comfort of their homes.

Work and family are two dynamic fields with which every fibre of our being is connected and from which we derive our sense of security. The first pair of brothers demonstrate that following Jesus, serving God, may mean giving up earning one's daily bread. The second pair of brothers indicate that it may mean leaving the safety of the family. Isn't life more than worrying about food and clothing? Isn't an individual more than his or her parents' child? Son of God, daughter of God, that's what we are.

'I will make you fishers of men.'

They aren't to go out and win souls, catch people in their nets. But safe in time and eternity they're to stretch out a saving hand to those who are in up to their necks, to those in peril on the sea.

Elisha, the countryman, was called to be a prophet cultivating the fields of Israel. Moses, the shepherd, was called at the burning bush to lead his people out of Egypt, so that he too could continue what he was doing: being a shepherd. The four men on the shore are also to remain what they are: fishermen. Their job simply takes on another dimension, becomes humanized. They still need the qualities so indispensable to the ordinary fisherman: patience, perseverance, courage, vigilance and a knowledge of the fishing grounds.

'And a little bit of luck,' exclaimed one of my congregation when I read out that list.

4

A DAY IN CAPERNAUM (1)

MARK 1.21-28

What did Jesus say, and what did he do, that these men on the shore gave up all that they had simply to be near to him? Could Mark tell us that?

Yes he can, in a rapid sketch. He compresses Jesus' preaching in word and action into a period of twenty-four hours, a sabbath in Capernaum.

In the synagogue of the fishing village the people of God gathers round the scriptures, and the service goes as the service always goes: it's all very familiar. So the only difference makes a difference: someone has come with Simon and Andrew, a man from Nazareth. Not a well-known place in those days. But when after the reading from the Torah and the Prophets, according to ancient custom they ask whether anyone wants to say anything, this stranger, of all people, stands up to expound the scriptures. The people who hear him will never forget it all their lives. Silence falls on the house of God. *They were astonished at his teaching, for he taught them as one who had authority, and not as the scribes.*

The man from Nazareth talks about Moses and Elijah, so impressively and compellingly that it's just as if Moses and Elijah were there in person. Sabbath by sabbath the people sit here, in their synagogue. That's their custom: it's tradition, and it's a good tradition. Always the same group: the rabbi, the cantor, the caretaker and the schoolmaster, the fishermen, the craftsmen and the tradespeople, the women, the children – and of course there's also the village fool, who now and then shouts out something but then is quiet again. Everyone knows everyone else, and they all know the Torah and the Prophets. Here words from the old days are spoken; it's good to hear them again, and people comfort themselves with the old promise: one day the Messiah will come; one day the messianic kingdom will dawn. And of course they believe that, firmly and truly. Or has some of the passion gone? Is this still news?

But now! It seems as if this stranger has seen heaven open. What a fabulous child of God he is! They've never heard anyone speak with such warmth about the Eternal One and about human beings; they drink in the words of the man from Nazareth. Everyone feels, 'This is about me, this is about us.' Who is this man? His voice, his words, his eyes are all so different. The scribes talk about God. This man has a touch of God himself! *They were dumbfounded and said, 'What is this? A new teaching!'*

A shock went through Capernaum; their teaching had suddenly grown old, because a new teaching had come. Or is it still the old teaching, but experienced and told afresh, so that a healing power goes out from it?

Teaching always has an element of danger, whether it's Jewish teaching, Christian teaching or any other kind. Faith never begins with teaching. Teaching sometimes puts an end to it. Faith begins, as with Moses, when life becomes a burning bush, or when, like Elijah, we hear God in the rustling of a gentle breeze. Faith begins with people on our way who give us eyes to see with and ears to hear with. We always get faith from someone; it comes over us, just like love, and it sparkles, it lives. Later it's codified and congeals into doctrine. Perhaps that has to happen, but it's dangerous, and before we know it, the life seeps out of it, and it only speaks to our heads and no longer to our hearts. Then we get scribes who know nothing about burning bushes and have never sensed the rustling of a gentle breeze, but who set themselves up as defenders of the faith. They can't conceive of God being different from what they think. They build walls round their faith: originality is their enemy and dogmatism their weapon.

Ask Copernicus and Galileo, who with their new teaching tampered with the bastion of faith. They were apostates, possessed by the devil. Even more dangerous is someone like Jesus, who strikes at the heart of doctrine from within, by disregarding the rules of life hallowed by tradition. He talks about God with the same fervour and reverence as a son talking about his unforgettable father. He goes new ways. He too is a 'scribe', but for him life is more than teaching.

Mark will mostly be using the world 'scribes' in his Gospel in a negative sense. Of course that's a generalization; it suggests that all the scribes in Capernaum and in Jerusalem were exclusively legalistic. The picture that Mark paints of them is clearly coloured by the tragic conflict which brought Jesus to the cross and by the bad relationships which in Mark's days were making a rift between synagogue and church inevitable. It's good to keep this in mind whenever we hear mention of 'the scribes' in the stories which follow.

A dead silence has fallen in the synagogue of Capernaum. The scribes never talk like this! *They were dumbfounded and said, 'What is this? A new teaching?'*

Hardly has Jesus begun his preaching than the difference between him and the scribes comes to light, and it's never made good again. Jesus was able to heal many sick people, but he had no medicine for hardened scribes.

What was it that made everyone so excited in this somewhat humdrum synagogue in Capernaum? It was as if this stranger had spoken with God himself, just as Moses had spoken with God. It was as if he'd been touched by God himself, just like Elijah. This Jesus didn't just speak about the kingdom of God; he also had it in him: he embodied what he preached. It was as if the people in Capernaum also saw the heavens open, as if a dove also descended on them and they heard a voice from on high: 'You are my child, my beloved, I love you.'

And who was the first person in the synagogue to hear that?

The village fool! It was the idiot of Capernaum who was the first to feel that something was afoot here. Or rather, the evil spirit which had him in its grip was the first to feel the power radiated by this man of God. He smelt trouble and immediately raised the alarm: *'What are you doing here, Jesus of Nazareth, have you come to destroy us?'*

Acute perception. Jesus has indeed come to destroy him and his minions. He will break the powers which enslave people.

A man with an unclean spirit. What it actually says is a man *in* an unclean spirit. This man doesn't have a demon, the demon has him; he's encapsulated him, taken him prisoner. The man's possessed. And we can hear it: one moment he says 'I' and the next moment he speaks in the plural: 'What have you to do with *us*, will you destroy *us*? *I* know who you are, a holy one of God!'

A man torn apart inside. How will such a man be made whole again?'

5

A DAY IN CAPERNAUM (2)

MARK 1.29-39

'Have you come to destroy us?'

The evil spirits have a sharp nose for the kingdom of God. They infallibly grasp that if *this* goes through, *our* kingdom will come to an end. 'You're a precious child of God,' says Jesus to the possessed man of Capernaum. If this tormented man can really believe that, he will no longer be a child of the demon. '*Have you come to destroy us? I know who you are, a holy one of God!*'

The coming of Jesus has unleashed a holy war on the shores of the Sea of Galilee. To whom will the man belong, by whom will he be possessed? By an unclean spirit or by the Holy Spirit? Will this man, sick with fear and self-hatred, be in the demon or in Christ? Battle commences, and Mark is our war correspondent.

'What are you doing here, holy one of God?'

Holy ones of God are mortals who have clearly seen God. Moses was a holy one of God, and so was Elijah. And now Jesus has entered the world of Capernaum. It is in a world possessed that his word of freedom rings out. On a sabbath, *the* day on which to celebrate freedom.

And Jesus rebuked the unclean spirit: 'Be silent and go out of him!' And the unclean spirit convulsed him and went out of him with much shouting.

The story gives the impression of some hocus pocus, and the question is whether such a healing could take place as quickly as that. Mark's brief report must be the account of a long process of healing; a victory over demons doesn't usually take place 'with much shouting'. Only after the necessary struggle can people free themselves from their evil spirits. It took 'forty years', almost a human lifetime, for Moses and his followers to rid themselves of the tyranny of Egypt, and now and then they still wanted to go back. One can be tossed endlessly to and fro between hope and fear, between fear and longing. Sometimes one manages to reclaim a new piece of land, but later on everything gets flooded again and hard pumping is needed in order not to drown.

In the end, the mentally ill man of Capernaum is healed. A miracle! That doesn't mean that the man from Nazareth did miracles. When soon afterwards he commands his disciples to drive out demons, heal the sick and raise the dead to life, he isn't asking them to practise magic. If they live trusting in God, as he does, and are equally infectious in bearing witness to that trust, people in a world possessed will be freed from their anxiety. They will be rescued from the sicknesses from which they suffer, the thousand deaths which they die. New trust in God – *a new teaching with authority* – and regained self-confidence will bring a person healing. 'Your faith has saved you,' Jesus then says. In this way the possessed man of Capernaum found healing, drawing strength from the very source from which Jesus lived.

And his fame spread like wildfire throughout the region of Galilee.

That same sabbath a woman also found healing. *Now Simon's mother-in-law lay in bed with a fever, and they told Jesus of her. He came closer and took her by the hand and raised her up. The fever left her, and she served them.*

Another story quickly told. What kind of an attack of fever was it which began with Jesus' arrival in Capernaum and disappeared like snow in summer when Jesus came into her house? Could it be that Simon's mother-in-law was sick of her son-in-law? On the spur of the moment he sells his ship to follow this strange miracle worker from Nazareth!

She was sick of that, sick to death. And he had promised so solemnly in the synagogue that he would take good care of her daughter. Not like this.

'Perhaps she'll understand when she's met you,' said Simon to Jesus. He can imagine his mother-in-law's reaction. Of course she's right. But with Jesus he's more right than he's ever been in his life. He just doesn't have the words to explain it to her.

And Jesus approached. Until he had got so close to the woman that there was no longer any room for the fever. *He took her by the hand and raised her up.* As if she was dead. And she stood up. This is a rebirth. She could say good-bye to all the fever, the pains and the anger. And she was deeply grateful to Simon for introducing her to this holy man of God. *And she served them.*

If we're to believe the evangelist, standing up and serving is what followers of Jesus, both men and women, are called to do. And if Mark told before this how the heavenly angels served Jesus, now he sees the task on earth transferred to Simon's mother-in-law. She too is an angel.

That evening, when the sun had gone down, people streamed to him, with all who were sick or possessed.

The sabbath is over, everyone may move around again freely. The people that walk in darkness, all those who are weary and heavy laden, throng before the house. The whole town is standing on the doorstep. Have mercy!

And he healed many of their sicknesses, and he drove out many demons. But he forbade the demons to speak of him. They knew him. They knew who he was.

Why weren't the demons allowed to speak about him? Surely it's a good thing that they already know who he is? They've found to their cost that the fever and the madness that they sow must yield wherever the holy one of God sets his feet. They're the first to get the message, while the scribes and the disciples still have no eyes to see, no ears to hear. Why does Jesus impose silence on them? Doesn't Mark want us yet to know who Jesus really is? Aren't we yet allowed to think that we know?

Jesus gets up in the middle of the night. He leaves the city and goes to a solitary place. Alone with himself and with his God he wants to gather new strength. He prays.

Thus Mark portrays Jesus to us as one who teaches, as one who heals and as one who prays. He's a man who loves God and his neighbour with all his being.

Then the disciples appear on the scene. *They followed him.* This is rather different from the following to which they've been called. Why don't they leave Jesus in peace? Jesus is going on a way which takes him through solitary places; how long will it be before the disciples begin to understand that mystery?

'Everyone's looking for you!'

Simon is speaking. In the Gospel stories he represents the disciples. In him they all speak. 'Everyone's looking for you!'

Yes, but who are they looking for, Simon? Are they looking for the servant of the Eternal One or are they looking for the miracle man? Do they have ears to hear what this holy man of God is teaching? Do they have eyes to see that his signs can't be given to order?

'Everyone's looking for you. We must go back to Capernaum.'

'No, Simon, we mustn't go back to Capernaum. We must go on.'

Strengthened by his prayer, Jesus wants to go his way. The gospel of God which has resounded so clearly in Capernaum, first in the synagogue and then throughout the town, now must go into Galilee. And as far as Mark is concerned, still further.

6

THE HEALING OF A LEPER

MARK 1.40-45

And a leper came to Jesus.

The story takes place outside Capernaum. People in the inhabited world prefer to keep lepers at a safe distance, and you can't blame them. Any lepers who want to approach must rattle their rattles and cry 'Unclean, unclean.' The village fool of Capernaum may sit among the people in the synagogue, and the sick lie at home in their beds, surrounded by family and friends. But those who are afflicted with leprosy are driven out of the land of the living and have to camp outside society, on the edge of civilization. People avoid them. They're already declared dead during their lifetime.

And a leper came to Jesus.

He will find healing with Jesus, otherwise Mark needn't tell this story. But what does he mean by it?

It was said that Miriam was healed of her leprosy after the intercession of Moses. Thanks to Elisha, Naaman was healed of the same complaint. Is that why such a healing has to be included in the story of Jesus, the second Elisha, the second Moses?

The leprosy can also be understood symbolically. In that case this man stands for all the outcasts who find their friend and healer in Jesus.

Perhaps here Mark is thinking of a skin disease which has its origin in a sick soul. In that case the skin becomes whole and sound again when 'the sores on the soul' are healed.

Or is this man suffering from leprosy and is the healing power of Jesus greater than we think possible?

And a leper came to Jesus and, beseeching him earnestly, fell on his knees before him: 'If you will, you can make me clean.'

There's always something enigmatic about sickness. One moment you're healthy and the next you're sick. Is that chance? Do you bring it upon yourself? Is it God's will, a punishment for sin?

We rebel against this last thought, but there's also something in it. There can be a connection between our health and the way in which we live, between our affliction and what we inflict on ourselves. 'You must change your lifestyle,' a wise doctor may say. 'What you're doing now is bad for your stomach or your liver or your heart – be glad that your body is telling you that you can't go on like this.'

However, the idea that sickness is a punishment for sin is just as cruel a notion, which is suggested by fear. Surely a person can't just be smitten with leprosy! Can such an abominable disease strike arbitrarily? It's an intolerable thought, which suggests another thought to people: better God than fate. Please let sickness be a punishment for sin! Then we understand God just a bit and we're in control. So let's agree that leprosy strikes only those who've sinned grievously. This thought reassures us: the sickness will pass us by, since after all we're well-behaved people. If the sickness attacks our good neighbour, then we justify the system by showing that our neighbour has apparently sinned secretly. It's no good his denying it. 'Just look, it's all lies!'

But if *you're* the neighbour and the sickness strikes *you*, with what answer can you live and with what answer can you die? Those smitten by the sickness talk differently. So does the leper. *'Lord, if you will, you can make me clean.'*

This man clings to Jesus. He doesn't yield to his sickness. He refuses to believe that it's God's will that this leprosy struck him, and he trusts that the holy God is on his side. *'If you will...'*

Moved with pity, Jesus stretched out his hand, touched him and said, 'I will, become clean!'

Jesus wants to rid him of all the uncleanness in his skin and under his skin, of his sores and his wounds. 'Let it go. That's what God wants and that's what I want, and you want it too. Otherwise you wouldn't have come. Your will be done! Know that you're a good child of God. Be such a child. Become clean.'

Immediately the leprosy left him and he became clean. Jesus said: 'Go, show yourself to the priests and offer for your healing the sacrifices which Moses prescribed. Let that be a witness to the priests.'

The man must show himself in the house of God as God has created him, and it is for the priests to declare him healed and to lift the curse.

After the man has reported his healing to the priests, he must continue to keep silent. *'See that you say nothing of this to anyone,'* Jesus tells him. Strange, the evil spirits in Capernaum were also sworn to secrecy.

'Jesus doesn't want it to leak out prematurely that he's the Messiah,' is the traditional explanation. But it's very questionable whether Jesus saw himself as the Messiah. He felt called by the Eternal One to say what he had to say and to do what his hand found to do. That he is the Messiah, the Christ, the Anointed One, is a confession by his followers made after his death.

So we must say that it's the evangelist who wants to keep up the tension in the story and puts the request for secrecy on the lips of Jesus. For the Messiah to whom he bears witness is such a different Messiah from the one that people expect. They envisage a triumphant Messiah, not a suffering Messiah. Granted, in the first sentence of his Gospel Mark has already confessed Jesus as the Messiah, but he wants to keep open the definitive answer to the question who Jesus is until he has also told of his suffering. He wants his readers is to prick up their ears. They mustn't be too sure that they know who Jesus is. Nor must they be too sure that they know what it is to be his disciple. The answer to the question who Jesus was will become clear in his Gospel bit by bit.

But hardly had the man left than he trumpeted it all around, so that it was no longer possible for him to enter the town openly and he had to stay outside in solitary places. But they came to him from all sides.

Mark, who is who? Are you deliberately writing in such an ambiguous way? Who could no longer enter the town openly and had to stay in solitary places? Do you mean Jesus? It looks as if *he* is a leper, banished to the periphery of society, while the former exile can dwell in human company again. Are the roles sometimes reversed?

7

THROUGH A HOLE IN THE ROOF

MARK 2.1-12

Jesus has returned to his house in Capernaum. The news quickly spreads through the town and the people stream in from all sides. The house is bulging and they're even standing in the doorway.

Jesus teaches. With a warmth and a simplicity which are new to people. That's how he speaks about heaven and earth, and about God! He gives God an intimate name, *Abba,* Father. Suddenly he has to stop speaking: people are busy breaking open the roof above his head.

Four men. They've put their paralysed friend on a stretcher and come with him to the man of God. But they couldn't get into the house; people were blocking the way to Jesus. They often do that. The friends then climbed up the outside staircase to the flat roof, broke it open and let down their paralysed friend from on high.

And Jesus saw their faith.

. They believe that the love of God has descended in this Jesus and they make their sick friend descend to Jesus' feet. He's already lying on his death bed unless the holy one of God raises up his paralysed body. Faith is faith that things can be different. Faith isn't held up by the barriers that people erect.

'Child, your sins are forgiven you.'

What's Jesus saying now? After all, this man isn't a child. And he didn't come to have his sins forgiven. He wanted Jesus to get him back on his feet again.

Yes, but Jesus clearly knows that the source of this man's trouble is inside him, and that therefore the healing must come from within. What is it that keeps him confined to his bed? Is this man paralysed with fear?

If we may believe Jesus, he's paralysed by sin. Which doesn't mean that he's a villain; he's only lost his way.

'Child,' Jesus says to him. How healing it would be if he rediscovered the

childlike trust that God is a Father with whom he can feel secure. *'Child, son of Abba, your sins are forgiven you.'* You're more than the mistakes in your life and God is great.

Jesus unconditionally loves this paralysed man, and for him that becomes a sign of the unconditional love of God. And the forgiveness of sins which has been announced to the paralysed man becomes a power which sets him on his feet again. The psalmist already knows about this miraculous connection when he celebrates the Eternal One as the God *who forgives all your iniquity, who heals all your diseases.** The paralysed man of Capernaum is a child of this God. Again he has a whole life in front of him.

However, the faith of the scribes sees it differently. *'How can this Jesus say such a thing? He blasphemes God. Who can forgive sins but God alone?'*

But Jesus isn't God. He isn't even his agent. Where does he get the right to play God like this from? Can he give any proof that he's authorized to do so?

No, Jesus can't. And of course the scribes are right: anyone can claim that someone's sins are forgiven. But Jesus can do something else, something which moreover can be verified. He can make a paralysed man walk again. *'What is easier, to say to the paralysed man, 'Your sins are forgiven you', or to say 'Arise, take up your bed and walk!' To show them that the Son of Man has power on earth to forgive sins, he said to the paralysed man: 'Arise, take up your bed and walk.' And he arose, took up his bed and went outside in the sight of them all.*

He had come through the roof; he went out through the door. He could walk again. The Son of man had announced forgiveness to him, the Son of man had healed him.

The Son of man?

That was an old dream in Israel, that one day a Son of man would descend to earth with the clouds of heaven,* as it were through a hole in the roof, so that heaven and earth would no longer be at odds. Mark believed that this Son of man had become flesh and blood in Jesus. Where this man came, the possessed regained their freedom, the lepers were cleansed, the lame walked. Wasn't all that to happen with the breakthrough of the messianic kingdom?

8

THE CALL OF LEVI

MARK 2.13-17

Jesus walked by the sea and all the people came to him and he taught them.

Mark once again says that he went by the sea. For that's where the man of God has his sphere of work; that's where he goes, along the dividing line between life and death, salvation and doom.

And all the people go out. Except Levi. Levi sits in his custom house, like a spider in its web. He's a minion of the Roman forces of occupation. He gets rich at the expense of travellers who have to clear their goods at his office. Levi sits behind his cash books and his money chest.

How can a man opt for such a job? What led up to it? Had he nothing to lose when he applied for the vacancy of a toll collector? Had he become alienated from people, and at that time was he thinking of the need to make a virtue of necessity by profiting from his isolation?

And Jesus saw him sitting there and said, 'Follow me.' Levi arose and followed him.

Mark gives the impression that it all took place in a flash. In reality there must have been a longer process. Something must have led up to it. It didn't just happen because a prophet happened to be walking along the sea when Levi happened to have no client in his office. A conversion is like a dam bursting – discontent has to pile up, and there needs to be a longing for change. However, there is also fear of change, and this holds everything back. Until Jesus sees Levi and his voice breaks through the dam of fear. 'Levi, follow me!'

What had led up to this? Who had led up to this? Had Levi heard John the Baptist's preaching of repentance? Did the prophet in his camel-hair coat make him think, while outwardly unmoved he collected his tolls and endured people's contempt? Did the voices of the prophets from a long-distant past also sow unrest in his soul? Did his mother appear to him in his dreams? 'My son...' Perhaps he'd already picked up fragments of Jesus' teaching from passers-by along the seashore, for example that you can't serve God and mammon, the god of money.

Jesus saw him sitting there. He saw through him. With a loving gaze, for otherwise Levi would never of course have opened up. You'll never get anywhere with those you despise.* Jesus saw not so much Levi's actions as his suffering. He saw his unease, the void behind all those riches and the fear of giving them up. As Levi sat there, he was really as much a leper as the pariah we've just met, and as paralysed as the man in Capernaum. *'Follow me.'*

And Levi arose.

So this is another resurrection story. Levi arose from the dead. The Lord has seen him and unexpectedly he's reborn.* It's a rebirth, and of course that has to be celebrated. A feast is arranged in Levi's house. He invites his friends, toll collectors like himself, and other people with little concern for the Torah. Jesus would also come; he'd promised. For Jesus didn't just tell parables; he also acted them out. He entered the great house that Levi had acquired with his ill-gotten gains and sat at table with Levi's dubious friends, men and women. He ate with them as if they made up a family, children of one Father.

When the Pharisees saw that he sat at table with sinners and toll collectors, they said to his disciples: 'He eats with toll collectors and sinners!'

'Does just anything go with that teacher of yours? There are limits. What's right and what's wrong? Are the unclean now clean? He talks of God all the time, but scorns God's holy Torah!'

Mark constructs his story carefully. First he tells us that the scribes pondered this in their heart; now we hear them asking the disciples for an answer; in a little while they will go on to debate with Jesus himself.

Jesus heard it and said to them: 'Those who are well have no need of a physician, but those who are sick.'

Not without irony, Jesus says that he hasn't come for healthy people, scribes for example: *'I am here for people for whom things have gone wrong.'*

The world would prefer to abandon people for whom things have gone wrong, but Jesus takes up their cause.

The invitation is unconditional; grace is freely given. That's too much for many people. It's even going too far for Luke the evangelist, the man who put his story of Jesus in writing years after Mark. This unconditional open-handedness of Jesus which Mark relates so innocently puts Luke in a quandary. Is that on? Luke wants to take over Mark's story, but in order to be quite safe he adds three words to it: 'I am here for people with whom things have gone wrong – *to convert them!*'

If Luke had so much difficulty with this open-handedness, how much opposition did Jesus provoke from the scribes? The end of the story was that Jesus was crucified between two men for whom things had gone wrong.

The story goes that God took up his cause. And that his voice from above continues undiminished to keep on calling 'follow me'. The story goes that the Eternal One is arranging a feast there.

9

FASTING

MARK 2.18-22

The disciples of John the Baptist and the Pharisees were fasting.

Fasting, praying and almsgiving are the three classic actions by which believers can show their love to the Eternal One. Love takes shape in their prayer to God, in acts of compassion towards their neighbours, and by fasting for their own bodies and souls.

To fast is partially or wholly to abstain from eating and drinking for a period. In many places and in all centuries fasting has been, and is, seen as a powerful means of finding a way to the Invisible One. 'Let us give the wings of piety to our prayers through almsgiving and fasting.'* By detaching themselves from bodily desires, people make room for the desire for God. Those who are full are full, and can't receive.

That's why we see all the great religious figures on earth practising the art of fasting. Whenever there is tension in their lives, by fasting they find the spiritual strength they need to hear their calling again and to remain faithful to it.

No wonder that the Pharisees and John the Baptist and his disciples respected the ritual of fasting. And it's difficult to understand why Jesus, who himself fasted, didn't teach his disciples to fast. *'Why don't your disciples fast?'*, the Pharisees came to ask.

We're accustomed to using the word Pharisee to describe a hypocrite, someone who pretends to be pious but isn't. This negative picture arises from some of the Gospel stories. However, their account is tendentious, coloured by the bitter struggle which raged between Jews and Christians at the time when the Gospels were written.

The name Pharisees means 'those set apart' and is rarely used to denote a fixed group. The Pharisees belonged to a spiritual current which from the second century before Christ strove for a strict observance of the Law.

They were often wise and courageous men, who had to fight to preserve their tradition at the risk of their lives. They cherished and preserved what was distinctively Jewish, and it is above all because of their dedication and perseverance that this precious heritage didn't disappear into the powerful Graeco-Roman culture of those days like a drop in the ocean.

So there is no such thing as 'the Pharisee'. But in the conflict with Jesus, and later with his followers, he was above all the model of the type of believer who seeks his salvation rigidly and anxiously in ritualism and who, if necessary, sacrifices humanity to the system of faith. This Pharisaism poses a danger to any religion anywhere and at any time. It's good to keep this constantly in mind, when the evangelist mentions 'the Pharisees' in the stories which follow, like what was said earlier about 'the scribes'.

'Why do your disciples not fast?'

The Pharisees who are speaking here are horrified at such negligence. They themselves even add a couple of fast days, just as they always begin the sabbath an hour early, so as not to be late. They're afraid of change, afraid of losing God's favour, or the favour of the group from which they derive their security.

Jesus was convinced that this takes people further and further away from the Torah: then the letter of the Law kills the spirit which created the Law. God gave the Torah to the people to give form to righteousness, mercy and faithfulness. Aren't the Pharisees too preoccupied with their rules and regulations, rather than being concerned about this righteousness, mercy and faithfulness?

'Why do you not fast?'

'But surely there is never fasting at a wedding? Can wedding guests fast while the bridegroom is still in their midst?'

Centuries-old imagery. That's how the prophets depicted God, as a bridegroom, suing for the hand of Israel, his beloved. Isn't Jesus such a bridegroom, who follows a trail of love through Israel to meet his bride Jerusalem? The meal that he gives for the sick and the sinners is a foretaste of the great wedding feast that is waiting, when God's beloved are united with him for ever.

'Now is no time to fast. But other times will come. When the bridegroom is taken away from them, then they will fast. In those days.'

Mark, who by now knows that the love wasn't reciprocated and that the bridegroom was put to death, is alluding to Good Friday. Then will be the time to mourn and to fast.

But not yet. Now is the time to feast and to enjoy the sparkling wine that the bridegroom gives. Come then, for all things are ready! Three cheers for the freedom of the children of God, three cheers for love! Away with all formalism, legalism and fanaticism which infects the holy interplay of faith. The bridegroom is among us. He's sitting at the head of the table and inviting his fellow-guests to live again by the old treasures of faith.

And no patchwork, please; let the new be new.

'No one sews a piece of unshrunk cloth on an old garment, for the new piece will then tear away and the tear will become worse. And no one pours new wine into old wineskins, otherwise the wine will burst the skins and the wine will be lost from the sacks.'

10

HALLOWING THE SABBATH

MARK 2.23-28; 3.1-6

Do we live to work or work to live? Those who live to work, live in slavery. Those who don't want to be slaves or don't want to become slaves will do well from time to time to stand back from their work and celebrate their freedom. That's what Israel invented the sabbath for. People must know when to stop, and moreover that's precisely what the word sabbath means. The sabbath is a unique and precious gift from Israel to humankind. The word has remained untranslated in all languages of the world.

Remember the sabbath day, to keep it holy. Six days you shall labour, but the seventh day is the sabbath of the Lord, your God. On it you shall do no work, neither you, nor your son, nor your daughter, nor your manservant, nor your maidservant, nor your cattle, nor the stranger who dwells in your cities. For in six days God made heaven and earth, the sea and all that is in it, and he rested on the seventh day. You shall remember that you were slaves in Egypt and that the Lord your God led you out from there with a strong arm.*

You've been liberated from Egypt. Don't let yourselves become slaves again. Be very careful not to land up in new slaveries. Celebrate your freedom. Let all your fellow creatures share in it. Let there be one day when kings and slaves, your fellow countrymen and women and aliens, are equal. This day is for God. Honour this day. Enjoy it.

Jesus and his followers enjoy it. *And it happened that Jesus was walking through the cornfields on the sabbath, and as they went his disciples began to pluck ears of corn.*

These are the disciples who don't fast because the bridegroom is here. They aren't slaves of work, far less slaves of a pedantic and joyless sanctification of the sabbath. They pluck the harvest ears of corn and sample the good creation. In doing that, for some Pharisees they're nibbling away at the holy faith of the fathers: *'Just look what your disciples are doing on the sabbath – surely that is not allowed?'*

In good rabbinic tradition Jesus asks a question in reply: *'Have you never read what David did when he and his followers were in need and were hungry? He went into the house of God and ate of the showbread of which only the priests may eat, and he also gave it to those who were with him.'*

Is Jesus here putting himself on a par with the great David? Or is it Mark who is comparing Jesus with David, associating David's opposition to the violent Saul with Jesus' opposition to a religion in which the message of love inevitably comes off worst in the face of dogmatism, exclusivism, and slavery to the letter, and in which people are sacrificed for principles? What are we to do with a religion which depends on fear and guilt-feelings towards one another, which makes people dependent and immature and alienates them from themselves instead of leading them to freedom? Commandments are good as long as they serve God and neighbour. If they don't do that, then there's nothing against transgressing them. *'The sabbath is there for human beings, not human beings for the sabbath.'*

This same critical voice had been heard earlier in Israel. 'The sabbath is given to you, but you have not been handed over to it,' said the old rabbis. Jesus' opposition to the letter of the Law which kills the spirit of the Law isn't new.

It was the sabbath and Jesus again went into a synagogue.

Mark has another story about the sabbath. It takes place in a synagogue.

There was a man with a withered hand. The scribes kept a close eye on Jesus. If he were to heal this man on the sabbath, they could accuse him.

This hand is paralysed. The man can't pluck ears of corn, to mention just one thing; he has no part in the good creation out in the fields. In the beginning God saw that everything that he had created was good, indeed very good. Jesus sees that this hand isn't good.

'Is it allowed to do something good on the sabbath?' he asks.

That isn't an issue for him. For him the sabbath is *the* day for being close to people who are suffering, and if possible healing them. A religion which has lost its healing power is as withered as this hand. It's a religion that makes people sick.

'May one do good on the sabbath or do evil? May one save a person or kill a person?'

If you neglect the good, you do evil. If it isn't forbidden to save a person on the sabbath, then surely it isn't permissible to let a person perish? Jesus looks the theologians straight in the face. They're silent. Their hearts are hardened. They're calloused. Jesus is both angry and sad. The divines love religion more than people. Is there nothing that can melt their frozen feelings?

And Jesus said to the man with the withered hand: 'Arise and go and stand in the middle.'

Jesus brings the man whom people have shoved aside into the heart of the community. In doing this he also symbolizes that this man has his very own place in God's heart. Let him be told that once again on this, God's sabbath, and let him see that this has been said. There is no reason whatever why he should feel inferior to anyone else; he needn't be paralysed by anything or anybody. It's high time that he took his own life in hand again. *'Stretch out your hand.'* Live!

And he stretched it out, and his hand became good again, as before.

And Jesus saw that it was good.

Has Jesus now violated the sabbath?

No, he's saved a man. But there are Pharisees who see things differently. If things go on like this they may as well pack up. 'Have you come to destroy us?' cried out the demons in the synagogue of Capernaum. Now these Pharisees in the synagogue also see that their kingdom is tottering. Wouldn't it be better if this blasphemous healer rapidly disappeared from the scene? *And they went and immediately held counsel with the Herodians how they could do away with him.* *

Jesus has barely taken a couple of steps along his way and the shadow of the cross is already falling over him. *'Is it permissible to save a person on the sabbath or to kill a person?'*, he asked. Apparently saving a person isn't permissible, but planning to kill him is. To do that it is even permissible to enter into a monstrous alliance with the Herodians, supporters of Herod, Rome's vassal ruler who has the power of life and death. Herod certainly wasn't a man well known for his hallowing of the sabbath...

11

TWELVE DISCIPLES

MARK 3.7-19

Jesus travels on, and death travels on with him. The great lords don't want him to go on misleading the people with his heresies.

But people stream to him and follow him, to the sea of Galilee. From near and far, from every region of the land and even beyond its frontiers, they travel to the man of God. They always know where to find him, those 'in peril on the sea', the poor and the sick, the wretched in the water up to their necks. *Kyrie eleison!* So great is the throng, that to be safe Jesus asks his disciples to keep a boat ready.

Many found healing. And as soon as the unclean spirits saw Jesus, they cast themselves down before him on the ground. 'You are the Son of God,' they screamed.

'You are my beloved child,' the voice from heaven had said earlier. The demons can only endorse this. The people, too, seem to sense it. By contrast, the divines are quite certain that Jesus is possessed by the devil and not by God.

Mark, who do you say that he is?

Mark says nothing about it; he pays silent homage to Jesus. The evangelist is afraid of false inferences. Jesus is Messiah in such a different way from the Messiah who is expected. Jesus is an unexpected Messiah, a suffering Messiah. That he in particular is the Messiah is something that people must discover for themselves in the course of the story. It's a mystery.*

Jesus commanded them to be silent.

He didn't want them to bring to light at this stage who he was.

And Jesus went up the mountain.

This is the mountain where you are close to God. It's the mountain where God spoke to Moses as one friend to another. It's the mountain on which God appeared to Elijah in the rustling of a gentle breeze. The mountain lies where heaven and earth touch each other in a human life. Rising up from flatland there's a vertical in your life, and you will never get rid of it again completely.

Jesus went up the mountain. He's been called, and he's going to call in his turn, for he's looking for people to carry the gospel of God, disciples who soon will become apostles.

And Jesus went up the mountain and he called those whom he himself wanted and they came.

When we see which disciples Jesus called, it's clear that he didn't select them for piety or prosperity, or for virtue or reputation. But they're to be his authorized representatives. And they came.

What was it that made them leave behind their nets, their family, their work, their old existence? In Jesus they must have heard the voice of the Eternal One, and they too go up the mountain, above the lowland. Close to Jesus they know that they're close to God.

He appointed twelve disciples to be with him.

Father Jacob had twelve sons, and ancient Israel had twelve tribes. The Jesus movement, represented by twelve disciples, remained rooted in Israel and inextricably bound up with it. The old people of God isn't written off; the church doesn't take the place of Israel. Jesus never turned away from Israel; the rift which developed between Judaism and Christianity is the sad work of people of later days.

Mark dreams of a resurrection of the kingdom of twelve tribes, of an Israel which is no longer dispersed and divided in itself. So he makes Jesus choose twelve disciples. Let Israel rise again! And may the people around who walk in darkness see a great light on God's holy mountain!

Like the mountain, the number twelve must also be understood symbolically.* Moreover Jesus didn't celebrate the last supper with his followers as it is depicted, in a historicizing way, on paintings, with six men on his left and six on his right. Jesus and his followers were many, and they included both men and women.

He appointed twelve disciples so that he could send them out to preach, with the power to drive out evil spirits.

Jesus isn't Messiah alone; they're Messiah together. They have a common task. *'You shall all be sons of God through faith in the Messiah Jesus,'** Paul will say later. The great work of the Messiah is work for all of them: driving out devils. Jesus could do it and they can do it too, in love, with faith.

There's no magic here. Jesus doesn't make any new retinas and eardrums descend from heaven. He could pray God's dove down from heaven and liberate people from the demons that made them sick. He could give new ears and new eyes to those who though sighted were blind, and though hearing were deaf. To the man who lay prostrate, paralysed by fear, he gave new trust in God and self-confidence, so that he could straighten his back again.

In the psychiatric clinic for mentally-ill delinquents in which I worked, the different therapies were practised by some twelve healers, of whom I shall mention three. There was the psychiatrist, because he knows a great deal about evil spirits, so that their heads can be crushed more quickly. There was the priest, because like Moses and Jesus in former times he can commute up and down between the mountain and the lowland so well. And there was the woman who taught these men pottery, because she showed them that you can only make an attractive vase if you first sit up straight and then give the vase a balanced form around an invisible but indispensable central vertical.

According to the story, Jesus called twelve disciples. The narrator gives their names and nicknames. The nicknames in particular make us curious.

Simon will be called *Peter*, Simon Rock. Is that a title of honour for an unshakeable man? Has he been called to be like Abraham, the rock from which the people of Israel is hewn?* It could also be that the title could mean quite the contrary, namely that in his case the seed sown by God the sower falls on rocky ground, blossoms rapidly, but withers away equally rapidly for lack of depth.

James and John are to be called *Boanerges*, sons of thunder. We can only guess at the significance of the nickname given to these brothers.

Finally, it is told of Judas that he is the man *who betrayed him*. Thus incomprehension and opposition don't just come from outside. Enmity is also there in Jesus' own circle.

It's strange, but later we don't hear much more about the twelve disciples. Apart from Peter, after Jesus' death Paul and James, the brother of Jesus, are the ones principally named, and they didn't belong to the twelve.

That's how it goes down church history. There are always new women and men who feel called to preach and to drive out evil spirits. Martin Luther King, for example, who in the valley of racist madness testified with such fire about the mountain where God called him and gave him a dream to dream: *'I've been on the mountain top.'*

12

POSSESSED, BUT BY WHOM?

MARK 3.20-35

When they were back home again, there was such a crowd of people that Jesus and his followers could not even eat.

Taking care of the people demands all their attention. So now, after all, the disciples are fasting, together with the bridegroom.

Meanwhile, Jesus' family is terribly upset and has travelled from Nazareth, determined to seize Jesus and take him back home – if not willingly, then by force. This must be stopped. *'He has gone crazy.'*

What tumult around Jesus! The scribes are plotting against him, Herod Antipas is already involved in helping to liquidate this threat to the state, treachery is already brewing among his companions, and now here are even his own mother and brothers, who think him mad: *'He has gone crazy.'*

The other evangelists will not be taking over these offensive words, but Mark mentions them quite freely. After all, was it so remarkable that Jesus' family thought that he was mentally ill and had to be protected against himself?

Tradition has made Jesus a dear, civilized, rather soft man, a fragile figure in white with gentle eyes and a sweet voice who lays hands on people devoutly and tenderly. But that's a romantic caricature. In that house in Capernaum there must have been a stench of putrefaction and blood, of sores and of the sweat of those who had travelled for days to get to the man of God. There must have been wailing and moaning in pain and sorrow, and also in bitter disillusionment when Jesus did *not* seem to have the power to heal a sick person. How are we to imagine him in the midst of these wretched people? We are told that he was moved 'to his guts' on seeing this boundless suffering.* He was a tormented man, in a life-and-death struggle with the kingdom of the devil, fighting for the healing of God's precious children.

And he spoke with so much passion then, and with such fire, that it was as if the clouds opened and something descended from heaven to earth. And when he laid hands on the sick, praying his Father for mercy and deliverance from these demons, with all the power that was in him, he must have been in a trance. He was possessed by God.

Yes, or possessed by the devil. For who says that this man is brim full of God? Why not brim full of Beelzebul? A special theological investigating committee, which had come down to the sea from Jerusalem, leaves no doubt about it: 'This Jesus is possessed by Beelzebul.' That's the diagnosis made by the family, but in theological language. The divines can't deny the healings, but they can suspect the source of power on which Jesus draws. According to their expert opinion a serious warning is called for. 'Beware of this satanic man,' they report, *'it is in league with the head of the demons that he drives out the demons.'*

'How can that be?' Jesus retorts with a parable. *'Surely the devil cannot cast out the devil? Surely it is impossible for a kingdom that is divided against itself to stand? Will not a house that is divided against itself perish? That is also the case with the kingdom of Satan. If Satan rebels against himself and is inwardly divided, he cannot remain standing; he is on the way to destruction.'*

Amazing! Jesus makes the theologians immediately think of demons, and makes the demons immediately think of God, for they've experienced 'in the flesh' that this holy one of God has entered their devilish kingdom from the heavenly regions. *'What does someone do who enters a house to plunder it? First he binds the owner of the house, and then he can go his way and empty the house.'*

Jesus has entered the house of this world. In single combat he has resisted the devil to his face, bound him fast, chained him, gagged him. Now he's busy casting out those demons which are still in residence. And the people who were in the grip of these demons can breathe again; healthy, they can again go their way. Everyone can see that with their own eyes. The divines can't delight in this; all they see in Jesus is a minion of Satan.

'The children of men can gain forgiveness for all their sins, except for their blasphemies,' said Jesus. *'But those who blaspheme against the holy Spirit, those who claim that I am a minion of Satan and work in his spirit and not in the Spirit of God, will never ever obtain forgiveness. Their guilt is eternal.'*

Is this a furious outburst by Jesus? Or are these the words of the first Christian community reacting maliciously to the malicious charge that their master is a minion of Beelzebul? In that case they're using the same words as we do when, deeply grieved and vilified by others, we go on the offensive and exclaim: 'I will never forgive you this and God will punish you!'

Meanwhile Jesus' family has arrived; they send a message asking him to come to them. *'Rabbi, your mother is here with your brothers. They're standing outside; they want to speak with you.'*

They are indeed standing outside. They're outsiders. Jesus has become a stranger to his own mother and his own brothers.

The first Christian community knew all about this: following this Messiah could alienate people from their families, just as Abraham was alienated from his family and his father's house when the Voice had called him.

'Who are my mother and my brothers?' Jesus looked round the people who were sitting in a circle around him and said to the man in the opening of the door: 'These here are my mother and my brothers. Anyone who does the will of God is my brother, my sister, my mother.'

Jesus puts the will of God above the will of his family, spiritual relationships above blood relationships. 'Are they standing outside? Let them come in! Let them enter a circle which is broader and goes deeper than the family circle. *Anyone who does the will of God is my brother, my sister, my mother.'*

Strikingly enough, Jesus calls no one in the circle his father. That place is reserved for God, the Father in heaven. The people in the circle are his sons and daughters. One big family.

13

A SOWER WENT OUT TO SOW

MARK 4.1-34

Again Jesus began to teach by the sea, and such a great crowd thronged to him that he got on board a ship and sat in it on the sea. The crowd was beside the sea, on the land. He taught them by telling them parables. 'Listen... See....'

The people on land have to have ears to hear the parables and eyes to see through the images.

'Listen. See, a sower went out to sow...'

Of course, he himself is this sower. From a boat he's sowing his words on the land. They're words of God, words from the other side which come wafting over the water. Will the seed fall in good soil on the land?

'Part of the seed fell along the path and the birds came and ate it up. Another part fell on rocky ground, where it did not have much earth. Immediately it shot up, but when the sun rose it withered and was scorched, because it had no roots. Yet another part fell among the thorns, and the thorns came up and choked it and it bore no fruit. The rest fell in good soil and growing up and flourishing it bore fruit, thirtyfold, sixtyfold, one hundredfold. Those who have ears to hear, let them hear.'

Later that day, when they were together again, the eyes and ears of the twelve proved to be somewhat defective. They asked themselves what this parable might mean. 'I don't understand,' said Jesus. 'The mystery of the kingdom is given to you, but you behave like the outsiders who are blind though they see and deaf though they hear – so that they don't need to be converted.'

He says this with a mixture of anger and sorrow. His own mother and his own brothers belong among those outsiders! They see him sowing and declare him to be crazy; they hear his words and want to shut him up at home. Now it seems that even those who have followed him along by the sea cannot follow him.

Will the *readers* of Mark understand the parable? Or shall the evangelist explain it again, just to be sure?

Listen! See! Part of the seed falls along the path, where the ground isn't receptive to seed. It's immediately carried off by the birds. The unreceptive ground is the closed heart of those who never give the new a chance, those who have a monopoly of wisdom and show it. They're always looking for a duel, never a dialogue. Like those spiritual people who immediately hit out at Jesus.

Another part falls on rocky ground. This may mean the disciples, the twelve, depicted in Peter, the man of rock. When Jesus calls them, they follow him immediately, but when things get too dangerous they take flight. The seed of the kingdom quickly blossoms within them, but it can't put down real roots, and they fall away when they are persecuted because of the kingdom.

And the ground sown with thorns, that may stand for the people in whom the sower's seed flourishes until it's choked by weeds: the cares of the world, fascination with wealth and the other things that people pursue, all those weeds with which no aromatic plant can cope. Mark hasn't given us any examples; apparently that's still to come our way.

The seed doesn't do very well, and not much comes up. It dies a thousand deaths and there isn't much to harvest. What must that have been like for the sower? He himself has died those thousand deaths. Hitherto, this parable seems to be no more than the sad account of a life full of futility, a way of failures and defeats. One might ask why Jesus doesn't give up. Why doesn't he go back to being a carpenter, if no one sees what's in his mind, if no one has ears to hear what he is saying?

Because he passionately believes in the germinating power of the kingdom. *'Now take a grain of mustardseed. There is no more insignificant seed on earth, but once sown it grows into a shrub, bigger than all other garden shrubs, with branches so large that the birds of the air can shelter in its shade.'*

This is a self-fulfilling prophecy of Jesus. For after the threefold drama of the lost seed, there was finally a great harvest in the field: the rest of the seed bore fruit thirtyfold, sixtyfold, a hundredfold. Don't ask how what was sown bore fruit; a sower never knows that. He scatters his seed over the earth, goes to sleep, gets up again, night and day, and the seed germinates and comes up without his knowing how. God has given what is sown a body.

We may expect Mark to give us examples of this, too, of people in whom the seed fell on good ground. That's also still to come our way.

Jesus spoke to the people in many parables, so that they could hear. He did not speak to them other than in parables. But privately to his disciples he explained everything.

So these disciples are privileged people. What are they going to do with all these lessons? It would be a pity if they put the light that they have been given under a bushel.

14

SLEEPING IN THE STORM

MARK 4.35-41

The day came to an end, and it was evening.

It's been a day on which the light of the kingdom has shone brightly, like a flame on the lampstand. Now night is falling. The question then is always whether the light will hold, for at nights it can be rough. Especially at sea, and that's where Jesus wants to go now.

'Come, let us cross.'

The man in the boat wants to go to the other side, to the land of the pagans. There too he wants to make the light of the kingdom shine.

They left the crowd behind and went over the sea. Suddenly there was a great storm and the waves broke over the boat, so that it was filling. And Jesus was in the stern, with his head on the cushion. He was asleep. The disciples woke him: 'Rabbi, do you not care if we perish?' Jesus awoke with a start and rebuked the wind and said to the sea, 'Silence, be still!' And the wind immediately ceased and the sea became still again.

It would be good to be able to hear such a miracle story again with the ears of an innocent child who still understands the language of fairy tales, the language in which so many Bible stories are also told. At school, children haven't yet learned to think scientifically, and so such a story of wind and water can still speak this kind of language. Intuitively the child feels its deep meaning. This is above all a story to tell before going to sleep, before the child, all alone in a puny ship, begins to drift around on the deep waters of the dark night.

How did the people in Rome hear this story by Mark at the time?

They heard the psalms in it. They were only a small group and they were persecuted because they had gone to sea with Jesus, and in their distress they cried out with the pious of Israel:

Truly, for your sake we are killed all day long,
we are counted as sheep for the slaughter.
*Awake, Lord! Why do you sleep?**

In this they heard the battle of faith from previous generations and also the confidence that believers of former times were given:

Some went down to the sea in ships.
They saw the works of the Lord
and his wonders in the deep.
He spoke and raised the stormy wind,
which lifted up its waves on high.
They mounted up to heaven, they went down to the depths;
their courage melted away in their plight.
Then they called to the Lord in their trouble,
and he delivered them out of their distress.
He made the storm be still,
and the waves of the sea were hushed.
Then they were glad because they had quiet,
*and he brought them to their desired haven.**

They recognized the fears of so many before them in peril on the sea of life, but in the presence of Jesus they nevertheless felt safe and secure in time and in eternity.

Of course they also heard the story of Jonah in it, the prophet who like Jesus was called by God to go to the pagans. But unlike Jesus, Jonah fled in a boat in precisely the opposite direction. A storm wind arose, but Jonah slept. They woke him up: 'How can you sleep so deeply? Arise, call on your God to save us!' Only when they had thrown Jonah overboard did the storm subside.

The parallel between the two prophets is striking, and so is the difference: Jesus puts Jonah very much in the shade. That's also shown by the end of the story: when Jonah finally lands among the pagans, as a real prophet of doom he embarks on a real tirade. Jesus can also preach a good sermon, but the God to whom he gives form in word and deed ultimately looks different from the God with whom Jonah has so much difficulty: *a gracious and merciful God, long-suffering and of great kindness.**

It's stormy and the disciples are afraid. Jesus is sleeping peacefully in the midst of the raging waves. 'Wake up!'

His followers thought that they were safe and sound with Jesus. They had to become fishers of men, but to their great alarm they came to discover what dangerous work that can be. There's a storm in Jerusalem and in Rome; the little Christian community gets into trouble and Jesus has gone to sleep, Jesus is dead. 'Arise! It was for your sake that we embarked, don't you care that we perish?'

Jesus rebuked the wind and said to the sea, 'Silence, be still!'

With these same words he had called the raging demons in the synagogue of Capernaum to order. 'Silence, be still!' The demons obediently calmed down. Now the wind too becomes submissive and the sea again becomes as flat as a pancake.

The disciples aren't very good at following all this. Although they've been initiated into the mysteries of the kingdom, they remain outsiders. *'Why are you so afraid? Have you no faith at all?'*

For Jesus the opposite of faith isn't unbelief but fear. Why be so afraid when it's stormy? With God, aren't we in good hands? These are the hands which wove us in our mother's womb, the hands which bear us up day and night, and which one day will lead us to the other shore, our desired haven.

Jesus' trusting faith is still too much for the disciples to understand; they can't grasp it. *'Who is this, that even the winds and waves obey him?'*

Indeed, who could he be? Mark raises the question again, and again he gives no answer. He still prefers to keep secret what the messiahship of this man means and what it means to be a follower of this Messiah.

15

IN THE LAND OF THE GERASENES

MARK 5.1-10

And they came to the other side of the sea, in the land of the Gerasenes.

This is pagan land, and it smells of death, for Jesus enters the rocky, inhospitable region where the graves are. It would be better not to go there; drunkards and demons, crazy people and other scum live in the empty vaults. They're the living dead, drop-outs, addicts, slow suicides. The idiot with the chains lives there.

No one knows his real name. He's a dangerous madman who rushes around there naked. Sometimes he slashes himself with bits of stone until he bleeds. They've often put him in chains, but he's as a strong as an ox, and can always escape from his chains. Day and night his cry of lament resounds, but as soon as a human being appears, he hurls abuse at them: 'Go away,' he then screams, 'away from here, leave me in peace.'

When the people are far away he calls them, and when they come closer he hurls curses at their head. He's dead scared of what he so much wants: human closeness, the love of the living. But he dwells among the dead, caught up in a vicious circle, fighting everyone off, screaming for them to come near.

Who or what has banished him to the tombs and made him unclean? Where does this self-hatred come from? And how does one approach someone who won't have anyone near him? Unlike the other desperate people who are described for us in the Gospel, it seems as if this sick man doesn't want to be healed. Or does he?

And when he saw Jesus, he came rushing at him from a long way off, prostrated himself before him, and cried out as loudly as he could: 'What have you to do with me, Jesus, Son of the most high God? I adjure you by God, do not torment me.'

It's as though the mentally ill man needs his mental illness. Although he's bowed down under it, he's clearly also afraid of being healed, afraid of the truth about his life. In heaven's name, wouldn't it be more merciful to leave this man in his vicious circle? *'Do not torment me.'*

Jesus has landed. He's the man from the other side who has come in the name of the Most High to be near to people. And this sick man has immediately sized him up! We ask ourselves how he knows so immediately and so precisely that the Son of the Most High has landed. The razor-sharp intuition of the mentally ill? What does he feel, then?

Warmth, probably. Acceptance. Trust. Rest. And out of sheer anxiety about being annihilated by it he lashes out.

Of course things aren't very different inland, where the ordinary Gerasenes live, the 'normal people'. There and in Galilee anyone can really see precisely what can be seen writ large in the case of the mentally-ill man. There too they're fleeing from their own truth. Always and everywhere it's difficult to follow the voice of one's heart. We want to live a fuller life, live in a less superficial way, establish other priorities. But to do that we have to abandon our old life, and who dares to do that, who does it? How many people cling desperately to their past? How many people aren't wed to their rage or their pain? Petrified, they see the Son of the Most High approach, seeking to rescue them from their pain. Which will win, their longing for freedom or their fear of it?

See them standing there, those two, on the shore of the land of the Gerasenes: the possessed man, an anonymous exile, and opposite him the man from the other side, a beloved of God. And now battle must be joined. This is a fight between God and the devil, with this man as the stake.

Jesus wants to rescue this man from the world of his fear, but the thought of leaving this world arouses new fear in the man. *'Go away, do not torment me!'* He had come to cling to death. He wants to keep at bay the person who approaches him in friendship, so as to raise him from the dead and to restore life to him as a new calling.

This is abominably complicated. And so Jesus' first attempt to drive out the unclean spirit comes to grief. *'Unclean spirit, depart from this man.'* However, the unclean spirit will not yield: *'What have I to do with you?'*

Jesus has lost the first round of the contest. The words of power which he spoke return to him empty. What now? Must he give up this man as incurable, shake the dust from his feet, get back in his boat and begin the return journey? *'Leave me alone'* is what this man has come to say. But he *has* come to say it. There's more in his soul than just the demon, so Jesus won't capitulate to this demon. In despair, people often say the opposite to what they really mean. Moreover Jesus chooses not so much to hear his words as the unexpressed wish which lies behind them. After all, he *has* come. But how to address him? How to break down the barrier of his fear?

The people who came into this man's domain before Jesus tried to calm him with chains, but that failed. Jesus does it a different way. *If* the fear is to be checked, it must be without compulsion. Perhaps he must ask him his name.

16

LEGION WAS HIS NAME

MARK 5.10-20

And Jesus asked him, 'What is your name?'

Jesus doesn't ask what this man is called, he asks him his name. In other words, he asks him who he is or wants to become at the deepest level. One's name expresses one's being. So God couldn't really give any answer when Moses asked him his name. How could a mortal know the Eternal One by name?

'What is your name?'

That's always the question before the face of the Lord 'on the seashore', and it can be years before a person has found the beginning of an answer. Who are you? Where do you come form? Where are you going? Who or what is restraining you?

'*My name is Legion, for we are many.*'

No 'ego', that's clear. The man in the land of the Gerasenes can give no better answer to the question about his name than by revealing how torn apart he is. He really can't have a name. In himself he's nothing. He's possessed by a horde of demons who stamp through his soul in hobnailed boots. 'My name is Legion.'

Who knows his real name? The name by which his mother called him when it was time for a meal, or his father when they went fishing on the lake? But that's long past, a previous life... Now he's living among the dead. He's no longer himself, his name is Legion.

We aren't told what precisely happened between the man and the man of God. That's their secret. Perhaps it can be compared with what happens now when one damaged person asks another for help. Often they take a long and terrifying way, for these demons must be driven out one by one. Complicated and painful experiences are talked about there, and as long as you allow them to haunt you, they continue to rule you. You find all sorts of things when you descend into the depths of your soul. So much sorrow comes up, so many old sores. But we shall overcome. No, not back to the house of slavery; freedom is waiting over there! We won't allow ourselves to be put off by anything; we must tame all the wild beasts that appear before us, crush all the monster's seven heads, one by one. One day you shall be free, my child. Then you will know that you're loved by God and created for happiness.

Precisely what happened we do not know, but the legion had to yield. The man found healing. The last thing that we are told about him is that he sits next to Jesus as a free man, somewhat ill at ease in his clothes. What do they talk about? They laugh.

'Rabbi, last night I dreamed of those demons. They were scared to death that you would drive them out of the land. Now there was a cliff where a large herd of pigs were rooting around. And the demons begged you, 'Please send us into the pigs; we want to go into them.' For of course those demons were homeless, now that they could no longer live with me. And pigs were better than nothing. 'Please may we go into those pigs?' What an awareness, don't you think? Like seeks like! And you nodded. You thought that would be a good thing. So there they went, those demons, and one by one they entered the pigs. Then in my dream I saw the whole herd, around two thousand of them, rush down the steep slope and throw themselves into the sea. All the filth, all the piggery from all those years, all the uncleanness, all the stinking mess, went under. I saw it sink before my eyes, down into the depth of oblivion, into the sea of the past. Then the waters closed over it and the waves subsided. The last thing I saw was a warm sun appearing over the smooth surface of the water. Then I woke up.'

Jesus smiled. 'That was a nice dream,' he said.

'I also dreamed about those swineherds. Of course they didn't know what to do, all their trade down the chute! And all the people here who heard about it became afraid. They began to shout that you're a crazy fool who turns everything upside down. 'Go away,' they cried, 'away from here, leave us in peace!'

'Just like you, then,' said Jesus. 'You also became afraid and wanted me to disappear.'

Jesus fell silent. Was he already thinking about what people would cry out later?

Jesus took ship to return to Galilee. 'Take me with you,' cried the man who was no longer called Legion. 'Take me with you.'

He wanted to remain with his benefactor. He wanted to give his life to the man who had restored life to him. And of course he was also afraid to be alone again. 'Let me follow you.'

This is the only place in the Gospel where Jesus doesn't think that this is a good thing. With this pagan, unlike the disciples, the seed has already fallen on good soil, and without the sower worrying it will come to growth and bear fruit. 'Go home, to your family, and tell them what God has done to you in his mercy.'

The man did what Jesus asked him. He told his family not only about God, but also about Jesus.

That isn't surprising. How could he tell what God had done without telling what Jesus did? It was Jesus who had shown him something of the kingdom of God.

17

THE WOMAN WITH A FLOW OF BLOOD

MARK 5.21-34

This is a story about two women, an adult woman and a woman on the verge of adulthood; a girl of twelve, whose bleeding is beginning, and a mature woman, whose bleeding hasn't stopped for twelve years. Both women are bowed down under female powerlessness. The one suffers from being unclean and being banished from the land of desire. The other is scared to death of entering that land. Both women find healing in two stories which Mark has artistically woven into one whole.

When Jesus had crossed again from the land of the Gerasenes to Galilee, a great crowd gathered about him. And he was by the sea.

Then came one of the rulers of the synagogue, Jairus by name, and seeing Jesus he threw himself at his feet, and begged him urgently, saying, 'My daughter is at the point of death. Come and lay your hands on her, so that she may be preserved and live.' And Jesus went with him. And a great crowd followed him and thronged about him.

Suddenly this woman who has been bleeding for twelve years appears on the scene. We don't know her name or her story, but she's hurt, in body and soul. For of course that bleeding affects your whole existence, every day, every night, year in and year out. She's unclean, and people would rather see the back of her. This woman is a walking taboo, and those she wants to love she must avoid.

What has happened for her to have to bled so much? Who or what has hurt her so? Or has she done it herself?

Life is flowing out of the woman with her flow of blood and so is her money, since she keeps going to doctors. And as so often happens, no physician can diagnose the wound from which she's *really* bleeding. Her life is one constant loss; she's constantly losing blood, and money. Then Jesus comes into the town. *She has heard about him.* Mark knows that.

Clearly she has ears to hear, as she's on the track of his secret; she won't go on bleeding. She's heard about Jesus, and in her case the seed has fallen on good soil. Thinking about Jesus and the gospel of God, she begins, though hesitantly, to think differently about herself. Might she still be able to find healing?

They say that a healing power emanates from Jesus. How? She doesn't know that either, but she supposes that it has something to do with the power of the love of God, the love of a God before whom one doesn't need to feel guilty, the love of a God before whom one doesn't need to be ashamed either: about one's past, one's desires or even one's wounds. This is a God who doesn't count our foolishness, a God who loves us, a God who wants no more for this woman than that she too should walk free along the Lord's ways. This is a God who isn't disgusted, a God who's like a father. He tears open the heavens and says: 'You're my daughter, my beloved, I love you, so love yourself. You're clean, do you hear, you're clean!'

If only God were like that! And God is like that, if she's heard aright. Her longing flares up, she begins to hope again. Can it be?

But no! How often she's had illusions!

And immediately the old anxiety has begun to seize her again. She mustn't dream. There's no way back to the world of men and women; she needn't even try. Moreover she doesn't even know whether she wants that. What must she do in a world which is so hard-hearted, a world in which men humiliate women, sometimes their own wives and their own daughters? She'd better stop wanting anything. No more dreams of healing. That prevents any disappointment. She's only a woman, and an unclean woman at that. Jesus is a man, a holy man. How will she ever get him to notice her?

What if she didn't come face to face with him, and simply touched him from behind, when he was passing by? What if she could see him without his seeing her? And if she could touch him, just touch him, if only the hem of his garment? Then *he* would be unclean. But would that upset him?

The woman with a flow of blood is anxious, shy. But she dares to go into the crowd and when Jesus is passing by – Jairus, the ruler of the synagogue has asked his help for his little daughter – she stretches out her hand. Briefly, very briefly, she furtively touches the hem of his garment from behind. And she finds healing.

A miracle?

Who will claim that something like this can't happen? A touch can change a person's life. One look can open up a world for a person.

The moment that the woman touches the hem of Jesus' garment, the source of her bleeding dries up and she becomes a different person. Is it the power that has gone out from Jesus? Is it the power that she herself mobilized, the courage to leave her home, the trusting faith that made her stretch out her hand, her wordless prayer? It could well be both. Power streamed out of her and power streamed back into her. It's as if this power has stemmed the stream of her blood.

'Who touched me?' asks Jesus. 'Someone touched my garment.'

'What do you expect,' say the disciples, 'you can see for yourself that all these people are thronging around you – and then you ask who's touched you?'

But Jesus looks round to see who it was. And the woman knows: now she must come forward from the mass of people. Now she must really overcome all her fear and show herself in the midst of all these people. Because Jesus wants to see *her*, the inconspicuous one. He wants to give her his blessing. She may become what she was meant to be: a free woman, walking along the Lord's ways, a reborn child of God, daughter of the Father.

Moreover that is precisely what Jesus says to her: *'Daughter, your faith has saved you. Go in peace and be healed of your disease.'*

Daughter. With that one word a long-drawn-out history of sickness is concluded, and a new future is opened up. Daughter. As if the heavens were opening up. 'You're my daughter, my beloved, I love you, so love yourself, you're clean!'

Her faith has been her salvation. Without faith the man of God can do no miracles; without good soil the sower brings forth no fruit.

While Jesus was still speaking, a messenger came up to Jairus: *'Your daughter is dead. Why trouble the rabbi further?'*

Too late. They're too late. What a wretched delay, caused by the unclean woman. That wasn't urgent; she'd been bleeding for so long. How bitter it is that while one daughter finds healing, the other daughter finds death.

Jairus had come to Jesus in the faith that he could save her. Will he now lose his faith?

'Fear not,' said Jesus. *'Only believe.'*

As in the boat, Jesus sees fear as the opposite of faith.

18

JAIRUS' DAUGHTER

MARK 5.35-43

Jairus, ruler of the synagogue, has waylaid Jesus: *'My daughter is at the point of death. Please come and lay your hands on her.'*

Jairus' daughter. Under this name she's gone down in history, because under this name she had almost gone *out of* history: not as a woman with a name of her own, but as a girl who never made womanhood but remained a child, simply taking her name from that of her father. Jairus' daughter – a girl on the verge of adulthood, twelve years old, marriageable – with her life before her. But at the threshold of life she finds herself on the threshold of death. *Please come!*

In the Gospel stories it's usually the mothers who appear for their children, but here the mother plays no significant role; here it's the father who appears for his child. Has the child's illness something to do with a sickening father? Does Jairus know that deep down?

He was ruler of the synagogue. So his child grew up in a glass house. 'Are you Jairus' daughter?' Everything that she does and everything that she doesn't do indirectly has some impact on her father's position. Jairus calls her *my daughter*; it sounds tender, and indeed it is tender, but it's also possessive. There's a parental concern which robs children of their freedom and prevents them from growing up. Then a girl remains 'the daughter of'. She never becomes herself, and so it becomes difficult for her to attach herself to someone else. She gets mixed up, in her life, in her body, in her love.

Jairus' daughter is lying deathly pale on her bed. Jesus will soon say that they must give her something to eat. Is it too rash to suppose that she had problems with eating? That wouldn't be surprising for someone who had problems with life. Those near to despair can hardly get a bite down. Or too much goes down their throats.

Be this as it may, Jairus' daughter is sick; she's only a shadow of her former self. Doesn't she want to go on living? In that case the girl is strangely right: she *has to* die as the daughter of Jairus if she wants to live.

Father Jairus has gone to get help. *'Please come and lay your hands on her.'* He's scared to death that he'll lose his daughter. But he will only be able to hold on to her if he can let her go. That's the paradox of love. And that strange delay, half-way, because of the woman who's been bleeding for twelve years, it's as if that bizarre postponement has been something like an exercise for father Jairus in letting go. In a sense he must stop being father Jairus: only then can his daughter stop being Jairus' daughter. If he can stop being a dictatorial father, she can stop being a submissive daughter. And whether he can do that, this story seems to say, is a question of faith. This is a faith which is seriously put to the test, for a messenger comes from the house to say that he needn't trouble Jesus longer. His daughter has just died. At that precise moment Jesus tells him that he must let go of his anxiety. *'Fear not. Have trust.'*

In other words: 'My dear Jairus, you aren't God. Why are you so afraid of life, why are you so afraid of death, and why have you made your daughter so afraid? She's a child of God, Jairus, and only if you can "give her back" to God will she be able to live. The poor child can't take a step – she's dead to life. Don't be afraid, Jairus. Believe.'

They came to the house. The girl lay motionless on her bed. 'She's dead,' the people lamented.

'No,' said Jesus, 'she's sleeping.'

The people laughed. First they were lamenting, now they have to laugh. It's like Sarah's scornful laugh when God promised her that she would become the mother of a son. 'Sleeping? Don't make me laugh.' It's the laugh of unbelief. But unbelief keeps things as they are, and therefore Jesus throws out the mockers. He can't bear these foolish people. Not now. Not there. Out with them! Out of the room and out of the house!

'My daughter is at the point of death. Please come and lay your hands on her.' That's what Jairus had come to ask.

Does Jesus do that now, lay hands on her? No, he doesn't. He doesn't lay anything on her. He takes her hand. For years Jairus' hand has lain on the child, protecting her and stifling her. Now she's raised up by Jesus' touch. In a chivalrous way the bridegroom takes her by the hand and draws her into the dance of life. Without fear, without guilt feelings, no longer ruled by anger, no longer sick of her father and mother but truly loved by them, she can begin on the great journey of her life. Not knowing where she'll get to, trusting that God is going with her. As God also went with Abraham and Sarah through time and through the lands.

Jesus took the child by the hand and said to her, 'Talitha cumi', 'Little girl, arise.' And immediately the girl got up and walked. She was twelve years old.

'Stand on your own feet. You can do it. Get up. There's no time to lose. You're twelve!'

There she goes. Jairus' daughter takes the first steps in her own life. She steps into the world.

Jairus and his wife laugh and cry with pleasure. 'All the best. Good-bye. Here's some food for the journey. Don't forget to eat.'

'Yes, I know now.'

Parents! Always anxious and upset. But they also love you. 'Good-bye. I'll be back. No, I can't say precisely when. I'll see. Don't be afraid, I can look after myself. A Dieu.'

19

A PROPHET IN HIS OWN COUNTRY

MARK 6.1-13

The miracles aren't yet finished. Three times the seed has fallen into good soil: the possessed man in the land of the Gerasenes has found healing, the woman with the flow of blood has returned to a full life and Jairus' daughter may embark on her freedom. Here Mark has at the same time shown how faith can transcend all social, cultural and religious frontiers. The good news is there for all: for Jew and for Gentile, man and woman, great and small, famous and inconspicuous. Together they all form God's big family.

How are things meanwhile with Jesus' family in Nazareth?

Jesus went away from there and came to his home town.

How will he be received there in remote Nazareth? Will they be proud that their little village has produced such a great son?

When the sabbath had dawned, he began to teach in the synagogue, and the many who heard him were bewildered: 'Where did this man get all this, and what wisdom has been given him! And then those miracles that have been done by his hand!'

Up to now, everything is going well in Nazareth. People come out and are impressed by Jesus' words and actions. Could he be a prophet of the Most High?

But his origins are lowly! He's a son of Joseph and Mary, he's trained as a carpenter, they know his brothers and sisters.* There are still people there who sat next to him at school, who played hide-and-seek in the workshop, knocked up huts out of old planks and stole oranges from the next-door orchard. Does this Jesus come from God? Look, he's just like the rest of us!

Jesus is from too close. And he comes too close. If *he's* a holy one of God, then *they* are, too!

Amazingly enough, that's precisely what Jesus is preaching. That they're children of God, even more than children of their parents. And that they must love the other children of God as their brothers and sisters with a love which knows no bounds. The healthy and the sick, the good and the bad, Jews and Gentiles, friends and enemies, may share in this love.

Nazareth is alarmed. No one has ever spoken about God and human beings in their synagogue as Jesus does. This is new. Is this what they want? He may claim that he's saying only what's in the Torah and the Prophets, but they venture to doubt that. Does the one who as a boy still rode his donkey through their streets and who then went away because he wanted to seek God now want to come and tell his old fellow villagers how to believe and live? Who does he think he is? He should know his place; he's no better than they are. The best thing would be for him to leave Nazareth again quickly and let normal life resume its course.

However, Mark doesn't mention Nazareth by name in his story. This is deliberate. He prefers to talk about his *home town*, with a word which can just as well mean his *homeland*. Nicely ambiguous, for in Mark's days Jesus' preaching is finding a hearing all around, while most people in his homeland remain deaf to it. Pagans want to follow him, but his own people reject him. That's a great sorrow for Mark. Jesus was already sorrowful about it in Nazareth at that time.

Jesus was amazed at their unbelief. It's as if they don't want what he has to offer. Nor could Jesus do any miracles in Nazareth, since two things are always necessary for a miracle: without trust there are no healings and without good soil there is no fruit.

Jesus was amazed. But it isn't all that amazing; in those days it was already proverbial that *a prophet is never honoured in his own country.*

Then Jesus shed the dust from his feet and left his home town to go to the surrounding villages. Later, after his death, Jesus' followers would leave his homeland to go to the surrounding countries. If his disciples are to be charged with this particular task, then they need to gain some experience during Jesus' lifetime.

He called the twelve and sent them out, two by two. Two are less vulnerable than one, two know more than one, two believe more than one. Testimony is confirmed by the word of two.

He gave them power over the evil spirits. How many lives are inhibited and afraid in the face of the uncleanness in the world and the uncleanness in their soul! Taboos govern daily life: keep away from the dead, from menstruating women, from lepers, from this and that. And there is also so much that people are shy of in their own souls: they've been given a light side and a shadow side by God, but they prefer not to see their shadow side, and when this becomes visible in their neighbour they reject this neighbour. They're haunted by it all; in heaven's name let the disciples drive out these evil spirits!

But if the disciples want to be able to free others from their fear and their inhibitions, then they will first have to free themselves. *'Take nothing with you on your journey but a staff: no bread, no bag, no money in your belt. Wear sandals, but do not put on two sets of clothing.'* So many exercises in trusting God.

The journey isn't without dangers. And just like Jesus, they will encounter opposition: the gospel of God forces people to make a choice. *'When you enter a house, stay there until you go on further. And if any place will not receive you and they refuse to hear you, when you leave, shake off the dust that is on your feet and depart.'*

The disciples went out and proclaimed that people must repent. They cast out many evil spirits, and anointed with oil many who were sick.

The oil has the scent of paradise. Kings were also anointed with this oil. 'Arise, sick person. You're clean, you're a royal child.'

In this way they brought healing.

20

SALOME DANCES

MARK 6.14-29

How will the disciples fare on their journey? And how will Jesus fare on his? Will his fate be like that of John the Baptist?

It's to be hoped that it won't be, for John the Baptist has been put to death by king Herod. Mark hasn't yet reported that to us; it's as if he was afraid of doing so. But now this story has to be told, and Mark does that with great skill. He weaves it into the kind of horror story that was told in those days, and he also brings in motifs from the stories of Esther and Elijah.*

What crime did John commit? He had mentioned the king's crimes out loud. This man was called Herod, like his father, the child murderer from the Gospel of Matthew. Herod junior had divorced his wife in order to be able to marry Herodias, the woman whom he had stolen from his half-brother Philip. 'A scandal!,' the prophet cries, for if the king does not act in obedience to the commandments and in faithfulness to the Torah, the people also degenerates.

But Herodias won't listen: 'Herod, I want you to silence that man!'

The king has John seized and throws him into prison.

That isn't enough for Herodias. 'Herod, I want that man silenced *for ever!*'

But the king thinks that that's going too far, since suprisingly enough he likes him. In the evening, when work is done and silence has fallen on the palace, he has John brought from his prison to talk with him. *He heard him gladly.* With a good glass of wine in his hand he likes listening to this ascetic from the wilderness.

This is bizarre. Herod lives in a world of decadence, intrigues and violence, while the prophet represents a world of righteousness and faithfulness and self-control. Does the king still hope that one day John's world

61

will become *his* world? Or is it because power always seeks justification and the king wants to win the prophet over?

'No, Herodias, I will not silence this John for ever. Why should I? Surely he can't do any more harm?'

Herod is no monster; he's a weakling. In the evening, when he's alone and summons the man in the camel-hair coat, he plays the game of the king and his prophet, a game of good and evil. It's a diversion.

It doesn't change anything.

In the meantime Herodias is sulking in the women's quarters. She's staked everything in her life on this Herod, and finally she's won him. But she doesn't own him, for John is in her way, that locust-eating trouble-maker in his rough coat who grudges her love, who thinks that he's God in person. And this husband of hers even listens to him. He enjoys it, instead of spending those hours with her. John is destroying her happiness and ruining her life. He must go. Herodias is out for revenge.

It's Herod's birthday, and there's a feast in the palace. The king prepares a banquet for the great lords of the court, the army leaders and the notables of the land. Herodias senses her opportunity.

She calls Salome. She herself couldn't seduce Herod into liquidating the man from the wilderness, but perhaps her attractive daughter will be able to. 'Dance, Salome, dance. Weave flowers in your hair, sprinkle yourself with fragrant oil, put on your veils and dance! The drink has flowed in abundance, the men are cheerful, the musicians are playing like a dream, let the men enjoy your splendid body, Salome, let your veils fall, dance!'

Salome danced, the lure of the woman behind the scenes whose beauty was fading. Swept up by the music and by the cries of the men, Salome danced her bewitching dance, and one by one the veils fell.

'Splendid!,' cried Herod, aroused and befuddled. 'You may make a wish, Salome. Ask what you like and I'll give it you, even if it's half my kingdom.'

'Mother, what shall I ask for?'

'Ask for John's head, my child.'

'Father, I want John's head. Immediately. On a plate.'

What is there about this girl that she not only accedes to her mother's wish but even adds a further touch? Does Salome know of the tensions which John is introducing into her parents' marriage, and is she trans-lating her longing for their happiness into a lust for murder?

Herod has John beheaded. In Herod the seed of the kingdom of God has fallen among the thorns. He's heard the word, even gladly, *but the cares of the world and the fascination of riches and the many other desires choked the word and it remained without fruit.*

John's disciples heard of his death. They went to the palace, took his body with them and laid it in a tomb.

End of story.

Mark clearly wants to prepare us for the fact that John was Jesus' fore-runner not only in life but also in death. He makes us share in his sorrow that those who want to live a righteous and holy life in the world come up against resistance and have a good chance of losing their heads.

When John was already long dead and buried, Herod received reports about one Jesus of Nazareth. This prophet also came from the wilderness and also seemed to be a righteous and a holy man. The man on the throne was terrified. He was still troubled by a guilty conscience. Could John have risen from the dead?

Before long, Jesus too will be taken prisoner. He will be led before the governor Pilate. This man on the throne will also know that he has a righteous and holy man in front of him. He too will be able to offer no resistance to the desires of those around him, filled with hatred. Again blood will flow.

Then Jesus too will be laid in a tomb. But that isn't the last thing that is told of him. The story goes that he was raised from the dead.

21

YOU PREPARE A TABLE FOR ME

MARK 6.30-44

'Let us go to a quiet place, to rest there a while,' Jesus said to the apostles, who had returned from their mission. *For so many people were coming and going that they had no time even to eat.*

Here the disciples are called apostles, those who are sent, for they are to be sent when Jesus has gone the way of John the Baptist. Then too they will need to rest from time to time. Those who keep talking away, who are afraid of silence, who neglect to talk with themselves and with God, in the long run have nothing more to offer these people who keep coming and going. *'Let us rest a while.'* The apostles have sown; the rest is up to the Lord of the field. *And they went away in their ship to a place where they could be alone.*

But the people knew what course this ship was taking, and they hastened there on foot. They arrived even before the boat. Jesus landed and, seeing the crowd, was moved with compassion. *They were like sheep without a shepherd.*

Those are words of Moses, when at the end of his journey he pleaded with God for a successor to lead the people, 'for otherwise they will be like sheep without a shepherd'. 'Take Jehoshua,' said God. Joshua. And so it would be: from then on Jehoshua was Israel's shepherd.

Like Moses at that time, Jehoshua of Nazareth looked on the crowd with compassion. They're sheep without a shepherd; who will lead them to green pastures, and give them still waters? *And he began to teach them,* for there was so much that he wanted to say to them, and how much time did he still have left? He gave them bread for their hearts, provisions for the way.

But the stomach also needs bread, and it was already late. The disciples thought that it was time for the people to go. 'The day is ending, they must go home or to the villages around here to buy food.'

'You give them something to eat.'

'Us? Do you want us to buy two hundred denarii worth of bread to feed so many people?'

'How many loaves do you have?'

'Five, and two fishes.'

Five loaves? That matches the story of David, the shepherd boy who had to flee before Saul. When David arrived at the priest of Nob half starving, he received from him five of the twelve holy loaves from the temple.* Five is the number of Israel. For four is the number of the wide world and One is the number of the Eternal One. Israel is called to bear witness to the One to all points of the compass. Four plus one is five.

'Make the people sit down on the green grass.'

The green pastures of which this same David sang.* Mark's purpose is clear: he sees Jesus, the son of David, as the good shepherd who leads his sheep to green pastures. Herod holds a banquet and blood flows. Jesus holds a feast with his followers and everyone revives.

Jesus took the five loaves and the two fishes, raised his eyes to heaven, and spoke the blessing, broke the loaves and gave them to his disciples to set before the people. He also divided the two fishes among them. So they all ate and were satisfied.

Again in this one story we hear an echo of many others. Mark calls to our mind a world of miraculous signs. When Moses raised his eyes to heaven in the wilderness, didn't manna then descend, with quails, enough for everyone?* And the widow of Zarephath shared her last loaf with Elijah, the holy one of God, but the meal in her pot never ran out, nor did the oil in the jar.* And the prophet Elisha commanded a great crowd to be given food from the few loaves of barley bread that someone had given him. 'But that is not enough for so many,' exclaimed his servant. Elisha nevertheless made him share the bread, and look, there was still something over!*

> *The Lord is my shepherd, I shall lack nothing.*
> *He makes me lie down in green pastures,*
> *he leads me beside still waters,*
> *he restores my soul.*
> *He prepares a meal for me,*
> *my cup overflows.*

However, it isn't just words from olden times which resound in the evangelist's story; there are also the words which Jesus speaks at the end of his life, when he's holding a farewell meal with his followers. There are the words which since then have resounded everywhere and always when Jesus' followers have met in his name and held a meal: *and he took bread, spoke the blessing, broke it and gave it to them.** Then they're sharing their abundance, in remembrance of him, and are gratefully celebrating his presence in their midst.

Mark dips his pen in the ink. In his thoughts he's with the persecuted Christian community of Rome which Sunday by Sunday meets to break bread. He wants to strengthen the little flock. He will support them with the story of the loaves and the fishes.

The desert setting for this miraculous event will speak to the people there. They mustn't forget that in earlier days the manna of God's goodness descended in such a forsaken place for Moses, for Elijah, for Elisha. And these saints of God, apostles of Jesus Christ in the dispersion, will also lack nothing. They mustn't be discouraged by the little that they have, but from their wretchedness must raise their eyes to heaven, and they will be filled.

Jesus took the five loaves and the two fishes; he broke the loaves and gave them to his disciples to distribute to the people.

He gave them bread, he who is called the bread of life. He also gave them the fish. He who on the tomb of the first martyrs in Rome is depicted as a fish because he had made his way like a fish through the waters of death. In a play on the letters of the Greek word for fish, ICHTHUS, a confession of faith formed itself automatically: *Iesous CHristos THeou Uios Soter,* Jesus Christ, Son of God, Saviour.

So they all ate and were satisfied. They even had some over: twelve baskets full. And those who had eaten of the loaves were five thousand men.

Five is the number of Israel, and so is twelve. All Israel is fed, and there is more than enough for all.

22

AN UNSUCCESSFUL CROSSING

MARK 6.45-56

Immediately Jesus made his disciples get into the boat and go before him to the other side, to Bethsaida.

Jesus sends his disciples out again. As good apostles they must now take the story of the kingdom to the other side in their own strength. The gospel of God must go to the world.

But they would rather not. They're afraid of embarking on their own, afraid of the other side. Jesus has more or less to force them.

He himself goes up the mountain to pray. He doesn't go with them. The disciples must learn to be alone on the wide sea of the world. Soon they will also have to do things alone. As long as they know that Jesus doesn't lose sight of them and on the heights prays for them.

The disciples are sitting in the ship, night falls, the wind gets up and becomes a gale, and whatever they try they make no headway. Their boat is constantly driven back by the storm wind and the waves. They'll never get there! They shouldn't have listened to Jesus; they shouldn't have gone.

No disciple remembers that the wind and sea obey him. They're poor fools, who don't know how to pray and don't dare to trust that someone is praying for them. And Mark only hopes that his readers will do better.

Jesus prays on the mountain for his friends below, who are tossing up and down on the sea. He sees their fruitless efforts, their fight against the elements, the despair in their eyes. They can't cope; he has to go to them. They seem to have left all their trust in God behind on shore, on the land where not long ago he fed them with bread and fish, the sign that they will never lack anything. But now that the wind and the tide are against them, their courage sinks again. He really must go to them.

And Jesus went down from the mountain, set foot on the waters, and walked on the sea.

Sometimes I ask people what their favourite Bible story is. Then they mention The Good Samaritan, or Rebecca at the Well, or The Prodigal Son. If you put the question in prison, then very often you hear something quite different: that he walked on the water. Outside the walls of the prison almost no one chooses that story; inside the walls it scores highly.

That isn't strange when you think about it. Prisoners know better than anyone else how terrifying life is, how dangerous and unpredictable. You can be haunted, the tide is against you, the wind is raging, you feel power-less, you sink deeper and deeper and the water comes up to your neck.

'I like it that he walked on the water,' they say. 'Don't think that I believe it, of course,' they say immediately afterwards, 'because it's impossible to walk on water. You sink.' You hear the sorrow in their voice and their longing. How marvellous it would be if you could, for then it is possible.

Jesus sets foot on the waters. As if he's God himself! For that's what is written of the Eternal One in the book of Job. He tramples the waves of the sea. And that's also how the Eternal One is celebrated in the psalms and by the prophets, as *One who makes a way through the sea, a path through mighty waters.**

Mark refers back to these mythical images to express what the encounter with Jesus has done to him. Jesus set his feet on the flood and walked on the sea; there was a power which bore him up. So this man of Nazareth strode over the sea of life in the firm conviction that nothing could separate him from the love of God. In so doing he was anticipating the future, for this is an Easter story. Jesus treads death underfoot; he walks where there is no way. Thus he goes before his followers to the other side.

Jesus came to them and meant to pass by them.

That's how the Eternal One passed by Moses and Elijah.* That's how the Eternal One went before his people through the water, towards the promised land. Jesus wants to go before his followers so that they follow him.

But they can't. They're deadly afraid. *When they saw him walking on the sea they thought that he was a ghost and cried out.*

They don't expect him, so they see a ghost and become even more afraid than they already were. They don't see that it's Jesus who wants to go before them and so they can't follow him. Then Jesus climbs into the boat. *'Take heart, I am here, do not be afraid.'*

I am here. The messenger of the God with the name *I am*, who made a way for his people through the sea. Don't you remember?*

No, they don't know it, they remember very little.

The wind and the waves begin to subside, but there is no longer any question of sailing to the other side. Weary and deeply disappointed, the disciples go back to Gennesaret. The crossing has failed.

23

MAN-MADE

MARK 7.1-23

Pharisees and scribes come from Jerusalem to Jesus. Are they on a tour of inspection to question Jesus?

'Why do your disciples transgress the tradition of the elders? Why don't they wash their hands before eating?'

This tradition of the elders isn't old; the commandment about washing hands before food is quite late and moreover doesn't appear in the Torah. The commandment really applies only to pilgrims on their way to the temple and in it, but there are Pharisees who make a daily practice of it. They see themselves as 'pilgrims for life', and clearly they're the ones who criticize Jesus because he and his disciples don't observe this commandment.

According to Jesus, however, obedience to scripture takes precedence over the practice of the Pharisees. 'Shall I tell you something? You're hypocrites. Isaiah would say: 'You honour the Eternal One with your lips, but your heart is far from him, your fear of the Lord is useless, for what you teach as holy commandments are simply human rules.'* You observe human tradition, but meanwhile you abandon God's commandments. Let me give you an example. Moses said: Honour your father and your mother. And also: Whoever curses his parents must be put to death.* He said that because in their old age parents are dependent on their children. But you allow people to dedicate their money and possessions as an offering to the temple, to avoid having to do anything for their father and mother. So these are left to their fate. You use the tradition, which is man-made, to evade the word of God. And that's only one example!'

On another occasion Jesus said to the crowd: *'Hear me, all of you, and understand. There is nothing outside a person which by going into him can defile him. Only the things that come out of a person defile him.'*

For according to some Pharisees you become unclean by consuming food that has been touched by an unclean person. And Jesus is just as opposed to this new regulation as he is to the regulation about washing hands. Even the disciples are amazed at this. When they got home they asked him what his words meant.

Jesus said: 'Do you too understand so little? Surely it isn't difficult? Whatever goes in from outside can't defile a person; it doesn't end up in the heart but in the stomach, and from there it lands in the cesspit. But what comes out of the *heart* makes a person unclean.'

In saying this Jesus declared all foods clean.

In all probability these last words are Mark's. That Jesus abolished the food laws of the Torah is improbable in itself, but in particular it can't be reconciled with the preceding story, in which Jesus actually criticized the Pharisees for abolishing the biblical commandment.

So it must be Mark's messianic community which declares all foods clean. Why?

To avoid a complicated problem. In those days the gospel was spreading everywhere and there was a need to tackle the burning question whether the pagans who had come to believe in the God of Israel also had to accept Israel's food laws.

Along with the majority of the first Christian community, which was for the most part Jewish, Mark judged that these laws mustn't form a barrier for the Christians from the pagan world who were going to belong to the people of God. In his judgment the gospel could also be proclaimed in the world without these laws.

24

CRUMBS FOR THE DOGS

MARK 7.24-30

All food is in principle clean; the food laws may no longer form a barrier; the gospel of God can enter the world freely. In fact it took a long time for the followers of Jesus to assimilate this notion, and perhaps there was even a development in the thinking of Jesus himself. We could at least infer this from the following story, the story of a woman from the pagan world.

And Jesus arose and went from there to the region of Tyre.

Jesus is again entering pagan territory. He isn't doing so in order to turn to the pagans. He's in search of peace and quiet and wants to spend some time anonymously on foreign soil. But there he doesn't remain unnoticed; a Greek woman recognizes him, the mother of a daughter who is possessed. *She heard of Jesus.* For Mark, believing ears are needed if that is to happen; he immediately makes us aware that in this region the sower's seed has fallen on good soil.

'*Sir, my daughter is possessed. I want you to drive this devil out of her.*'

'*First the children must be fed, for it is not right to take the children's bread and throw it to the dogs.*'

What now? Is Jesus annoyed because his rest has been disturbed? Does he retort so roughly because the preaching in his own country is already a heavy burden on his shoulders? And why does he use that disparaging word *dogs*? Does he still see a pagan as unclean, as someone who lives like a dog? Of course the bread which the Eternal One gives is first given to the children of Israel. But isn't Israel called to go to the end of the earth to share it? Is Jesus so weary and battered by what he has to endure in his own land that he has nothing more to spare for this pagan woman and her child?

'*Woman, it is not right to take the children's bread and throw it to the dogs.*'

'Yes, sir, yet even the dogs under the table eat the children's crumbs.'

The Greek woman won't be put off. She fights for her sick child and she fights for her sacred conviction: 'All right, I'm one of the dogs, sir, I don't dispute it. But why don't you let some crumbs drop from the table so that the children don't go short? Surely God's love for Israel doesn't grow less if we pagans also share in it.'

Jesus uses the metaphor as a weapon to ward off the woman. Now she beats him at his own game. In theological disputes he won't give way, but this woman from the pagans surprises him and he confesses himself beaten. As if he was only now beginning to understand his own gospel properly, now that he's told it by another.

'Go home, the devil has already gone out of your daughter.'

When she gets home, the Greek woman finds her child lying in bed. The evil demon has disappeared.

A special story. Jesus' initial, point-blank refusal alarms us. Must even Jesus be cured of a prejudice? In Mark's days it was difficult for Israel to turn towards the world of the pagans. Does the evangelist want to show that Jesus too had difficulties here and only gradually arrived at the insight that God has to do not only with the sheep of Israel but equally with the 'dogs' across the border? Perhaps Mark hopes that his Jewish readers, just like Jesus in his time, will begin to realize through this Greek woman that God's mercy knows no bounds.

25

EPHPHATHA

MARK 7.31-37; 8.1-9

Thus a pagan woman and her sick child are freed from their suffering. In now adding a story about the healing of a pagan man, Mark is giving a good illustration of how salvation is destined for the whole human family.

Jesus travelled via Sidon to the heart of the land of the Ten Towns. There people brought to him a man who was deaf and also could hardly speak; and they begged Jesus to lay hands on this man.

What does Isaiah say again, dreaming of the messianic time? 'See, your God will come and save you. Then the ears of the deaf shall be unstopped, and the tongue of the dumb shall sing for joy.'*

Jesus took the man aside, away from the crowd.

In each of Mark's miracle stories there are some striking, apparently unimportant, details. They are never just there. They always tell something of the suffering of a person and of the special way in which Jesus deals with that person.

Jesus takes the man aside. It's as if he must first also be detached physically from the human world, from which he has cut himself off spiritually with his deafness, because he prefers to live in silence rather than in the world of hard human words. 'It's safe here, no one will disturb us. There's just the two of us, together before God's face.' Only in this way will this man be able to come to himself.

Jesus took the man aside, away from the crowd. He put his fingers into his ears, formed spittle and touched his tongue with it.

Jesus speaks body language; the ritual takes place in silence. Jesus puts his fingers into the deaf ears of this man, as if he's cautiously feeling for a way through. Then he transfers spittle from his own organ of speech to the man's tongue. It's an intimacy which does the man good.

And Jesus looked up to heaven and sighed.

Heaven is the source from which he draws comfort. May God grant that this man, too, can also find strength there to get rid of his fear of other people. Jesus sighs. The whole creation sighs, and Jesus sighs with it. 'Father, look down on him in grace, have pity.'

And he said to him, 'Ephphatha,' 'be opened.' And immediately his ears were opened, his tongue was released, and his speech was good.

Ephphatha! Be opened! Roll the stone from the tomb! Even before the word went through his ears, the man had already understood it. And he spoke. His speech was good. And Jesus heard that it was good.

It happened *immediately.* In our world it can take time for a person to find healing. In stories like this, in which time is concentrated, healings happen immediately. Eternity knows no time.

Again Jesus commands secrecy, but that's far too much to ask of this man. At last he can speak again, so how is he to keep silent? Radiant, he trumpets it around and a new song is born in the Ten Towns. However, really it was the old song of Isaiah's all over again.

> *He has done all things well;*
> *he makes the deaf hear,*
> *to the voiceless he gives a voice.*

So a man, a woman and a child from among the pagans have experienced God's goodness. The bread of life is there for the children of Israel, and it is just as much there for the peoples. And in order to emphasize that once more, Mark tells another story of a miraculous multiplication of loaves. The second story is as like the first as two peas, but there are a couple of striking differences. In the second story not five, but seven loaves are shared, and not five thousand people, but four thousand are fed. And it isn't twelve baskets that are left over but seven.

Anyone who thinks logically must conclude that Jesus' magical power is diminishing. But those who know that there is more to this than meets the eye, those who have been initiated into Jewish number symbolism, will sense that God's good gifts are infinitely multiplied. For in Israel four is more than five and seven more than twelve. If the five and the twelve stand for Israel, the four stands for the world and the seven for fullness. First salvation is given to Israel, and from there it spreads to the four points of the compass.

The first feeding took place in Galilee, on Israel's side of the sea. It will be clear that Mark sets the second feeding on the other side, in the land of the pagans. It is there that Jesus of Nazareth has also given the bread of life to the *goyim.*

26

SLOW LEARNERS

MARK 8.10-21

Immediately after that, Jesus went on board ship with his disciples and he came to the region of Dalmanutha. The Pharisees came out and began to dispute with him.

They're back in Galilee and the conflict with the spiritual leaders of the people is flaring up again. The Pharisees ask themselves where Jesus gets these miraculous signs from. However, this isn't a real question; they can't see Jesus as a holy one of God and so his arts have to come from the devil. *And they asked of him a sign from heaven.*

Jesus sighs deeply. What drives them is not a desire for God; they simply want to tempt him. They challenge him to convince them with a sign from heaven. Only in this way will he be able to gain recognition in their world. As if Jesus would ever use his power to do this! As if he would ever leave his world for this, and as if in their world they would immediately understand a sign from heaven! Their world is the world of unbelief, of the age-old longing for a God who irrefutably demonstrates that he is with us and who frees us from the burden of being human with a wave of his wand. *'Truly, I tell you, it will be a long time before a sign is given to your type of person.'*

Jesus turned round and went back on board ship.

Do the disciples sense what is up here? If they don't understand it now, how will they be able to later, when Jesus is no longer in their midst and they have to stand up to temptations like this in their own power?

'Be careful to keep your eyes wide open. Look out and beware of the leaven of the Pharisees and of the leaven of Herod.'

Beware of Herod, for although he may listen to you now and then, you can end up beheaded. And beware just as much of the theologians who spread themselves and begin to get in the way between human beings and

God. Look out for the leaven with which these men make themselves great, the yeast with which they make themselves rise.

Do the disciples hear Jesus' words?

No, the disciples are only half listening. They're preoccupied with something else. Not with leaven but with bread. They've discovered that there's only one loaf on board, and good heavens, what are they to do?

Mark's story begins to assume the form of a farce. For the third time the disciples have taken ship with Jesus, for the third time there's a shortage of food, and for the third time they're anxious about this. As if Jesus hasn't already multiplied the bread twice! To say that the disciples of Jesus are slow learners is putting it mildly. They travel over the water with the bread of life on board, bread for the hearts of both Jews and pagans, but they still can't see it.

'Why all this "We have no bread" talk? Hasn't it dawned on you yet? Is your heart hardened too? You've eyes in your head but you see nothing; you've ears but you hear nothing. When I broke the five loaves for the five thousand, how any baskets of fragments did you gather up?'

'Twelve.'

'And from the seven loaves I broke for the four thousand, how many basketsful did you gather up then?'

'Seven.'

'And you still don't see it?'

No, they still don't see it. They know the good news, but it hasn't become a power in their souls.

The question arises whether we, the readers, see it. Fortunately the book isn't yet finished. And the Gospel teaches that blind men can come to see.

27

THE BLIND MAN OF BETHSAIDA

MARK 8.22-26

And they came to Bethsaida. And some people brought to him a blind man, and begged him to touch him.

Bethsaida is on the other side of the sea of Galilee, in pagan country. It had already been the disciples' destination earlier, but they failed to cross and never reached the village then. Fortunately for the blind man they now set foot on the shore.

Twice Jesus has stilled a storm. Twice he's multiplied loaves. Twice he's touched a deaf man in the territory of the Ten Towns. Ephphatha! And this man's ears were opened.

It can only be that Jesus will now also touch the blind man of Bethsaida twice. The disciples are deaf and blind, so it's best to say everything twice; perhaps it will slowly dawn on them.

And Jesus took the blind man by the hand and led him out of the village.

The story is the spitting image of the story of the deaf man. To all appearances this man, too, has had to cut himself off from a reality which he could no longer see. Eyes closed, door closed, he no longer wants to see anyone; he becomes blind, and the wicked outside world magically disappears. Therefore Jesus takes him by the hand and leads him out of the village, outside. May God grant that, set apart, far from human gaze, together with Jesus before the face of the Lord, he will rediscover himself. Then it will no longer be intolerable for him to be looked in the eyes and to look others in the eye.

Jesus put spittle on his eyes and laid hands on him. 'Can you see anything?'

The actions are as simple as in the case of the deaf man earlier. Again Jesus acts like a mother who strokes her sick child and smears the painful place with spittle. Just as she reassures her anxious child with mouth and hands that it's as safe and sound as if it were still in her warm womb, so too Jesus is near to this blind man, with mouth and hands. He strokes him and smears with spittle his eyes, the place where the pain of his life is. In that way he wants to get through to this human child that he's a child of God, safe and sound. Jesus' own mission had also begun with such an experience of happiness: 'You are my son, in you I am well pleased.'

But it's difficult for a blind man to gain sight from one moment to the next. It has to grow, and that takes time.

'Can you see anything?'

'I can see people, they're like trees, walking trees.'

Truly it's beginning to dawn on him. But people aren't trees. He can't yet see the people as people, as brothers, sisters. He still stands apart, and isn't yet one human being among others. But in the presence of Jesus he will gradually be able to sharpen his gaze without immediately falling victim to fear again. Gradually his sight will become clearer.

Again Jesus laid his hands on his eyes, and now his sight was good again, just as before.

This man has looked on the light of life again. He's been born anew. So Jesus makes him first go home and not immediately into the village. It's better first to get used to the world a bit in the intimacy of the family circle before again going back into the bustle of people. Small beginnings.

28

WHO DO PEOPLE SAY THAT I AM?

MARK 8.27-9.1

Jesus went with his disciples to the villages around Caesarea Philippi.

Jesus is now north of Israel's northern frontier, again in pagan territory. So he's steadily getting further from home. But surely he was sent in the first place to the children of Israel? Really he should be going in precisely the opposite direction, south, to Judah, to Jerusalem, to the heart of Israel.

But that will become one great way of suffering; death awaits him there. Must he take it?

Jesus is in two minds, on the frontier between two worlds. Shall he turn away from Israel and remain here, or shall he go? What is he to do? Who is he? And if he goes, then will he have to go alone?

'Who do people say that I am?'

'Some say that you are John the Baptist, others Elijah, yet others one of the prophets.'

A question then and a question for all times. Who is he? Time and again this question, and always different answers. John the Baptist. Elijah. A prophet. King of the Jews. Lamb of God. Good Shepherd. Blasphemer. Son of David. Son of Beelzebul. Redeemer. Bread of Life. Judge. The Way, the Truth and the Life. Man of Sorrows. Lord of the Dance. Mystic. Revolutionary. King of Glory. Superstar. Mediator.

He conjures up so many notions, so many images, the patron of those who escape the world and those who seek to improve it. There is the Jesus of Rembrandt and Chagall, of Bach and Elgar, of Julian of Norwich and Calvin, of Francis and Teresa of Avila, of Renan and Schweitzer, of my mother and my neighbour's child.

'And you, who do you say that I am?'

Peter replied. He's the spokesman of the disciples, and in him they all speak. *'You are the Messiah.'*

The great word is out. Peter confesses what the first Christian community confesses, and what Mark has already confessed in the first line of his Gospel: Jesus is the Messiah.

But Jesus impressed on him that he should say nothing about this to anyone.

Does Peter know what he's saying? Jesus isn't the kind of Messiah that people expect. If Jesus is to go to Jerusalem, it isn't to drive out the occupying forces; his kingdom is of another order. He will go, faithful to his calling, to portray the love of God in the heart of Israel. Do Peter and the others sense what awaits him there?

He began to teach them openly that he must suffer many things and that he would be rejected by the elders and the chief priests and the scribes.

Peter isn't prepared for that. Is Jesus to be a suffering Messiah and not a triumphant Messiah? Peter is afraid of following a Messiah whose way will be a way of suffering. *He took Jesus aside and began to protest vigorously.* 'Surely you aren't telling us that...'

This provokes just as vigorous a reaction from Jesus, for this is a temptation, a diabolical temptation. Peter wants to divert him from his high calling and to bring him back to the human world, where all suffering must be avoided at any cost. Peter wants to bar his way to Jerusalem. He mustn't do that. He must just follow him on this way. *'Get behind me, Satan! You are not guided by God's plans but by human plans.'*

Jesus didn't speak to Peter only about his approaching suffering; he also said that *he would rise from the dead on the third day.* That can prove surprising: a person on the stage who in the first act describes how he will be murdered in the second act in order to rise again in the third act. As if Jesus so to speak already knows about Easter on Good Friday. But of course in a story that's possible.

In the Bible *on the third day* isn't an indication of time but a stereotyped formula which indicates that after a time of suffering, salvation from God will dawn. In other words, when Jesus speaks of his approaching death, in the same breath he also bears witness to his trust in God. He believed – a belief which he shared with many – in the resurrection of the dead. He goes his way in fear and trembling, at the same time trusting that God will have mercy on him.

The evangelist adds a few words for anyone who wants to follow Jesus on this way: *'If anyone would come after me, let him deny himself, take up his cross and follow me.'*

Mark is all too well aware what kind of way that is; in those days it is dangerous to follow Jesus. Many are tempted to deny him. Those who do not want to deny Jesus must deny themselves, take up their crosses and follow him.

Self-denial isn't the opposite of self-fulfilment. Jesus doesn't call for a self-denial which deforms people in their growth, which makes them sick. What he wants to open their eyes to is that God can ask people to abstain from merely satisfying their own desires for the sake of the kingdom.

'Whoever would save his life will lose it, and whoever loses his life for my sake and the gospel's shall save it. For what does it profit a man to gain the whole world and harm his soul?'

Those whose main concern is to save their skins can easily miss their calling. Those who trust in God and abandon a self-centredness which is governed by fear will be blessed in life.

'Whoever is ashamed of me and my words in this adulterous and sinful generation, of him shall the Son of man be ashamed when he comes in the glory of his Father with the holy angels.'

Does this terrifying saying come from Jesus, or is it Mark who is putting pressure on his readers and impressing on them that they mustn't fail when they stand before their judges? Those who remain faithful to the One in a world full of adultery, who stand up for Jesus and his words, will find Jesus standing up for them when they appear before the throne of God and his holy angels. Above all they mustn't lose heart. The kingdom can come at any moment, it won't be long...

'Truly, I tell you, there are some standing in our midst who will not taste the cup of death before they have seen the kingdom of God coming in power.'

Jesus lived in the expectation that the kingdom of God would dawn speedily. The first Christian community had to get used to the fact that the kingdom had failed to materialize. Did Jesus make a mistake? And who says that it will ever come?

29

THE TRANSFIGURATION
ON THE MOUNTAIN

MARK 9.2-13

Jesus will take the way to Jerusalem. It will be a long and lonely way, as the disciples won't be good at following him. Jesus is reminded of the great Moses and how he persisted, sent by God to be in the midst of a people that didn't understand. And where did the prophet Elijah get the power from to accomplish his task? Jesus lifted up his eyes to the hills. Where would his help come from?

Six days later Jesus took Peter and James and John with him and led them up a high mountain.

This must be Moses' mountain, the mountain where heaven and earth touch. Moses met God there. *The glory of the Lord rested upon the mountain and the cloud covered him for six days. On the seventh day God called to Moses from the midst of the cloud.** After that Moses went down again, with God's holy Torah in his hand. He shone. His face radiated such heavenly light that he had to veil himself when he approached the people who were waiting for him down below.*

This mountain is also Elijah's mountain, that other figure from the high hills of the spirit. Didn't Elijah also seek his salvation there on the heights in an hour of desperation? And hadn't God also revealed himself to him there, in the rustling of a gentle breeze?*

Jesus led them up a high mountain. And his form was transfigured before their eyes; his garments shone with glistening whiteness, as no fuller on earth could whiten them. And Elijah appeared to him, along with Moses, and they were talking with Jesus.

Jesus has gone up the mountain. He is seeking to be near to God. And look, Elijah and Moses, his shining examples, appear to him. They appear to him because he so wants them. He summons them, as it were, himself. From childhood he's had dealings with them; he's constantly been in conversation with the two of them, with the Torah and the Prophets. Wherever he went, people were reminded of Moses and Elijah. 'Moses is again in our midst,' they would then call, or 'Elijah has returned.'

Now they appeared to him on the mountain of God. As if the Eternal One had sent them to strengthen him. The two figures who have been so close to him from the cradle will accompany him to the grave.

Moses is there to put heart into him. He died in sight of the promised land, and there the Eternal One buried him with his own hands. Like a mother, God had pity on him and covered him, and no one to the present day knows where his grave is. He's safe with God.

Elijah is there to strengthen him. He went up to heaven in a fiery chariot, borne up by the breath of the Eternal One. He too is safe with God.

Jesus beamed when he saw their familiar faces. Suffering and death awaited him, but on this mountain it was already Easter. Jesus knows that he should persevere, like Moses and Elijah before him. His garments will be drenched with blood, but in God's glory they will be shining white, whiter than a fuller on earth could make them.

A vision. A peak experience. The Torah, the Prophets and the Gospel meet. Time no longer counts; the clocks stand still; God's clock stands at eternity. And Peter wants to perpetuate this heavenly scene. *'Rabbi, how good it is that we are here! Let us set up three tents, one for you, one for Moses and one for Elijah.' For he did not know what to say, they were so afraid.*

Afraid that this beautiful dream will come to an end, afraid to go to Jerusalem. He just says the first thing that comes into his head.

Then a cloud overshadowed them and a voice resounded from this cloud: 'This is my Son, my beloved, listen to him.'

This is the voice with which it all began on the bank of the Jordan, the voice which Jesus heard when he was being baptized: 'You are my Son.' Now the voice addresses his followers. Anyone who wants to hear God must listen to his Son. Just like his Father.

Then, looking round, they no longer saw anyone with them but Jesus only.

They aren't to build tents on the mountain; they have to go back to the valley. Jesus will pursue his way.

And as they were coming down the mountain, Jesus charged them to tell no one what they had seen, until he had risen from the dead.

We may not say too early that Jesus is God's Son. What that means can be understood only in the light of the cross. Only gradually will the meaning of the saying that Jesus is Messiah be disclosed. Until then it's better to be silent.

Peter, James and John tried to understand what this might mean: rise from the dead.

These are the same three disciples who were there to witness the raising of Jairus's daughter and who on the mountain were there to witness how Moses and Elijah appeared in glory. And yet they ask what rising from the dead may mean!

Jesus will indeed have to go his way alone.

30

THE POSSESSED MAN IN THE VALLEY

MARK 9.14-29

Jesus and the three disciples who accompanied him have come down from the mountain. Peter wanted to remain up there, but that was impossible. True mysticism never leads to flight from the world as long as there are people living in the valley who also long for a glimpse of heaven, a word from the heights, an act of love. *The people hastened to Jesus and welcomed him.*

He comes as if he'd been sent for; the disciples who've been left behind are entangled in a vigorous dispute with the scribes. It seems to have something to do with a sick child.

'What are you arguing about?'

A man comes forward. *'Rabbi, I have come to you with my son. He has a spirit which prevents him from speaking. Whenever this spirit seizes him – and that can happen at any moment – it throws him to the ground; the boy foams at the mouth, gnashes his teeth and becomes quite rigid.'*

Here's another story about a father and a son. If the previous story was set in high glory, now we're in the valley of a possessed world, a universe away.

The boy is clearly suffering from a form of epilepsy, and the father is suffering from his son's suffering. There's a tormenting spirit inside him which attacks unexpectedly and no one can prevent this happening. *'I asked your disciples to drive him out, and they were not able.'*

Jesus sighs. Surely the disciples know that faith can heal people? *'You unbelieving generation, how long have I to be in your midst, how long can I go on bearing you? Bring the boy to me.'*

They brought him to Jesus. And as soon as the demon saw Jesus, it convulsed the boy so that he fell and rolled about on the ground, foaming at the mouth.

'How long has he had this?' asked Jesus.

'From his childhood up. More than once the demon has driven him into the fire or into the water to destroy him. If you can do anything, help us; have pity on us.'

'If you can do anything...? Everything is possible for the one who believes!'

Faith is always faith that things can be different. And the father understands that unless he is completely open to that and entrusts himself completely to Jesus, no healing can be expected. *'I believe. Help my unbelief.'*

The father stops being anxious and gives in: *'I believe.'* But these words trigger off new fear. Isn't he saying too much, too quickly? How ever will he be able to go this way of self-surrender without help? *'Help my unbelief.'*

Belief is always about unbelief, and with this confession this father has comforted countless people for centuries. 'Lord, I trust you. Help me with my lack of trust.'

Jesus rebuked the evil spirit: 'I, Jesus, command you: go out of this boy and never return to him again.'

With a loud cry and a vigorous convulsion the demon went out of him, but it seemed that he had taken all the boy's liveliness with him. The boy lay on the ground like a corpse. 'He's dead,' said the people. But Jesus took his hand and made him arise.

Fear can make a person sick and faith can heal a person. Through the Son of the Father, the father of the son could let go of his fear and free his faith. The child was healed.

'Why couldn't *we* drive out that demon?,' asked the disciples that evening in dejection.

'You can only do it with the power of prayer,' said Jesus.

It can only be done in solidarity with God. Only those who themselves trust in God can awaken trust in God in others and bring them healing.

31

A CHILD IN THE MIDST

MARK 9.30-50

Jesus and his followers travel through Galilee in the direction of Jerusalem. They avoid the main roads and the villages; now teaching the disciples has priority. It won't be long now before they're on their own. Do they see the seriousness of the situation?

Jesus said to them: 'The Son of Man will be delivered into the hands of men and they will kill him. Three days after his death he will rise.'

Hasn't Jesus already told them that?

Yes. But that he seems to have chosen to go the way of suffering is so strange and incomprehensible to the disciples that it has to be said more than once. Perhaps now it will get through to them.

That's a vain hope. Again they can't grasp the meaning of these words and, afraid of what the answer could be, they daren't ask Jesus about their meaning. They prefer to get round to another question: *which among them is the greatest?*

The greatest in what? The boldest, the richest, the most powerful, the most pious? Perhaps a little bit of everything.

'What were you discussing on the way?' Jesus asks when they arrive in Capernaum.

The disciples are silent. Do they feel trapped? Jesus knows all too well what they were discussing with one another on the way. He's going to Jerusalem, and they're talking about who is the first. That's the last thing you need to bother about on this way.

Jesus went to sit down, called all twelve together and said to them: *'If anyone will be the first, then he must become the last and the servant of all.'*

All twelve have to be told that the kingdom of God isn't about power but about service. God is different.

God is different. With him the last become the first. God is served by serving the least, people without form or majesty. *And Jesus took a child and put it in the midst of them and embraced it. 'Whoever receives such a child in my name receives me. And whoever receives me receives not me but the one who sent me.'*

You must receive such a child *in my name*. Not for yourself, not to boss it around or to relieve your loneliness. Solely *in my name*.

Now one might expect a long silence in that house, to allow this thought to sink in. But John thinks it advisable to change the subject. 'Talking about *in my name*,' he says, 'we saw someone who isn't one of us busy casting out evil spirits in your name. We quickly intervened, for this exorcist isn't one of us.'

There's chutzpah for you! The disciples are pretty average when it comes to driving out demons, but they obstruct someone who is good at this because he isn't *one of us*. Clearly John expects to earn Jesus' praise for this vigorous intervention.

'Leave this man alone,' said Jesus. 'Anyone who has done a miracle in my name won't be quick to speak evil of me afterwards. Anyone who isn't against us is for us.'

And so that soon the disciples don't think in a narrow-minded way when they have to take over from Jesus, Mark adds another saying of Jesus: 'Look, you will be persecuted and will have to flee. Know that anyone who gives you a cup of water in my name because you belong to me will surely be rewarded.'

We can find something of God in people who indiscriminately help those who have no helper. The exorcist just now, and the person with a cup of water, make something of the kingdom of God visible on earth.

Mark has another saying of Jesus about children which deserves to be recorded. This is a good moment to listen to it.

'Whoever causes one of these little ones who believe to fall would do best to put a millstone round his neck and throw himself into the sea.'

It's possible that this saying isn't about children but about grown-ups who are as small and defenceless as children when they're being persecuted and tortured for their faith. Mark knows those benevolent outsiders who offer a persecuted Christian a cup of water, and the malicious bystanders who set out to make the followers of Jesus stumble. However, the temptations can just as easily come from within. What's to be done then?

'If your hand threatens to bring you down, cut it off. It is better for you to enter life maimed than with two hands to go to hell, to the unquenchable fire.

If your foot threatens to bring you down, cut if off. It is better for you to enter life lame than with two feet to be thrown into hell.

And if your eye threatens to bring you down, pluck it out. It is better for you to enter the kingdom of God with one eye than with two eyes to be thrown into hell, where the worm does not die and the fire is not quenched.'

To many people, these sayings suggest primarily sexual transgressions, but on the way to the kingdom there are many kinds of temptation, certainly in times of persecution. Mark impresses on his fellow believers that they must be strong at all times. In order to remain on course it can sometimes be necessary to cut into one's own flesh. For Mark, that's the way of the kingdom. It's the way which Jesus also went. This way ends up with God.

According to Mark, on the other side of death a person can land in either heaven or in hell. He doesn't dwell further on the matter, but that needn't prevent us from doing so by way of a postscript.

Let's presuppose that we *know* nothing, either about a heaven or about a hell. But we may brood on the matter.

We dream of a heaven. Is that wishful thinking?

That goes without saying. We don't want to believe that with death it's all over. Beyond doubt the wish is father to the thought. But that isn't the point. The question is whether we may believe that we have a Father who has the same wish in his thoughts. There comes an end to the love and care that one human being can devote to another: death intervenes. Does it also intervene with God, the God who invented loving care? Do things also stop with death for God? That's hardly credible.

Then is there also such a thing as a hell?

We also fantasize over that, and of course this fantasy isn't as crazy as all that. The God who gave us life will certainly also want to ask us what we've done with it. No, we still don't *know*, but it's hard to imagine that God is indifferent to the way in which we've used our talents. So it isn't so strange a notion that there is some reward in heaven for those who fed the hungry and clothed the naked and stood up for a child. In that case should the villain also get what he deserves, or does he have an advantage over his victim not only in time but also in eternity? Is it a purely human desire for vengeance – however understandable – that makes us sketch out a hell?

If we're responsible people – and we all want to be that; who wants to be said to be of diminished responsibility? – then God does a person justice once he holds that person responsible. That's a terrifying but also a mature thought.

So the images of heaven and hell introduce some tension into life here below. This can be a healthy tension; it can also be a pernicious tension. There is belief which makes people sick and belief which heals them. The thought of it can maim a person; it can also form a person.

Someone once asked Pope John XXIII: 'Holy Father, does hell exist?' 'Certainly,' said the pope in reply. 'But there's no one in it.'

The Holy Father isn't playing around with the tradition; he thinks that hell is a valuable fantasy of faith. But hell is empty. That happens with a God who loves people. So don't be afraid. And don't be vengeful either.

32

WHAT GOD HAS JOINED TOGETHER...

MARK 10.1-12

Jesus arose and went to the region of Judaea and beyond the Jordan.

Up to Jerusalem, the heart of Israel, *the* place for God and his people to meet each other. It's there especially that the Eternal One of Israel bears witness to his love and faithfulness and it's there that the 'Yes' of his beloved can resound. Jesus goes up to Jerusalem, like a bridegroom on the way to his bride's house.

Speaking of love and faithfulness: some Pharisees once had a dispute with Jesus there. It seems to Mark that this is a good moment to relate it. It's a story about the alliance between husband and wife, but that alliance is also a model of the alliance between God and human beings.

Pharisees came to Jesus, and to test him they asked: 'Is it lawful for a man to put away his wife?'

That was a disputed question in those days. The question whether a wife may put away her husband hasn't yet been raised; the thinking is exclusively in terms of the husband. According to the Torah of Moses, the husband is justified in giving his wife a letter of divorce if she's done something *unseemly,* but the rabbis differed over precisely what was unseemly and what wasn't. *'What has Moses commanded you?,'* asks Jesus.

'Moses allowed a man to write a letter of divorce and to put away his wife.'

'You know very well that Moses wrote that commandment because of the hardness of your hearts.'

The letter of divorce was legally regulated in such a way as to limit the arbitrariness of the husband and to protect the wife as the weaker party because she had no rights. Here this rule is used by some Pharisees to confirm the right of the husband. But what does sacred doctrine teach? What did God have in mind when he created man and woman?

'Let me take you back to the beginning, to the garden of paradise of which the Torah tells. God created humankind, male and female created he them, two human children who long to be one together. That's what God had in mind: these two are one. Why are you so rigidly and lovelessly busy with all these laws and regulations? Where's your concern for the woman who can be sent packing without so much as a penny in her purse? Truly, God was dreaming of something else when he created heaven and earth. He was dreaming of a man and a woman who find warmth and protection with each other. Don't forget that we're talking about a mystery from God's garden, we're talking about God's gift of love. *What God has joined together, no human being must separate.*'

Later this saying of Jesus was again made into a new law to condemn men and women who couldn't hold their marriage together. But initially Jesus wasn't talking about what we now call divorce, namely the adult decision of two people who have grown so far apart that their marriage is no longer worthy of the name. Moreover, Jesus isn't giving an irrevocable commandment; his words are more a pastoral admonition to human beings not to break apart what God has joined together. A faith community may never commandeer such a statement. Nowhere is it said that what *the church* has put together, human beings may not separate.

'What God has joined together no human being must separate.'
Jesus is speaking about a great mystery. For doesn't the relationship between man and woman also have something to do with the relationship between God and human beings? Doesn't earthly love point beyond itself to a Creator who created human beings, man and woman, out of love?

It's precisely in order to depict this that Jesus is on the way to Jerusalem, his beloved. With a last effort he shows that God wants to join together what human beings have separated. He can't remain separated from Zion if he wants to be faithful to the love of God. Faithful till death.

33

BECOME LIKE A CHILD

MARK 10.13-16

And they brought children to Jesus for him to touch them, but the disciples rebuked them.

Why? Why were the disciples so hard on those fathers and mothers who so wanted the man of God to touch their children? Is faith only for grown-up children, those who behave in an orderly way?

Jesus sees that in their zeal the disciples are again missing the point and reprimands them: *'Let the children come to me, do not hinder them, for the kingdom of God is for precisely such children.'*

The kingdom of God isn't something which is *also* for children; it's *primarily* for children. And for adults who become like children. A child is still completely dependent on receiving. A child's heart beats full of expectation. A child isn't bothered about power and wealth, and as yet has no achievements of its own to appeal too. A child has no cares, because father and mother take care of it and will also do so tomorrow. We love children simply for being there.

'Truly I say to you, whoever does not receive the kingdom of God as a child will certainly not enter into it.'

So a person must change decisively if he or she wants to become a child of God. Grown-up people's longings for wealth and power must be set aside. We have to rediscover a childlike simplicity. We have to give up fantasies of greatness in exchange for the stronger feeling that we're already accepted, weakness and all, that we're loved, simply because we're here.

Jesus is firmly convinced that 'the children' of this earth, 'the little ones', are God's real favourites. Did Jesus have a psalm in mind when he called on grown-up people to become like children, and when he embraced children, laid hands on them and gave them the blessing?

Lord, my heart is not haughty,
my eyes are not too proud,
I do not occupy myself in great matters,
or in matters which are too marvellous for me.
For I have calmed and quieted my soul,
like a child that has drunk at its mother's breast;
like a child that has drunk,
so is my soul within me.*

34

A FAILED CALLING

MARK 10.17-31

Adults can very well enter the kingdom of God, but they will find more obstacles in the way than children, because they're really too big for it. And a rich man will find more obstacles than a poor man, because he has so much to lose.

Just listen.

Jesus is pursuing his way. A man rushes up to him, falls on his knees before him and asks, *'Good master, what must I do to obtain eternal life?'*

No longer a child, a well-to-do man. But also an anxious man, uncertain about the way to go. Apparently he has all that his heart desires, but in kneeling he confesses his pain because real life is passing him by. 'Good master, what must I do to share in it?'

'Why do you call me good? No one is good but God alone. You know the commandments: "Do not kill. Do not commit adultery. Do not steal. Do not bear false witness. Do not defraud. Honour your father and mother."'

Why so anxious, my friend? No one is good but God alone. God *is*, and God is *good*. Let this thought free you from all your uncertainty and all your anxiety. And just observe the commandments.

'Master, all these have I observed from my youth.'

Jesus looked on him and loved him.

This man is so honest in his restlessness and in his striving for the good. Despite his efforts, the kingdom of God has remained an alien and distant reality for him. He's a seeker, but he can't find what he's looking for, nor can he buy it, either with his money or with his virtues. What is there between this child of man who is no longer a child and the kingdom of God?

'One thing you lack, go, sell all that you have and give it to the poor, and you shall have a treasure in heaven. Then return and follow me.'

God *is*, and God is *good*. If that's at the heart of your life, you needn't cling on to your money and your possessions. You've found your security in God; the Eternal One is your wealth and the ground of your existence. *The Lord is my shepherd, I shall lack nothing.* Those who know that God holds them fast can let go of everything else without losing anything. Then they're like children who have no trouble parting with their toys because they've grown out of them. 'Go, sell all you have and give to the poor.'

His face fell and he went away sorrowful, for he had many possessions.

A failed calling? At all events for the moment, the sower's seed has fallen among the thorns, *where it is choked by earthly cares and the fascination of riches.**

Just imagine that this man had done what Jesus asked him. Then the world would have been richer by a poor man and an eccentric: someone who opted for poverty as an expression of the highest freedom and a deep security. But he didn't. He couldn't make it. He went away sorrowful.

The disciples, too, are defeated. In desperation they look at Jesus. And Jesus looks at them.

'*Children, how hard it is to enter the kingdom of God. It is easier for a camel to go through the eye of a needle than for a rich man to enter the kingdom of God.*'

Jesus calls them children. Children of the one Father who *is,* and is *good.* Brothers and sisters who find among one another the riches of a new sense of security when, following Jesus, they've given up their former support: family, money and possessions. Isn't their reward great, already now and soon in eternal life, when the first shall be last and the last first?

The children are afraid. All doors on earth open before those who have money and possessions, but not the door of the kingdom of God. '*Who then can be saved?*'

Jesus looked at them.

'*For human beings it is impossible, but not for God. For all things are possible with God.*'

Not only must a rich man give up a great deal; everyone must become detached, and so it's difficult, if not impossible, for anyone really to become poor in spirit. But if the power of the spirit of God comes over a person, it *is* possible.

Jesus' followers felt extremely uncomfortable about this, and that has never changed.

35

BLIND THOUGH SEEING

MARK 10.32-45

They were on the way, going up to Jerusalem, and Jesus went before them, and those who followed became very uncertain. They were afraid.

For where does this way lead? Where does it end up? And why is Jesus taking it?

It's the way of the Messiah. But it will be a way of suffering, and that is such a terrifying thought that people would rather block it off. So Mark makes Jesus speak about it for the third time.

Jesus took the twelve aside: 'Look, we are going up to Jerusalem, and the Son of man will be handed over to the high priests and the scribes. They will condemn him to death, and deliver him to the Gentiles, and they will mock him, and spit upon him, and scourge him, and put him to death. And after three days he will rise.'

It's just like a Greek tragedy: we know precisely what's coming; the hero is going to meet his doom and there is no one who can avert this evil. But in contrast to Greek tragedy, God can turn the evil to good; on the third day the hero rises again from the dead.

Now Jesus has told three times of the way that he is taking and of the doom that people will prepare for him. He's also borne witness three times to his faith that this way doesn't come to a dead end, and to the salvation that God will prepare for him. Will the disciples have understood him at long last?

James and John, the two sons of Zebedee, detach themselves from the twelve, so that they can have a confidential conversation with Jesus. At last something of Jesus' words seems to have got through to them. Not about the great suffering that he was talking about – that passes them by completely – but they've picked up something about the glory of God which awaits Jesus on the other side of death.

'Master, we want to ask you to do something for us.'

'What do you want me to do for you?'

'Grant that we may sit next to you soon in your glory, one on your right hand and the other on your left.'

The sons of Zebedee have an eye on the places of honour at the messianic banquet. After all, they haven't followed Jesus from the first hour for nothing.

But what they ask for cannot be. They want to be on the heights with him; they won't grasp that the way there goes through the depths. They want to have the one without the other. That can't be. 'You do not know what you ask. Can you drink the cup that I drink or be baptized with the baptism that I am baptized with?'

The cup is the cup of suffering that he must drink. He will be submerged in the dark water of death.

'We can.'

That sounds very easy. Do they know what Jesus is talking about? As if he's looking into the future, we hear the prophet of Nazareth accept their words without further ado: 'The cup that I drink you too will drink, and the baptism with which I am baptized you too shall be baptized with.'

Mark's first readers know by now that this prophecy has been fulfilled, at any rate for James. He's been imprisoned by Herod Antipas, tortured and beheaded, so he has indeed drained the cup to the dregs.*

'But to sit at my right hand or my left is not mine to grant; that is for God.'

When did James and John see the foolishness of their question about places of honour on either side of Jesus? Was it when they saw how two robbers were crucified beside Jesus, one on his right hand and one on his left?

When the other ten disciples heard what James and John had been talking about with Jesus, they reacted indignantly. If one among the followers of the Son of man begins to exalt himself above another, where are we?

Jesus called them together: 'You know that those who are supposed to rule over the Gentiles lord it over them; you know that their great men have the supremacy over them. But it shall not be so among you. Whoever would be great among you must be the servant of all, and whoever would be first among you must be slave of all. For the Son of man came not to be served but to serve, and to give his life as a ransom for many.'

Mark is talking about the ransom for which slaves are redeemed. Hasn't

Jesus with his life of love redeemed many people from the slavery in which they were imprisoned: the obsessive striving for places of honour, for riches and power?

Any of his disciples who want to aim high will have to seek lowliness. Just like the Son of man, who came to serve, giving himself for the life of many.

Will those two and those ten finally grasp that, or will they continue to be blind though they see?

36

SEEING THOUGH BLIND

MARK 10.46-52

The way takes Jesus and his followers by Jericho, from time immemorial the last stop for pilgrims on their pilgrimage to Jerusalem. One more day's journey to go.

And as he was leaving Jericho with his disciples and a great multitude, Bartimaeus, a blind beggar, was sitting beside the way...

He's made a living from his misery and moreover he plays no part in the human traffic; he sits *beside* the way. But it's this blind man who sees what those who are following Jesus on the way don't see.

When Bartimaeus heard that Jesus of Nazareth was coming along, he began to cry out.

His hearing is still good. And he cries out. He has heard about Jesus, that messianic man through whose divine power the blind and the deaf, the lepers and the paralysed, find healing. *'Son of David, Jesus, have mercy.'* All eyes wait on you, mine in particular.

Son of David: no one has yet addressed Jesus with these messianic words. How does this blind beggar know the secret of the Son of man?

Many rebuked him, telling him to be silent.

They want him to keep his mouth shut. They want to keep their world manageable. Jesus is for people on the way, not for people beside it.

But Bartimaeus doesn't keep his mouth shut, for Jesus is coming along, that royal man from the house of David, come to serve and to seek the lost. At least, that's what he's heard, and if he's heard it right, then this man of God will certainly see him and perhaps, perhaps, he will see the man of God. Again he cries above the noise of the crowd: *'Son of David, have mercy.'*

He believes that his life can take a new turn, and that belief is his salvation. Jesus stops. He thinks the veneration of the many who are following less important than the cry for help from this one man by the roadside. *'Call him.'*

They call the blind man: *'Take heart, arise, he is calling you.'*

They can talk! First they think that this man must keep his mouth shut and stop bothering Jesus, and now they're encouraging him to go to Jesus. Their larynxes keep producing different sounds. Who knows, tomorrow they'll be crying out hosanna and the day after that something different again.

Bartimaeus throws off his mantle, leaps up and runs to Jesus.

'What do you want me to do for you?'

Jesus recently put the same question to James and John: 'What do you want me to do for you?' 'We'd very much like to receive the places of honour soon,' they said to him in their blindness. And what does the blind beggar say? *'Rabbi, that I may see again.'*

Jesus gets the right answer from Bartimaeus. He's thrown off his cloak, his beggar's garment, the image of the old life with which he wants to break.

'Go, your faith has saved you.'

Immediately Bartimaeus gained his sight. And he followed Jesus on the way.

So amongst the many who follow Jesus on his way there's at least one who isn't blind, but sees clearly.

37

LOW ON AN ASS

MARK 11.1-10

The Son of David prepares to enter the city of David, together with the many pilgrims who come to celebrate Passover there, the feast of Israel's liberation.

But does Israel still know what it's freed for? Not according to Mark. Where is the inspiration of former times? Where is the justice for the least important? Where is the radiance of God's love for all peoples? To put it in the language of fairy tales, the fair maid Jerusalem is under the spell of an evil demon, a dragon holds the daughter of Zion captive, she's bewitched. Isn't there a prince who can free her?

Mark knows that there is. For four hundred years the people has been without a prophet, but now he's standing at the door, knocking. 'Open up, my beloved, let me in.' The King's son requests an audience with lady Israel, his bride. He's already reached the foot of the Mount of Olives. God grant that new life may blossom from this new covenant.

The Mount of Olives is the place where according to the prophet Zechariah God will reveal himself at the end of times, so Mark's Jesus must go there first.* The Son of David will enter the city of David from the Mount of Olives.

How will he enter it? At the moment when Mark is writing his Gospel, it isn't long since the Roman warrior Vespasian entered Jerusalem, after the conquest of the city, with prisoners of war and the temple treasure which he had plundered. So not like that! Jesus won't enter the city as a triumphant general, high on a horse. Better as the messianic figure of whom Zechariah dreamed: a shabby king,* low on an ass.

Yes, that's how Mark will stage Jesus' entry on to the scene, as the fulfilment of Zechariah's vision. In times of bitter war and violence it was this prophet who in the spirit saw a king riding into Jerusalem, a prince of peace, righteous, meek, not in a chariot with well-tried horses, but on a young she-ass which no one had ridden before. Mark needs that ass, now that the Son of Man is going the way that no one has even taken before.

> *Rejoice greatly, you daughter of Zion,*
> *shout aloud, you daughter of Jerusalem!*
> *Look, your king comes to you,*
> *righteous and victorious,*
> *humble and riding on an ass,*
> *on a colt, the foal of an ass.*
> *Then I will cut off the chariot from Ephraim,*
> *and the battle bow shall also be destroyed.*
> *He shall proclaim peace to the nations;*
> *his dominion shall extend from sea to sea,*
> *from the Jordan to the ends of the earth.**

Did Jesus have this picture in mind as he travelled through Galilee, journeying up to Jerusalem? The evangelist cannot illustrate better how he sees the Messiah Jesus than by putting him on Zechariah's ass.

Jesus sent out two of his disciples: 'Go into the village opposite you. Immediately you enter it you will find an ass standing, tied there, a young animal on which no one has ever sat.'

Jesus knows from a distance that the ass is there. It's been there for ages, patiently waiting until the Lord needs it.

It's a young animal, which no one has ever ridden. That's also appropriate: a person may never use for other purposes what is destined for the temple. It's indeed a holy ass.

'Untie it and bring it here. And if anyone says, "What are you doing?," say, "The Lord has need of it, and he will send it back immediately."'

The disciples went and found the colt, tied firmly by the wayside, and they untied it. 'What are you doing?'

'The Lord has need of it, and will send it back immediately.'

They brought the animal to Jesus, put their garments on its back, and Jesus sat on it. The people spread their garments on the road, and green branches, which they cut in the fields.

Those who went before him in the procession, and those who went after him, began to shout: *'Hosanna, blessed is he who comes in the name of the Lord, blessed is the kingdom, the kingdom of our father David. Hosanna in the highest.'**

Ancient words from the psalms sing the praise of the Son of David who goes in to his bride.

How will his beloved fair maid, Jerusalem, greet this royal man who seeks to woo her as his bride?

38

A FIG TREE WITHOUT FRUIT

MARK 11.11-25

Mark summed up Jesus' first steps on his way, the beginning and at the same time the principle of his words and actions, in a single day: a day in Capernaum.

Now that Jesus has come to the end of his way, and Mark therefore to the end of his story, the evangelist puts Jesus' last words and actions in a time-span of seven days: a week in Jerusalem.

On the first of these seven days Jesus made his entry on an ass. The animal knew the way; it had already known for centuries where it had to bring its burden: to the temple area in the heart of the city of peace. *And Jesus went into the temple and looked round at everything.*

You can see him looking. Not with a carpenter's eye but with messianic eyes. Not as a builder with an interest in construction and good architecture, but as a prophet who is looking for God's presence.

What does he see? He sees religious practice in full swing: the priests in their long garments busy with the holy silverware, the money-changers behind their tables, the merchants with the sacrificial animals and other trade, the whole show. He sees only Jews there; not a foreigner can be seen in any of the courts or corridors. What's left of the dream of Israel's prophets?* Mustn't this house be a house of prayer for all peoples, a sanctuary in a city where righteousness dwells?

And when he had looked round at everything, as it was already late, Jesus left the city and went to Bethany, he and the twelve.

Jesus doesn't take up residence in Jerusalem, but in Bethany, *the house of the poor*. If all is well, it's always from *the house of the poor* that prophets see the temple; they hold the state and religion against that light.

The second day dawns, and Jesus leaves Bethany to return to Jerusalem. *And he became hungry.*

Just left home and already hungry?

This is no ordinary hunger, for this is no ordinary story. Jesus is hungry for a temple in which the poor receive their rights, in which seeking souls are given a warm welcome, the grieving comfort and the battered forgiveness, and in which the stranger feels at home. A house of prayer for all peoples.

Those are the fruits which the Eternal One would like to see on the fig tree of Israel which he himself has planted by the streams of the Torah. Sadly, Israel's prophets have all too often had to note, with anger and sorrow, that Israel doesn't bring forth these fruits because it is diseased.*

Jesus saw in the distance a fig tree with leaves on it. He went over to see if he would also find fruit there, but when he came closer he found nothing but leaves. It was not yet the season for figs.

In that case, why was he looking for figs?

Once again, this is no ordinary story and therefore this is no ordinary tree. It's a dream tree: one day, as the prophet Joel saw in a dream,* one day, in the messianic age, the fig tree of Israel will again bear fruit, as much as twelve months in the year. So with this dream tree in mind it wasn't so strange that Jesus was looking for that fruit.

He looked in vain: leaves everywhere, but there wasn't any fruit to be seen. It was like the temple: activity everywhere, but what has this place to offer to those who come from the house of the poor with a hungry heart?

And Jesus said to the fig tree: 'No one will ever eat fruit from you again.'

The tree is cursed and thus doomed to destruction. Jesus isn't telling a parable here, he's acting a parable. The tree stands for the temple – the temple which in Mark's day was in fact destroyed. Mark can only see its destruction as a divine judgment. He makes Jesus announce that judgment in his Gospel.

And Jesus entered the temple and began to drive out those who sold and those who bought in the temple, and he overturned the tables of the money-changers and the seats of those who sold pigeons; and he would not allow anyone to carry the holy incense through the temple.

And he taught and said: 'You know that it is written, "My house shall be made a house of prayer for all peoples"? But you have made it a den of thieves.'*

The old prophetic anger is lurking in Jesus: 'What deceptive words are in your mouth: "This is the temple of the Lord, the temple of the Lord, the temple of the Lord." Hypocrites! Thus says the Lord: because of their evil deeds I shall drive them from my house.'*

Israel doesn't fulfil the promises which it bears. Anyone who comes from Bethany and walks into the temple area can see how here the holy is being frittered away. Here the God of Abraham, Isaac and Jacob isn't served, but Mammon, the god of money. The traders in sacrificial animals do good business, as do the money-changers. Every pilgrim has to pay his temple tax at Passover, but not with a coin which bears the image of the hated Roman emperor. The money must be old Jewish money that hasn't been minted for a hundred years and therefore is costly. Through the priests the antique coins come back to the money-changers; it's a lucrative trade for both parties. The pilgrims are shamelessly exploited.

This is an abomination to Jesus, and just as in Galilee he drove out the demons from sick bodies, so now in Jerusalem he drives the trade out of the diseased temple. Mark can only see this as a warning which is to no avail, a foreshadowing of the destruction of the temple.

Thus the evangelist has once again summed up what Jesus stood for and what moved him. Israel's temple must be a hospitable home for all God's children, for the love of Israel's God extends to all peoples. That's why the evangelist makes Jesus declare all foods clean. That is why Jesus censures the men who get rid of their wives, the great men who no longer take any notice of children, the rich who give the cold shoulder to the poor, the selfish who want to rule instead of serve, and his followers who regard others as 'not one of us'.

The high priests and scribes heard what Jesus said and sought how they could do away with him.

They feel threatened. Every day they serve in God's temple in Jerusalem and honour the tradition of Torah and Prophets, and then a crazy man comes from Galilee to tell them that they've barely understood the Torah and the Prophets, and that the grace of God must be given to everyone as freely as the air and the sunshine. How can one silence such a man?

If we read such a story simply as a history from former days, then we keep out of harm's way. Then we hear only how the religion and temple worship of Israel had been debased under a priesthood which lusted for money and a scribal learning which was not of this human world.

But once again: this is no ordinary story. More than being a story about

Jesus and the Sanhedrin of his days, more than being a story about Israel's prophetic self-criticism, down the ages it's a story about people of all times and all places. For in all places and at all times love of gold infects love of God, and servants of God obscure the view of the Eternal One. In our tendency to seek support we externalize religion; we make a community of faith a closed club, righteousness gets lost and the poor starve.

The story illustrates how torn apart we are. There's a voice from within which welcomes with hosannas such a defenceless figure on his ass, since he radiates God's love. And there's a voice from within which cries out that he must be crucified, for there are limits.

Who doesn't long for the messianic kingdom? But who wants to lose themselves for it?

In the meantime Jesus has signed his death warrant with his cursing of the fig tree and his violent appearance in the temple. Night falls. Before the gates of the city are closed, he leaves Jerusalem to return to Bethany.

The third day dawns.

As they passed by early in the morning, they saw the fig tree withered away to its roots.

The disciples shudder. Only yesterday Jesus had cursed this tree, and look, there's nothing left of it: roots and branches are withered. A miracle. What a display of power!

'Look, rabbi, the fig tree which you cursed is withered.'

'Have faith in God.'

Faith does miracles. Everything is possible for those who believe. If only you trust, like God, that what you say will also happen.

'Truly, I say to you, whoever says to this mountain, "Be taken up and cast into the sea," and does not doubt in his heart, but believes that what he says will come to pass, it will be done for him.'

'Therefore I tell you, whatever you ask in prayer, be confident that you have already received it, and you will receive it. And whenever you stand praying, forgive, leave behind any grievances that you have against any one; then your Father who is in heaven will also forgive you your trespasses.'

39

FINALLY HE SENT HIS SON

MARK 11.27-33 AND 12.1-12

For the third time Jesus enters the city limits of Jerusalem; for the third time his way leads to the heart of the city; a clash with the chief priests, scribes and elders can't be put off much longer. We're approaching the denouement. This false prophet from Nazareth, who stirs up the people and desecrates the sanctuary, must go. Now they must remove him from the scene as quickly as possible.

'Who has given you the authority to do these things?'

They want to see Jesus' credentials. To come forward as a prophet without authorization is a capital offence* – if Jesus knows the Torah, he will know that. But Jesus is imperturbable.

'I will ask you a question; answer me, and I will tell you by what authority I do these things. Was the baptism of John from heaven or from men?'

Asked about the origin of his authority, Jesus asks them about the origin of John's baptism. Hadn't they *all* had themselves baptized?*

They deliberate among themselves. If they say that John's baptism was from heaven, there's no reason to doubt Jesus' authority. If they say that his baptism was from men, then the question arises why they had themselves baptized, and then they must also fear for the people, for John lives on in their memory as a true prophet, a man of God.

The chief priests and scribes hesitate. The best answer is no answer.

'We do not know.'

Indeed they know even less than Herod, who had John beheaded! Herod knows that John the Baptist is a righteous and holy man; he knows that he's silenced a voice from heaven.* The men of the Sanhedrin act dumb.

Jesus said: 'Neither will I tell you by what authority I do these things.'

Words are no longer any use; their ways are parting. Or will Jesus make one last attempt? To outsiders he always tells parables.* He will tell one more parable to these outsiders in a last attempt to make it clear to them that John and he are not just troublemakers, but stand in a long tradition of prophets whom God sent to Israel to ask for the fruits of his vineyard.

A man once planted a vineyard.

Jesus' audience immediately knows what he is talking about. They know the song of God's vineyard that the prophet Isaiah sang.*

> *Let me sing for my beloved*
> *the song of my beloved concerning his vineyard:*
> *My beloved had a vineyard on a fertile hill.*
> *He digged it and cleared it of stones;*
> *he planted it with noble vines;*
> *he built a watchtower in the midst of it,*
> *and hewed out a wine press in it.*
> *He expected it to yield good grapes,*
> *but it yielded wild grapes.*
> *He expected good government,*
> *but look it was blood government;*
> *he expected law making,*
> *but look it was law breaking.*

A man once planted a vineyard. He set a hedge around it, and dug a pit for the winepress, and built a tower, and let it out to tenants, and went abroad. When the time came, he sent a servant to the tenants, to get from them some of the fruit of the vineyard. But they took him, and beat him, and sent him away empty-handed. Again, he sent another servant, and they struck him on the head, and treated him shamefully. And he sent another, and him they killed. So it went on: some they beat and some they killed. Finally the owner had only his beloved son.

His beloved son? Those are the words which resounded from on high when Jesus was baptized by John. It was a voice from heaven, not a human voice: 'You are my beloved son.'

Finally the owner of the vineyard sent his beloved son to them. 'They will respect my son,' he thought. But those tenants said to one another, 'He is the heir, come, let us kill him, then the inheritance will be ours.' And they took him and murdered him, and cast him out of the vineyard.

Jesus knows that death awaits him and that he won't even be granted a grave.

What will the owner of the vineyard do now? He will come in person and destroy the tenants, and give the vineyard to others.

Who are these others?

As long as the answer you give isn't that these others are the church, all is well. As if this attractive vineyard in this parable stands only for Israel and not just as much for the whole wide world! As if only Israel has failed and has killed God's prophets! As if, for example, good government in Christian hands doesn't degenerate just as much into blood government and law making into law breaking.

Be this as it may, if we may believe the story, that's what happens to the vineyard and that's the point of telling this parable: not as a prediction of how things will turn out but as a warning, so that things *don't* turn out like this.

'Do you not know the word of scripture:
The stone which the builders rejected,
has become the cornerstone?'*

The rejected stone has been chosen by God to be the cornerstone of a new building. Clearly Mark is alluding to the resurrection from the dead of the beloved son who was murdered by the tenants. He dreams of a new temple, now that the old one has been destroyed.

By now the chief priests and scribes had a good grasp of the parable. However, good isn't the word, since they were all too eager to do what the tenants did in the story: *they wanted to arrest Jesus, but they were afraid to because of the crowds. They had understood that he had told the parable against them. They left Jesus and went away.*

Now the ways part irrevocably. It isn't that the leaders of the people don't understand Jesus; they understand him very well. But they're afraid, and hatred fills their heart. *They left Jesus and went away.*

So this is precisely the opposite of what the disciples did and what disciples need to do. The disciples left their own life behind them and followed Jesus. The chief priests left Jesus behind them and returned to their old life.

It happened and it happens. For time and again Jesus is crucified. He will be in agony to the end of the world.*

40

SHOW ME A SILVER COIN

MARK 12.13-17

And they sent to him some of the Pharisees and the Herodians, to entrap him in his talk.

In the parable of the vineyard the owner sent servants, prophets, to the people, with an honest question. In this story Pharisees and Herodians are sent to the Son of Man with a false question.

The Pharisees and the Herodians have joined forces. The latter fear the intervention of the Roman occupying power if the people who see Jesus as their king stage a rebellion. The former regard Jesus as a dangerous innovator who is trampling on the Torah.

'Rabbi, we know that you are an honest and upright man. You take no account of appearances, but teach the way of God in truth. Is it lawful to pay tax to Caesar? Must we pay or not?'

A believer couldn't have put it better; the question is attractively packaged. Whether it's *lawful* is a theological question, which is a matter for the Pharisees. Whether it *must be* done is more a political problem, typically a question for the Herodians.

What answer shall Jesus give? If he says yes, then he's taking the side of the authorities and he will lose his grip on the people. If he says no, then he's calling for resistance and they can hand him over to the Romans.

But Jesus saw through their hypocrisy and said: 'Why are you putting me to the test? Show me a silver coin, so that I can look at it.'

As if Jesus had never seen such a silver coin! But he wants them to take this coin from their own purses.

One of them gives him the coin. It bears the image of the emperor Tiberius with the words DIVUS AUGUSTUS, the divine, the exalted, on it. Blasphemy for a right-minded Jew. But each of them carries this image on their person.

'This likeness and this inscription, whose are they?'

'The emperor's.'

'Then give to the emperor what is the emperor's. And what is God's, give to God.'

The image of the emperor is minted on the coin. This coin comes from the emperor's world. An emperor imposes taxes.

But human beings are obligated to pay tribute above all to God. The creator has minted his image upon them. Human beings bear the image of God; they're the property of the Eternal One.

And they were amazed at him.

Anyone reading this story centuries later is equally amazed. Jesus is threatened from all sides, his mission seems doomed to failure and a cruel death awaits him. But he answers those lying in wait for him in a magisterial way and with lofty humour. In the midst of a world filled with hatred and fear, he proclaims God's goodness to anyone who wants to hear it: 'You and I, we're God's possessions.'

41

A GOD OF THE LIVING

MARK 12.18-27

The Sadducees also came to Jesus – they are the ones who assert that there is no resurrection – and they interrogated him.

The Sadducees are the senior clergy of Jerusalem, the well-to-do priestly nobility. We all know their kind. Really they've everything a man could wish for. They can only become worse off as a result of change, so they're very conservative people. It will be much more peaceful for them if the carpenter's son from Nazareth, the supporter of the poor who preaches revolution and has just gone through the temple making arrogant remarks about the activity in it, is quickly silenced. Then, in their view, he will have been silenced *for ever* – the Sadducees don't believe that there is anything after death. For where in God's holy Torah is it written that anyone will rise from the dead? It's just as absurd in their eyes as the existence of angels. No Sadducee believes in that.

'Rabbi, Moses has prescribed that if a man dies childless...'

They're talking to Jesus about levirate marriage, marriage with one's brother-in-law. If a man dies without leaving children, then a brother-in-law of the widow has to father descendants by the woman in the name of his dead brother, *so that his name is not wiped out from Israel.** Levirate marriage is a *human* duty, performed so that the blessing of children is not withheld from the widow; it's a *social* duty, so that children are there to provide for her old age; and it's a *religious* duty, so that she too is fruitful before God and a link in the chain of generations in which one day the Messiah will be born.

'Rabbi, Moses has prescribed...', and the Sadducees conjure up a bizarre example of a woman who is barren after entering into marriage and sharing a bed with seven of her brothers. Which of the seven will be her husband in heaven?

Of course the Sadducees could have left it at a woman with two husbands, but for fun they make it seven. In their view there's no better illustration of the sheer nonsense of something like belief in the resurrection than the number of perfection.

Why do they want to ridicule Jesus' belief in resurrection? After all, he shared it with many people in Israel. Is an underlying motive that they want to rob him of his consolation? If so, they won't succeed. That he can peacefully let the hatred of others roll over him is also a fruit of his belief that nothing can separate him from God's love.

However, Jesus won't allow them hard-heartedly to rob ordinary people of their consolation. He's a man of the people, people in need. People dreaming of angels who one day will lead you to paradise, the land on the other side, where poverty and hunger will be no more, where all suffering is past. Please may a victim hope that injustice will not rule for all eternity?

Or do we do the Sadducees who have come to Jesus an injustice? Under their absurd question may there be a longing for a faith like that of Jesus? Do they silently hope that he can rid them of their doubt? Who doesn't know this doubt? Is paradise perhaps the product of our own imagination? Have we thought it up ourselves?

No doubt we have. But Jesus believes that the Eternal One has also thought it up. Many have gone before him in that faith.

'You are wrong. You do not know the scriptures; far less do you know the power of God.'

It isn't that the Torah and the Prophets speak of resurrection in so many words,* but according to Jesus those who haven't unearthed the resurrection in them haven't understood them. 'Have you read scripture properly? The whole book is a book of resurrection, brim full of God's mercy. There's a predominance of life over death. But don't think that in heaven we shall still be like man and wife. There we shall be like the angels! How did you arrive at the short-sighted idea that the other world is simply an extension of this one? Of course we dream of seeing our loved ones again one day, and images are part of these dreams – we can't fantasize without pictures. But at the same time we sense that the other world is completely different. How different it is, we confidently leave to the Eternal One. The grain of corn that goes into the earth disappears completely. But the miracle is that God gives it a new body.'

'You don't know the scriptures and you've gone completely astray. Where is your love for the Eternal One and the mortals whom he created? Why didn't the burning bush set your life on fire when God called you, as he once called Moses? Do you still remember? *'Moses, Moses, I am the God of Abraham, Isaac and Jacob...'* When Moses heard these words, Abraham, Isaac and Jacob were already long dead and buried. But God reminded Moses of his love and faithfulness through time and eternity. He was the God of Abraham, Isaac and Jacob, and he's still their God. He's not a God of the dead; he's a God of the living. Friendship with the Eternal One is eternal friendship.*

A footnote:
Many Christians derive their belief in the resurrection from the bodily resurrection of Jesus. Of course that's possible, but the Jewish tradition already teaches the resurrection earlier. Jesus, too, already believed in it, and he shared that belief with the Pharisees. So belief in the resurrection of the dead isn't typically Christian.

It will be good to keep this in mind when we go on soon to talk about the resurrection of Jesus. For many people, the fact that someone doesn't believe in the bodily resurrection of Jesus but does believe in the resurrection is a new idea, and one that is difficult to follow.

42

THE TWO COMMANDMENTS

MARK 12.28-37

Pharisees have laid their trap for Jesus, Sadducees have put him on the spot with his faith in the resurrection of the dead – it would be nice if on this third day in Jerusalem there was also an encounter in which two people had a heart-to-heart conversation.

One of the scribes who followed the discussion thought that Jesus had given a good answer. He accosted Jesus and asked, *'Which commandment is the first of all the commandments?'* The man wants to know what Jesus thinks that life is all about.

Jesus answered, 'The first is: Hear, Israel, the Lord is our God, the Lord alone. You shall love the Lord your God with all your heart and with all your soul and with all your mind and with all your strength. And the second commandment is this: you shall love your neighbour, he is like you. There is no greater commandment than these two.'*

Hear, Israel, *Shema, Yisrael,* is the beginning of the Jewish confession of faith. Jesus may have his doubts about the way in which Pharisees and Sadducees stand in the tradition, but he leaves the age-old confession intact: God is unique; nothing, no one, may be deified. The Lord is God, the Lord alone. Human beings are to love him. And you must love your neighbour – he goes on to say that in the same breath. Your neighbour is like you. He too has his tricks, and he too depends on forgiveness. He too longs for a place in the sun and for some warmth. Love this neighbour.

'Which commandment is the first of all the commandments?' was what this scribe had come to ask.

One commandment is the first, but it's divided into two: to love God and your neighbour, neither one without the other.

The scribe is glad to hear this answer from Jesus: *'Indeed, rabbi, in truth you have said that only the Lord may be our God. And to love him and our neighbour with all our heart and with all our soul and with all our mind and with all our strength is more than all burnt-offerings and sacrifices.'*

These last words come from Hosea. It's as if with that old prophetic testimony the scribe is taking Jesus' side in his opposition to the sacrificial practices in the temple area, the day before. And Jesus in turn is glad to hear that answer: *'You are not far from the kingdom of God.'*

Two people have spoken with each other openly before God. Where that happens, the kingdom is near. At the same time it means the end of all theological disputes. All who witnessed this conversation seem to have sensed that. *And no one dared to ask Jesus any more questions.*

The people in the temple area had listened intently. *Most of the people heard him gladly.*

That sounds ominous. Herod also heard John the Baptist gladly. But that didn't prevent him from having the prophet killed.

43

THE WIDOW'S PENNY

MARK 12.38-44

This is a story about conspicuous lords and an inconspicuous woman.

The conspicuous lords are those who've been entrusted with the control of the treasury of faith. 'Beware of them,' says Jesus, not without bitterness. *'They like to go about in long robes, and to be greeted respectfully in the market place. They prefer to sit in the front row in the synagogue and at the top table at feasts. For the sake of appearances they make long prayers, and in the meantime they are devouring widows' houses.'*

It must be made clear that of course this doesn't apply to every scribe. As if we hadn't just encountered a scribe with no ambition, avarice and hypocrisy, someone who, of one mind with Jesus, confessed the age-old *Shema Yisrael, Hear, Israel.*

In this short comment by Jesus, Mark isn't concerned with a regrettable episode in Israel's history in which vain divines lay down the law and poor widows are left to their fate. He wants to point to a danger which threatens faith always and everywhere, the danger of debasing religion. This lurks everywhere and keeps claiming new victims.

Faith and religion are remarkable things. They can arouse the best and the worst in people. Their grandeur is as indisputable as the misery that they can cause. The most noble deeds have arisen out of faith, the most exalted thoughts and poems, the most beautiful cathedrals, the most splendid paintings and sculptures, the finest music. But in the name of faith and religion stakes have also been set up at which people have been burned alive, and dirty wars have been fought, and still are. Faith can bring reconciliation between people, but it can also alienate them from one another permanently.

There's healthy faith and there's unhealthy faith. Religion can be a liberating game before the face of the Lord, and it can just as easily kill all fantasy and power of imagination. There's a faith which turns away from the world, and there's a faith which works indefatigably for this world. There's a faith which in order to remain pure sets itself up alongside culture, and there's a faith which takes part in the struggles of this culture, with dedication and with pain. There's religion which wants us to hand over our minds, switch off our thought, and obediently and unquestioningly fit in with the tradition. There's also faith that isn't afraid of any question, at the same time knowing that the final answer can never be given because we're talking about mysteries, and because the Eternal One, praised be his name, dwells above the roof of our thought.

To find words for faith, to write these words down, to give them voice in a song, to order them in a doctrine, to depict them in rituals and gestures – you may, you must do this; you can't do it without a temple or without scribes, without a synagogue and without rabbis, without a church and without ministers. People must celebrate and feed their faith; this faith must be articulated and protected from running wild or being stifled; and it must also be handed on to the next generation. But we have to watch closely to ensure that it doesn't go cold or grow rigid. If inspiration fails, rituals shrivel into routine, liturgical forms lose their content, and words and symbols of faith cease to be evocative. Before we know it, faith has been made into a thing, something that we can embrace. Before we know it, the sabbath again comes before people instead of people coming before the sabbath. Doctors of divinity begin to obscure the divine, scribes become slaves to the letter, bishops put shutters on the windows of their palaces, and no one cares for the widows. One day we shall have to take responsibility for this.

Talking about widows, this is a good moment for Mark to let Jesus tell the story about the widow:

'I was sitting opposite the chest for offerings in the temple area. Many rich people threw a great deal of money in. And a poor widow came along, who threw in two copper coins, which makes a penny. Truly I say to you, this poor widow has thrown more into this chest of offerings than all the rest. For they all contributed out of their superfluity, but she threw in out of her poverty all that she had, her whole livelihood.'

Two copper coins. Had this women thought 'one for God and one for me, let's share it all fairly,' she would still have been extraordinarily generous. But she gives both coins: her whole *bios,* as the Greek puts it. So she gives all that she needed to live on. In so doing she portrays the true people of God, confessing that all that she has, all her possessions, belong to God, and she entrusts herself to him. Those who lose their lives...

This story is about more than just mercy. In contrast to the aloof men against whom Jesus has just been issuing a warning, this woman bears witness to her complete surrender to God. It isn't without significance that Mark has put this story at the end of his Gospel, just before he tells of Jesus' suffering. By it he wants to indicate that Jesus saw faith in its finest and most noble form in this woman. It was this widow, with her self-offering and trust in God, who now strengthened Jesus, too, to give his *bios*, his life.

If we don't read the story as a historical encounter in the temple area but as a parable, then we can say that in the portrait of this widow Jesus depicted faith in its finest and most noble form, and that to the last moment he remained true to this story.

44

ON THE LAST THINGS

MARK 13

Jesus leaves the temple, for good. Instead of being a house of prayer for all peoples, where love of God and neighbour is proclaimed and celebrated, because of the abuses of those responsible for it this place has become a den of thieves, where widows' houses are devoured. Jesus turns his back on the place.

One of his disciples looks back once more: *'Rabbi, what wonderful stones and what wonderful buildings!'*

Jesus said to him: 'Do you stand looking at this mighty building? Not one stone of it shall be left standing on another.'

For Jesus this is a monument of petrified faith, which has no future.

The evangelist wrote these words after the year 70, after the destruction of the temple, when not one stone was left upon another. For many Jews this was such a shocking experience that they saw it as the prelude to the end of the world. When *your* world falls apart, you're inclined to think that the *whole* world is going to pieces.

Will the end come quickly? The Jews who went along with the Jesus movement hoped so, because then they would be saved from their suffering. A bitter struggle was going on between the Christian Jews and the Jews who could only see the way of Jesus and his followers as a delusion, an attack on sacred doctrine. Families were breaking up, Jesus people were being persecuted and tortured. A prey to despair, they were asking themselves how long it would be before the kingdom of God dawned, the last day, the end of time. 'Lord Jesus, save us, we perish, return!'

The people of the Jesus movement couldn't imagine God's future without Jesus' 'return': the Son of man will return on the clouds, with the kingdom of peace and happiness. So they expressed their faith by saying that the kingdom which Jesus dreamed of would soon dawn in full splendour. But when? 'Why are you delaying? Come, Lord Jesus, come quickly.'

It's with these persecuted and despairing people in view that Mark writes down sayings of Jesus about the last things. This is Jesus' testament, a last message to his followers before he has to bid farewell to them, and before they too will go the way of suffering, for a servant is no more than his master. Disasters will come, and wars, cruel persecution will be their lot. But it isn't the end. These are the birth-pangs of a new age. Soon the Son of Man will appear. *This* generation will experience it. Be of good courage, be watchful!

And where does Jesus speak these words? *On the Mount of Olives, opposite the temple.*

According to an old prophetic saying, God will reveal himself to the nations there.* Popular piety is sure of this: it will be on the Mount of Olives that the Messiah manifests himself and the great liberation begins.*

Jesus sits down on the Mount of Olives, *opposite the temple.* Just as Moses lies buried in the land of Moab opposite the temple of Baal, as an abiding witness given by Israel to paganism,* so in the Gospel of Mark the Son of Man will bear witness until the last day, opposite the temple, that a house of God which isn't a house of God is doomed to destruction.

When Jesus was sitting on the Mount of Olives opposite the temple, Peter and James, John and Andrew asked him: 'Tell us, when will it happen and what is the sign that these things are being accomplished?'

The four first disciples are asking about the last things.

Jesus said to them: 'Do not be led astray by anyone. Many shall come in my name and say "I am he", and they will mislead many.'

It's inevitable that in their fear people cling to false Messiahs who cry 'I am he' and thus shamelessly take the name of God on their lips: 'I am from the God *I am.*' Beware of these people. They're playing God. They're will-o'-the-wisps.

'When you hear of wars or rumours of wars, do not be alarmed; this must take place, but the end is not yet. Nation will rise up against nation, kingdom against kingdom; here and there the earth will quake, there will be famine. This is only the beginning of the birth-pangs.'

These apocalyptic words of Jesus aren't meant to predict an unavoidable catastrophe; rather, they're meant to be an encouragement to persevere in all the pain and the divisions. Such things are birth pangs. Just as Jesus has come to share in new life through death, so too will his followers, who suffer for his sake.

'See to yourselves. They will hand you over to tribunals and you will be beaten in synagogues; you will have to stand before governors and kings for my sake, to bear testimony before them. And the gospel must first be preached to all peoples.'

Mark wants his fellow believers to be aware that perhaps the same fate awaits them as that of the Lord whom they serve, the same fate as the servants whom the owner of the vineyard sent to the tenants. What they mustn't forget is that by their witness the gospel will be preached far beyond the frontiers of Israel.

'And when they come to get you to drag you before tribunals, do not be anxious beforehand what you are to say. Say whatever is given you at that moment, for it is not you who speak, but the Holy Spirit.

Brother will deliver up brother to death and the father his child; children will rise against their parents and hound them to death, and you will be hated by all for my name's sake. But whoever perseveres to the end shall be saved.

When you see the abomination of desolation standing where it ought not to be – note this, reader! – then the people of Judaea must flee into the mountains.

An enigmatic term, this *abomination of desolation*. Daniel used it as a description of the idolatrous image that Antiochus IV had set up in the temple, a provocation which led to the Maccabaean revolt.* By this desecration the temple was destroyed, not as a building, but as a sanctuary. So too now, *many abominations of desolation* threaten the holy city, the holy temple and the holy faith. Flee then, flee to the mountains, as Lot once fled from Sodom. Flee and don't look back!

'Whoever is on the rooftop must not come down to take anything out of his house, and anyone who is in the country must not return to pack his clothes. Woe to the women who are pregnant or breast-feeding. God grant that it does not happen in winter.'

In the winter, when the rains fall and the roads become impassable, it's difficult to find refuge.

Those days shall be a time of terror, such as has never been from the moment when God began on his creation until today, and never will be. And if God had not shortened this time, no human being would be saved. But for the sake of his elect God has shortened these days.

This shortening of the time is a sign of God's grace. Just as we try to comfort someone who is having a terrible time. 'It will soon be over.'

> *You who called light, and light was born,*
> *and it was good, became evening and morning, to this day...*
> *Hasten the day of your righteousness.*
> *End the time when here and there in this world*
> *people are tortured, children are killed,*
> *we ravage the earth and steal each other's light.* *

'*And if anyone says to you "Look, here is the Messiah," or "Look, there he is," do not believe it. False messiahs will arise and false prophets; they will perform signs and wonders, to lead astray, if possible, the elect. But watch out: I have told you all things beforehand.*

After those days of terror the sun will be darkened and the moon will no longer give its light, and the stars will fall from heaven and the heavenly powers will come adrift. Then they will see the Son of man coming on the clouds with great power and glory. * Then he will send out his angels and gather the elect from the four winds, from the ends of the earth to the ends of heaven.*'

A cosmic upheaval is to be expected; heaven will fall down, the sun, the moon and the stars will be shaken, the first creation will perish. A new time is beginning; a new sun, a new moon, a new star is starting to shine: the Son of man. Throughout the cosmos there is only one shining example by which a person must be guided: the human figure of Jesus of Nazareth.

'*From the fig tree learn this lesson: as soon as its branches become tender and put forth leaves you know that summer is near. So also, when you see these things taking place, you know that it is here at the very gates.*'

As surely as the bitter winter must yield to the gentle summer, so this time with its deprivations will soon have to give way to the new time which God has promised.

'*Truly I say to you, this generation shall not pass away before all these things have taken place.*'

Jesus and Mark lived in the expectation that the end of the world age was at hand, but was a long time coming. Jesus preached the kingdom, but what came was a rift between the synagogue and the church. The church had difficulties because of the failure of the Son of man to return. The more people have to suffer, the more ardently they long for the end. Had Jesus made a mistake? Had *they* made a mistake?

But Mark's admonitions still keep their value. They form as it were the weight on the clock that keeps the world's time in tension. There can be no harm in living today as if the kingdom will dawn tomorrow. 'May peace come in our days,' say the Jews in their Kaddish prayer.

People in prison often ask whether heaven and hell exist. A brave question, which many good citizens never get round to asking. These prisoners ask themselves whether one day they will have to give a reckoning. They dread that tremendously, but at the same time they sense that it could help them to look into the very depths of their failure and guilt now and embark on the painful way of change. An answer to their question could be that it's always good for a person to prepare for an imminent encounter with the Son of man. Even if he doesn't appear, the work isn't in vain. In any case it will prove a blessing.

'Heaven and earth will pass away, but not my words. But of that day or that hour no one knows, not even the angels in heaven, nor even the Son. Only the Father knows it.

Look out, watch, for you do not know when the time will come. It is like this man going abroad and leaving his house in the hands of his servants, each with a particular task – and he commands the gatekeeper to be watchful.

Watch, then, for you do not know when the master of the house will come, in the evening or at midnight, or at cockcrow, or in the morning. If he comes unexpectedly, do not let him find you sleeping. What I say to you, I say to everyone: 'Keep awake!'

These are the last words of the speech about the last things with which Mark has interrupted the account of Jesus' passion. They aren't about the suffering of the Son of man but about the suffering of his followers. Jesus goes before them in that suffering. He also goes before them in the resurrection.

Watch, then. Mark admonishes his readers not to be like the disciples whom Jesus found sleeping, deep in the night. Nor must they take flight or be surprised by the crowing of the cock. Far less must they fall prey to despair, when Jesus is crucified and the sun is darkened. Didn't the women find the tomb empty, in the first light of morning? One day the great summer will come.

Keep awake.

45

YOU ANOINT MY HEAD WITH OIL

MARK 14.1-11

The fourth day dawns. Jerusalem is full of pilgrims; tomorrow will be Passover.

And the chief priests and the scribes were seeking an occasion to arrest Jesus by stealth and to kill him. For, they said, 'Not during the feast, lest there is a tumult among the people.'

Not during the feast. The masses could revolt and the Roman authorities could intervene, bloodily, as ever.

While the notables in Jerusalem are forging their evil plans, Jesus is giving a meal in Bethany. *The house of the poor.* And in Bethany *in the house of Simon the leper.* It would be hard to think of a more evocative place.

A woman comes into the house. In her hands she is carrying an alabaster jar with pure oil of nard. The slender neck ensures that the flask gives up its precious contents only drop by drop.

But what does the woman do? She breaks the neck of the alabaster jar and pours the myrrh straight over Jesus' head.

An age-old ritual. This was how Israel's kings were anointed at the hands of prophets. 'Be blessed, O king. Be king by the grace of God. You are a royal child.'

Not only were Israel's kings anointed with myrrh, but also Israel's dead. These dead, too, are royal children.

The unknown woman who entered the house of Simon the leper anoints a king doomed to death. She anoints him during his lifetime. After his death that will no longer be possible; crucified men aren't carried reverently to the grave. Unless she anoints him now, he will never be anointed again.

She's a prophetess. While men of name are planning Jesus' death, this anonymous woman is confessing that he's the Anointed, the Messiah. Like that poor widow with her two copper coins in the temple area, she too is giving herself utterly. She lavishes her most precious possession over the head of this royal child who is marked for death. Love is always abundant; it's never given in dribs and drabs, drop by drop.

For Jesus, this woman is an angel of God who with her fragrant pantomime has acted out Israel's most beautiful song:

> *You prepare a banquet for me*
> *in the face of those who seek my life.*
> *You anoint my head with oil,*
> *my cup runs over.* *

A few disciples who don't know about such love and don't understand her devotion exclaim that it's a waste: *'This myrrh could have been sold for more than three hundred shillings and we could have given the money to the poor.'*

But Jesus stands up for her:

'Let her alone. She has done a good work to me. The poor you will always have with you, and you can do them good whenever you will. But you will not always have me with you. She has done what she could; she has anointed my body beforehand for burial. Truly I say to you, wherever the gospel is preached in the whole world, what she has done will be told in memory of her.'

This woman has started something. Long after Jesus' body has been broken, long after Jesus' blood has flowed, this story will still be told in memory of her. This woman has set a faith in motion, and so she lives on.

Judas Iscariot, one of the twelve, went to the chief priests in order to deliver Jesus to them.

The picture changes; the woman has disappeared, as noiselessly as she came. We're back in Jerusalem and men are taking over the story again.

In this way Mark sets two types of faith over against each other.

'The woman' portrays honest faith in the Messiah. She's open and receptive to the love that the Son of man embodies: she gives herself wholly, as a bride gives herself to her bridegroom.

'The man' doesn't want to lose himself to the Messiah. He resists, and seeks to kill Jesus. The messianic way isn't his.

The great lords again appear on the scene. Their question was how they could do away with Jesus as inconspicuously as possible. They're given the answer on a plate: Judas will hand him over. Happy at this agreement, they promise to reward him with silver.

Silver for Judas, one of the men who thought it such a sin that that woman's myrrh wasn't turned into silver for the poor. Why did he want to deliver Jesus up?

We don't know what moved him. We don't even know whether he's a historical figure. The Judas whom the evangelists portray for us consists largely of Old Testament quotations: the friend who betrays, betrayal with a kiss, the thirty pieces of silver, the betrayer who commits suicide, all these are so many reminiscences of the Prophets and the Psalms.* Judas shows all the features of a personified anthology, and the more the formation of the legend progresses, the more his features take on malicious forms in the Gospels.

The question whether Judas really lived or has been called to life by the evangelist isn't so important. Judas lives in every human being of flesh and blood who wants to follow Jesus and go the way of love, but all too often betrays him and crucifies him. He could just as well have been called Adam, or Everyman.

The fourth day is over.

In another four days women – again women are first – will go to Jesus' tomb early in the morning with myrrh. The executed man has a tomb after all, and the women are going there to anoint him.

But that's no longer possible, because the tomb is empty.

However, he has already been anointed.

46

THE LAST SUPPER

MARK 14.12-25

On the first day of unleavened bread, the day on which the Passover lamb is slaughtered, his disciples asked him: 'Where do you want us to go to prepare everything for eating the Passover lamb?'

The fifth day of Jesus' stay in Jerusalem has dawned. It's the first day of the feast of unleavened bread, when Israel commemorates the exodus from Egypt, the hasty departure which meant that the bread had no time to rise.

When will Judas hand him over? If he does it now, then Jesus will die on the feast of Passover. That will be the precise moment when his blood flows, as the blood of the lamb once flowed. But isn't that precisely what the authorities want to avoid?' *Not on the feast day, lest there be an uproar among the people.*

In the Gospel story it will happen precisely on the feast day. If we are to understand the mystery of Jesus, we mustn't detach the evangelist's portrayal of the life and death of Jesus from Israel's liberation from slavery and Israel's expectation of the kingdom of God. A Jewish tradition has it that the Messiah will appear on Passover night.

Jesus sent out two of his disciples: 'Go into the city. There you will meet a man carrying a jar of water. Follow this man. And say to the owner of the house which he enters, "Our master asks, 'Where is the room where I can eat the Passover meal with my disciples?'" He will show you a large upper room furnished with what is necessary. Prepare everything for us there.'

What is Jesus up to? Only a few days earlier he sends two disciples ahead into the city and again he prophesies in detail who and what they will meet there. Whereas first it was the foal of an ass on which no one had ever sat, tied up by the wayside, now it's a man carrying a jar of water. The second prediction is, if possible, even more miraculous than the first. A *man* going down the street with a jar of water? You only see that kind of thing in a dream. Could this water carrier be an angel?

When it was evening, Jesus came with the twelve. And as they were reclining and eating, Jesus said, 'Truly I tell you, one of you will betray me, someone who is eating with me now.'

That isn't just a remark. These are words from a psalm:

> *Even my friend in whom I trusted,*
> *with whom I have shared my bread,*
> *has lifted up his heel against me.* *

It's a psalm of David, a psalm which according to tradition he prayed when one of his faithful friends went over to the opposition during Absalom's revolt.* Now David's Son meets the same fate.

Nowhere in Mark's story are there any casual remarks. The evangelist doesn't intend to give a 'historical' account of Jesus' life and death; he wants to give this life and death a precise place in Israel's story of God and humankind, and to interpret it in the light of God's liberating actions down the centuries.

'One of you will betray me, someone who is eating with me now.'

The disciples became sorrowful and said one by one, 'Is it I?'

Betrayal lurks in their own circle. Which of them will be the traitor? They look round the circle, and then they look at Jesus. 'Is it I?' There's some doubt in their voices. Is there a Judas in each of them?

'One of the twelve, one who is dipping bread in the dish with me, will betray me. For the Son of man goes as it is written of him, but woe to that man by whom he is betrayed. It would have been better for that man if he had never been born.'

Jesus' blood will flow; that's unavoidable. Prophets like him are put to death. One has only to read the scriptures.* But woe to the person through whose doing this actually happens.

It was their last gathering. At this meal Jesus, who had so often had meals with his followers, bade them farewell.

Later, when Jesus had gone from them and they were alone, they continued to hold these meals. As good Jews they went to the synagogue on the sabbath, but they also met to break bread, in remembrance of Jesus and encouraging one another. Meals consisting of bread, fish and wine. *And he took the loaves and the fishes, looked up to heaven, spoke the blessing, broke the bread, and gave it to his disciples.* Eucharistic language.

As they broke the bread they remembered how Jesus' body had been broken, and in pouring the wine they thought how his blood had flowed. But their gathering was not simply one at which they looked back in guilt and sorrow; there was also a joyful expectation. The grain of wheat which went into the earth had borne fruit, thirty, sixty, one hundred fold. And Jesus had promised them that one day they would again drink the fruit of the vine with him in the kingdom of God. Hadn't the Son of man been the Passover lamb which gave life to Israel with his death? They believed that the Father in highest heaven had taken up his cause, and *in* him the cause of the world which rejected him. Therefore the last word isn't left to guilt or death. And shouldn't they, his followers, celebrate all that together at a meal? They believed that in so doing they were acting in his spirit.

And as they were eating, Jesus took bread, spoke the blessing and broke it, and gave it to them, and said, 'Take, this is my body.' He also took a cup, and spoke a thanksgiving over it, and he gave it to them, and they all drank of it. 'This is my blood of the covenant, poured out for many. Truly, I say to you, I shall not drink again of the fruit of the vine until that day when I drink it new in the kingdom of God.'

This is profound and mysterious language. To translate it freely: 'Father, if I must die, let my death be like the death of the grain of wheat and the bunch of grapes. May my way of living and my way of dying be bread and wine for all people of all times.'

It was Jesus' farewell meal: 'This is my body.' Thus they received what from then on they themselves were to be: the body of the Lord. Before he was betrayed, Jesus had nothing to entrust to his disciples but his faith and his calling. It is for them to give further form to his dream. Here he will have had few illusions: they would betray him, they would deny that they were his friends, they would take flight. But above all they would know once and for all that a person can also love unconditionally and be faithful to death.

47

GETHSEMANE

MARK 14.26-42

They sang the psalms of praise and went out to the Mount of Olives.

They sang the songs which Israel sings at the Passover, century in and century out.

> *Who is like the Lord our God?*
> *He is seated on high, and sees to the depths.*
> *He raises the poor from the dust,*
> *and lifts the needy from the dirt.**
> *If God is on my side,*
> *what can man do to me?**

This night is different from other nights. Israel's sons and daughters commemorate God's great acts and feed the dream of the great acts of God that still await them.

After singing the psalms they went out to the Mount of Olives. Only Judas didn't go with them.

Why didn't Jesus escape, over the Mount of Olives, into the hill-country of Judaea? He would have had no difficulty in disappearing; many kings before him had sought escape that way.

But not this king of the Jews. If God is on his side, what can people do to him? He can only be faithful to his calling. His one wish was for people to live by God, in the face of all their fears. He would deny his own preaching if he gave up now.

Jesus said to them: 'You will all fall away.'

Jesus already talked about that in the parable of the sower, about followers in whom the seed of the kingdom fell upon rocky ground. Their faith blossoms quickly, but doesn't put down roots. When they're persecuted for that kingdom, they fall away.

'You will all fall away. For it is written: 'I will strike the shepherd, and the sheep will be scattered.' But afterwards, when I am raised, I shall go before you into Galilee.'*

In a little while there will be a shepherd without a flock and a flock without a shepherd. But that isn't the last thing to be said. 'When I am raised, we shall see one another again, in Galilee.'

A mysterious remark. We hear Jesus' trust in God sounding through, the faith that no power in the world will be able to quench his dream. He relies on the God who sits on high and sees into the depths, the God who raises the poor from the dust, the needy from the ash heap. Behind the sorry prospect of the scattered sheep the distant prospect of a happy reunion opens up. No human being, not even Jesus, can accept injustice and suffering without finding some meaning in it. Jesus derives this sense from the prophets who have gone before him:

> *The Lord has torn us and he shall heal us,*
> *he has stricken us and he will bind us up.*
> *After two days he will revive us,*
> *on the third day he will raise us up,*
> *we shall live before his face.**

Peter Rockyground meanwhile refuses to believe that they will fall away. He surely won't. *'Even though they all stumble, I certainly will not.'*

Jesus said to him, 'Truly, I tell you, this very night, before the cock crows twice you will deny me three times.'

Peter said all the more vehemently: 'Even if I must die, I shall never deny you.'

And so said all the rest.

They don't know Jesus well and they don't know themselves well. Has Jesus ever spoken nonsense? And just now at the table, they were still not so sure that they would never betray him, 'Is it I?' 'Is it I?' And now Peter suddenly knows that he will be faithful to Jesus to the death. He's shouting down his own uncertainty.

And they went to a place called Gethsemane and Jesus said to his disciples. 'Sit here and watch while I pray.' And he took Peter, James and John with him.

In this last hour Jesus chooses his three original disciples to accompany him. These are the three who were the witnesses to the raising of Jairus' daughter and the transfiguration on the mountain. These three have seen for themselves that life, not death, has the last word. On his last journey Jesus can't wish for better disciples beside him.

Jesus was seized with great distress, and fear came over him. 'My soul is very troubled,' he said, 'even to death. Remain here and watch.' And he went a little further on, fell to the earth and prayed God that if it was possible, this hour should pass by him. 'Abba,' he said, 'Father, everything is possible for you. Take this cup from me. Yet not what I will but what you will.'

The dark night of the soul. He breaks out in a sweat of agony. So as not to fall prey to despair, Jesus seeks support from his Father. 'Abba, everything is possible for you.'

Everything? Will God intervene? Jesus knows that God will not. He will go the way to Golgotha. Unlike the legend, the sun will not be darkened and the earth will not quake. The sky will be bright blue above the hill, birds will sing their song there, the farmer will go on ploughing, the earth seems unmoved.

Jesus sends his lament to heaven. 'Let this cup pass from me.' No desire for death moves him, nor the longing to be a martyr. Nor is he negotiating with a cruel God who wants his crucifixion. God doesn't want his death; human beings do.

Jesus wants this cup to pass him by. At the same time he wants to remain true to his calling. Will God abandon the work that he's begun? If God won't, then he, Jesus, may not abandon the work that *he's* begun. He won't let go of God. God won't let go of him. He's lived in God's spirit, and in this spirit he will now also die. Can his friends be with him in this spirit and be close by him?

He found them sleeping. And he said to Peter, 'Simon, are you asleep? Could you not watch with me one hour?'

Of course it isn't natural sleep that has seized them. They've closed their eyes to what moves the man of God; they're sitting in the darkness. They can't see his suffering, they don't share in his prayer. The sleep of the disciples is the sleep of all those who cut themselves off from the Son of man, who is constantly crucified afresh. 'Watch, so that the master of the house does not find you sleeping,' said Jesus, speaking of the last things.*

With the story of the garden of Gethsemane Mark hopes to encourage the persecuted Christians of his days. He rouses them to watch and to pray. In his story Jesus is the model of the person who relies on God, whereas Peter is depicted as the person who is overcome by fear and seeks flight in sleep. Peter, who was called Simon and is now addressed by Jesus with this name. 'Do you remember, Simon, that I called you when you were fishing and that you followed me, in faith and trust? Even just now you said that you would never deny me.'

'Simon, are you asleep? Could you not watch with me one hour? Watch and pray that you do not fall into temptation. The spirit is willing, but human nature is weak.'

Again he went away and prayed with the same words. And again he returned and found them sleeping, for their eyes were heavy. They did not know how to answer him.

And Jesus came to them a third time. 'Sleep now and rest. It is enough.'

Jesus has sowed, taught, comforted, healed, admonished, prophesied. In word and deed he has proclaimed the kingdom of God. Three times he's told them of his suffering and three times of his faith in eternal life, but three times they've failed to understand him. Not a word about his life of service, not a word about his suffering and not a word about his resurrection seems ever to have got through to them. Now he's found them sleeping three times, and that's enough.

'The hour has come. See, the Son of man is delivered into the hands of sinners. Arise, let us be going. See, my betrayer is near.'

Jesus has overcome his fear. He will follow the way to the end, trusting in God.

48

JUDAS' KISS

MARK 14.43-52

Hardly had Jesus finished speaking than Judas came, one of the twelve, and with him a crowd of people with swords and clubs, sent by the high priests, scribes and elders. The one who delivered him up had agreed a sign with them, 'He whom I kiss is the one. Seize him and lead him away under close guard.'

Why a sign? If Judas simply brings them to the place, then surely they themselves know who Jesus is? And why *this* sign?

Betrayal is related in its most macabre form. Thus once David's general Joab kissed his enemy while running him through with his sword.* It seems a tender sign of intimacy, but it's cold hatred. One of the twelve is Judas. He's been an intimate friend of Jesus. Now he hands him over to those who seek to kill him.

Mark is probably telling the story in such a way as to encourage his fellow-Christians. Didn't Jesus himself say, *'Brother will deliver up brother to death, and a father his child; you will be hated by all for my name's sake.'** So if you're betrayed by someone from your innermost circle, know that Jesus suffered the same fate.

And Judas came up to Jesus. 'Rabbi,' he said, and kissed him.

Mark doesn't say more about Judas. The traitor disappears into the darkness of history. As mysteriously as evil once entered the world, so now its bearer disappears again.

Why is evil here specifically attached to a man called *Judas*, man of Judah, Jew? Is that a coincidence, or is the wickedness of 'the Jew' depicted here? Be that as it may, for centuries the church made the Jews responsible for Jesus' death on the cross, punished them for it and then washed its own hands in innocence. Luther's words are shocking: 'Shut up the Jews in a stable. Let their young men do forced labour. Set their houses of prayer on fire. They are not human. Think what Judas did.'

If a great and erudite pastor like Luther was so blind, what can one expect from the sheep of his flock?

And they laid hands on Jesus and seized him. One of the bystanders drew his sword and struck the slave of the high priest and cut off his ear.

An impotent gesture, that sword-stroke, a grotesque attempt to do something now it's too late. The evangelist Luke is so sensitive that he has Jesus replace the ear, but in Mark from now on the young man has only one ear to hear with.

And Jesus said, 'You have come out as against a robber, with swords and clubs to capture me. Day after day I was with you in the temple teaching, and you did not seize me. But let the scriptures be fulfilled.'

In the temple area they didn't fight him with the force of arguments. Now, in the Garden of Olives, they fight him with clubs and swords. So the scriptures are fulfilled. Wasn't the suffering of the righteous regularly related in the Bible? The actors are new, but the play's an old one.

And the disciples all forsook him and fled. A young man followed him, with nothing but a cloth around his naked body. They wanted to seize him, but he left his garment behind in their hands and took flight, naked.

Who is this young man? No one knows. There are those who think that this is a little self-portrait of Mark, just as a mediaeval painter depicts himself in a corner of his painting. It may also be that in this one follower the evangelist is once again presenting us with 'the disciple': a tarnished figure who with his shameful departure plainly illustrates the failure of discipleship. All the disciples have been put to flight. They had gone some of the way with Jesus, but when persecution became too difficult, they only knew the urge for self-preservation, saving their hides. Here and there they looked for a good way out.

And so it happened as Jesus said it would: the shepherd is struck and the sheep are scattered.

49

IMMEDIATELY THE COCK CROWED

MARK 14.53-72

Mark takes up his pen again. Now he's going to write the ending to his story, about the last days of Jesus, his trial, his execution. Mark thinks of the people for whom he's writing all this down, his fellow believers who in Israel, in Rome and elsewhere in the Dispersion are handed over to tribunals, scourged in synagogues and sentenced by rulers and kings. How is he to tell these suffering people about the suffering Son of man so that they can recognize themselves in him and draw inspiration from him to take up their crosses as fearlessly as Jesus did?

Mark knows how. In his story Jesus will have to appear before both a Jewish and a Roman tribunal. He will be spat upon and tortured and condemned to death by both tribunals. He will be abandoned by everyone. He who himself always feels so close to the Eternal One will feel forsaken even by God in his last hour. That's how Mark will describe it, for that's what happened to the righteous sufferers to whom the psalms and the prophets bear witness, and now that's happening to their followers. That will also happen to Jesus. Mark hopes that the martyrs of his day can be as steadfast of those of former times.

And they led Jesus to the house of the high priest. All the chief priests, elders and scribes met together there.

The Sanhedrin, Israel's supreme legal body. Mark doesn't mention the name of the high priest, as if he isn't concerned with the person but with the institution. One constantly comes up against high priests of a rigid and institutionalized faith.

And Peter followed him from afar, to the court of the high priest's house, and he sat there with the servants, and warmed himself by the fire.

He'd followed him at a distance; he couldn't follow him properly. He left Jesus in the lurch.

The book of Psalms knows of this:

My friends and companions stand aloof,
and my loved ones avoid me. *

While Peter sat warming himself below, Jesus stood before his judges in the upper room. Many false witnesses appeared, but their statements didn't agree. There were those who claimed, 'We have heard him say: I shall raze to the ground this temple which has been made by men, and in three days I shall build another temple, not made by human hands.'

Had Jesus said that? He *had* said that the temple would be destroyed, but not that he would destroy it. He *had* spoken about what was going to happen on the third day, but that again had nothing to do with the temple. So Jesus' words have been torn from their context and twisted.

However, the irony is that the man who bore this false witness didn't know what truth he was speaking. He couldn't have given a more accurate account of the work of Jesus and its significance. Jesus could have said it, and in a certain sense he did say it: hasn't he overthrown the sacred houses of a diseased faith? And when he had risen from the dead on the third day, hadn't a new temple community been founded in his spirit, a house of prayer for all peoples, not made by human hands?

Meanwhile things aren't going easily in the judgment hall; it's time for the high priest to take matters in hand. He rises from his seat and comes forward.

'Why do you give no answer? Many accusations are being made against you.'

Jesus is silent.

'When they come to get you and drag you before the tribunal, don't be anxious beforehand about what you must say. Say only what is given to you at that moment, for then it isn't you who speak but the Holy Spirit,' he'd said shortly beforehand.

Jesus is silent. The Holy Spirit has clearly indicated to him that there is no point in defending himself. A psalm of David attests that the Holy Spirit does this from time to time:

I do not defend myself, I remain deaf and dumb,
I set all my hope on you, O Lord,
on your answer. *

The high priest is at his wits' end: the charge isn't weighty enough, the witnesses are contradicting one another and the accused is silent. Must he let Jesus go again? May this so-called Messiah continue to damage the faith of the fathers with impunity? As high priest, mustn't he protect the religion from heretics and heresies? This silent figure wants to tarnish all that is holy to him.

Then the high priest asked him directly: 'Are you the Messiah, the Son of the Most High?'

What is Jesus to answer? What does the Holy Spirit inspire him to say? What does Mark make him say now? Does he continue to keep silent or does now, at long last, the great statement emerge? Will he now finally say aloud that he's the Messiah?

'I am he. And you will see the Son of man sitting at the right hand of Power, coming with the clouds of heaven.'

The high priest can't believe his ears. With his question he'd hoped to get this deadlocked trial going again, but this one answer settles the matter. If this isn't blasphemy, what is? And not only does this foolish man openly claim to be the Messiah; he even sees himself as the Son of man who will come to hold judgment at the end of time. Hold judgment? That's what *we* shall do, immediately: '*What need have we of further witnesses? You, my lords, have heard the blasphemy. What is your verdict?*

Unanimously they condemned him to death.

Really Jesus' fate had already been sealed from the moment that he was taken into the high priest's house, but he has now sealed it himself: 'I am he.' In telling his story Mark has initiated his readers into the mystery of a suffering Messiah. For a long time it remained in the dark. Who is this...? Now, at the end of his story, the evangelist can let Jesus openly confess his messiahship.

And which of his followers will be the first to understand that mystery? Perhaps Peter, who's warming himself by the fire in the courtyard below?

The high priest is flabbergasted. 'Is God behind you? Do you claim an authority given by the Eternal One?' The man opposite him has answered in the affirmative. And as if that isn't enough, in his megalomania he's added that before long, at the end of time, the roles will be reversed: then the high priest will be summoned before *his* judgment seat. In other words, they can kill him, but that won't get rid of him. When the time comes, they will see him appear on the clouds of heaven.

The high priest tore his garments.

This is a sign of dismay at the shocking blasphemy that he's just heard from Jesus. At the same time he's relieved that this pseudo-messiah is so willing to contribute to his own downfall and has made it possible for him soon to bring this trial to a good conclusion.

However, the high priest's gesture can be interpreted in several ways. In Mark's eyes, in condemning Jesus the high priest has torn apart his truthfulness and his truth. As far as Mark is concerned, the faith that the high priest stands for is in shreds.

Unanimously they condemned him to death. And some began to spit upon him. They blindfolded him and struck him in the face.

Why blindfolded? Is it easier to strike when the other person can't look at you? Didn't they want to be recognized later?

'Prophesy!' they cried.

He's a false prophet in their eyes. But he's a great prophet in Mark's eyes, and that's why the evangelist has staged things like this. For all that they do, the judgments, the spitting and the striking, has already been prophesied by Jesus.

'Prophesy!'

Jesus was silent.

How is Peter faring in the meantime, in the courtyard?

He too is interrogated. One of the high priest's slave girls thought that she could recognized him by the flickering light of the fire. *'Were you not also with the Nazarene?'*

'I do not understand what you are talking about.'

He went outside, into the forecourt. In the distance a cock crowed.

While in the upper room Jesus said openly who he was, down below Peter denied both Jesus and himself. Jesus signed his death warrant, Peter escaped his.

When the slave girl caught sight of him again in the forecourt, she said to the bystanders: *'That man is also one of them.'*

Again Peter spoke to her, and his speech betrayed him.

'Certainly you are one of them, you too are a Galilean.'

'May I be cursed if I know what you are talking about. I swear to you, I do not know this man.'

Peter is lying. You can also say that he's speaking the truth. Indeed Peter doesn't know Jesus.

Immediately the cock crowed for the second time. And Peter remembered the word that Jesus had spoken to him: 'Before the cock crows twice you will have denied me three times.' And he began to weep.

He wept because he'd failed. Jesus knew his weakness better than he did.

So Mark has drawn two models. Jesus is the ideal for the persecuted believer: firmly trusting in God, he stands before his judges and will not yield. Peter can't manage this.

50

JESUS BEFORE PILATE

MARK 15.1-20

The sixth day dawns. It's now Friday. One day this Friday will be called Good Friday, but at this point it doesn't yet look like it.

Early in the morning Jesus is put in fetters and handed over by the men of the Sanhedrin to the governor, Pilate. It's for the Roman authorities to confirm death sentences and carry them out.

The name of Pontius Pilate is still mentioned by countless people every day, in the same breath as the Virgin Mary, when the creed is said in churches and chapels in every country in the world. What an irony! A second-rate governor, stationed in an outpost of the Roman empire, but his name is and remains on all lips because people constantly tell of another who suffered under him.

Who was Pilate? Historians portray him as a cruel and harsh man, a hated procurator, filled with antipathy to the Jews and their religion.

The evangelist shows us another Pilate. Although the man never paid any attention to the will of the people, in this story he puts the fate of Jesus into Jewish hands: whom shall he release, Jesus or Barabbas? It's an improbable scene – there is no mention of pardons on feast days at the time of his administration. The story gives more the impression of being a creation of Mark's. What for?

Probably for the advancement of preaching. If it is to be possible to proclaim the story of the crucified man publicly in the Roman empire of Mark's days, it's better for the role played by the Romans in this drama to be minimized. That means that the role of the Jews is magnified. Mark is afraid of giving new substance to the fear among Christians living under the Romans. Aren't these as dangerous to the state as their leader at that time? It's better for him to pin the guilt on Judas and have the Judaeans cry out that Jesus must be crucified – to Pilate's dismay, in Mark's reading. If the Roman authorities at that time didn't see so much evil in this Jewish rabbi, Mark may hope that the same authority will leave his followers untroubled.

Unfortunately, this propaganda of Mark's sowed the seed for the great disaster which later came upon the Jews, when non-Jews began to feed their hatred of the Jews from it and found in it confirmation of their ideas about a pernicious Jewish race. After Auschwitz, the passion narratives of Mark and the evangelists who wrote after him – who reinforced further the lines drawn by Mark – really can't be read or sung on Good Friday any longer unless we set alongside them the well-known passiontide hymn:

> Who was the guilty? Who brought this upon thee?
> Alas, my treason, Jesu, hath undone thee.
> 'Twas I, Lord Jesus, I it was denied thee:
> > I crucified thee.*

Back to the story. The men of the Sanhedrin bring Jesus before Pilate: 'This man claims to be the king of the Jews. Moreover he says that he is the Messiah, the Son of God.'

The last accusation interests Pilate less than the first. In this country there are always eccentrics claiming to be the Messiah, Jewish folklore over which a worldly-wise Roman shrugs his shoulders. But what is the meaning of his claim to be 'the king of the Jews'?

'Are you the king of the Jews?'

Just imagine that this strange man could really become a threat. Pilate above all wants peace and quiet in Palestine.

What answer must Jesus give? In Pilate's world of course he is no king, but rather a beggar. He's an itinerant healer who sees visions and hears voices. Pilate is a man who can think only in terms of power, but Jesus' kingdom isn't about power: for him, being a king is the same thing as serving; his kingdom isn't of this earth. Only in the realm of humanity could this man call himself king.

'Are you the king of the Jews?'

'You say so.'

Jesus doesn't contradict Pilate. Nor, however, does he say in so many words that he's king of the Jews; that would be a statement that the governor couldn't possibly understand.

The chief priests brought many accusations against him, but Jesus remained silent.

'Have you no answer?,' asked Pilate. 'See how many accusations they bring against you.'

Jesus was silent. Pilate wondered greatly.

Were the chief priests and the scribes also amazed? How nice it would have been had they recognized this scene with this still, silent figure who was allowing himself to be led to the slaughter. The scene is exactly like the messianic dream of the prophet Isaiah: *he was maltreated, but he accepted affliction and did not open his mouth; like a lamb that is led to the slaughter, and like a sheep that is dumb before its shearers, so he did not open his mouth.* *

But Israel's chief priests and scribes can't make this connection. The lamb will be led to the slaughter.

Or can Pilate still devise a plan?

Now when there was a feast, the governor used to release a prisoner, one for whom the people asked.

What if he now gives the people a choice between Jesus and Barabbas, a rebel with a murder on his conscience? Out of pity for Jesus, Pilate is actually becoming a democrat!

Bar-abbas. His name means *son of the father.* Mark couldn't have thought of a better name: which son of the father will the people choose? The liberation fighter who seeks to deliver his people by violence, or the man who wants to free people's hearts?

Pilate is convinced that the people will choose to release Jesus. But look, the people is turning against Jesus, prompted by the high priest.

'Barabbas! Barabbas!'

Not long ago, the leaders had been afraid of a rebellion among the people if they seized Jesus at Passover – 'not upon the feast' – but now they need to manipulate the people, who become a powerful help instead of a hindrance to doing away with Jesus. Brought from his quarters, Pilate again calls out: *'What then must I do with the man whom you call king of the Jews?'*

But they cried out all the louder, 'Crucify him!'

Just now Pilate had been convinced that the people would want what he wanted; now he's compelled to want what the people wants. The man standing before him is no criminal, but it would be politically unwise to go against the people and its leaders.

Pilate thought it advisable to give the people its way and he released

Barabbas to them. Jesus he had flogged and then handed him over to be crucified.

This flogging is a barbarous torture under which those condemned to death often collapsed even before their execution. Later the evangelist John will mitigate Pilate's guilt further by making it seem as if with this flogging the governor aimed at arousing the compassion of the people: 'Behold the man' – an addition which is absent from Mark.

The soldiers took Jesus inside the inner court of the house of judgment and called together the whole detachment.

They must all take part; they too must become perpetrators.

Look at the soldier. See how he hits out. See his fear. See his suffering and the suffering that he causes. Behold the man.

Look also at the defenceless human being before him, with his dream that the children of God should overcome their fear and come together in love. He had a vision that Jerusalem should be a place for all peoples, where people should be one with God and with one another. This dream is intolerable, that vision must be done away with. Jesus must die.

They clothed him in a purple cloak and put on him a crown which they had woven from thorns. And they solemnly began to salute him: 'Hail, king of the Jews!'

The Jews have made him the object of their religious mockery: 'Prophesy, then, prophet!' Now the Romans practise their political mockery on him. 'Hail, king of the Jews!' Without realizing it, they're speaking the truth about his life.

And they struck him on the head with a reed, and spat upon him, and they knelt down in homage to him. And when they had mocked him, they stripped him of the purple cloak and put his own clothes on him. And they led him out of the city to crucify him.

It's Friday, the sixth day. The day on which God created the human being. Look what's become of him. Behold the man.

51

THE CRUCIFIXION

MARK 15.21-32

They led Jesus out of the city to crucify him. And they seized a passer-by, a certain Simon of Cyrene – he was coming from his land, the father of Alexander and Rufus – and compelled him to carry the crossbeam.

The condemned man had to carry the heavy crossbeam himself, but the burden was too heavy for Jesus, who threatened to collapse under it.

Had that goat not escaped, Simon would have gone home a quarter of an hour earlier. Then he wouldn't have seen the man who was to be crucified and the soldiers. Or only in the distance. Then he would have remained a passer-by.

He'd never been with the man from Galilee. There was indeed another Simon who was with Jesus, but where is he? This Simon was a chance passer-by, but he had to go up the hill with Jesus. Later he understood who this man was whose burden he had carried, and then he became a believer. Alexander and Rufus, his sons, became believers too. It often happens that children come to believe because they see how their father and mother lighten people's burdens in life and thus indeed bear witness to God.

And they brought him to Golgotha, the place of the skull. They offered him wine to drink mixed with myrrh, but he did not accept it.

Wine mixed with myrrh is a sedative. However, Jesus refuses the drink; he doesn't want his mental powers to be diminished.

And they crucified him and divided his garments, casting lots for them to decide what each would take.

Anyone who is familiar with Israel's psalms can detect echoes here of the laments with which the innocent sufferers of all ages cry out their pain.

> *Dogs have surrounded me;*
> *a company of evildoers has encircled me;*
> *they pierce my hands and feet.*
> *I can count all my bones,*
> *they stare and gloat over me.*
> *They divide my clothes between them,*
> *and cast lots for my garment.**

It was the third hour when they crucified him.

The third hour after the rising of the sun, nine o'clock in the morning.

The superscription with the reason for his condemnation ran: 'The king of the Jews.'

As a deterrent to the people it was Roman custom to write the crime of the person condemned to death on a board and to hang it above him: 'Rebel leader', 'Runaway slave', and now, 'King of the Jews'.

And they crucified two robbers with him, one on his right side and one on his left.

An image from the prophet Isaiah: *delivered over to death, he was reckoned among the evildoers.**

Jesus hung on the cross and was mocked and reviled.

Passers-by shook their heads and derided him:* 'Aha! You who would destroy the temple and build it again in three days, save yourself.'

They mock, but in the meantime they reveal what Mark sees as Jesus' secret. In his eyes Jesus has destroyed 'the temple' – faith as it took form then and there. At the same time he wants to bear witness to the new messianic community which was built up after Jesus had risen from the dead on the third day.

The chief priests and scribes also mocked him: 'He has saved others, himself he cannot save. Let the Messiah, the King of Israel, come down from the cross, that we may see it and believe.'

The chief priests are right. Jesus cannot save himself from the cross; were he to do so, he would deny his calling and his teaching. This Messiah believes that the person who wants to hang on to his life at any price will lose real life.

The robbers who were crucified with him also reviled him.

Jesus is abandoned by everyone and surrounded by evildoers he will die in solitude.

52

AND HE YIELDED UP THE SPIRIT

MARK 15.33-41

And when the sixth hour had come, there was darkness over the whole earth until the ninth hour.

Yesterday at this time of day the sun stood high in the sky, but today it refuses to shine. It's the nightmare of the prophet Amos:

> *And it shall happen in those days*
> *– runs the word of the Lord –*
> *that I shall make the sun go down at noon*
> *and darken the earth in broad daylight.* *

Full of repugnance, God puts the world in darkness. This isn't what he had created the light for. Darkness everywhere,

And at the ninth hour Jesus cried out with a loud voice, 'Eloi, Eloi, lama sabachthani?', 'My God, my God, why have you forsaken me?

Again we hear words from the twenty-second psalm, that heart-rending lament of the innocent sufferer: *'My God, why have you forsaken me?'* *

That's how people cry out in the dark night of the soul, in the hours of the darkening of God. And what answer does God give? None. Heaven remains dumb. And that too is an age-old experience which is expressed by this psalm:

> *My God, I cry in the daytime and you do not answer,*
> *at night, and I find no rest.* *

In the story of Jesus' call the voice of God resounded on the bank of the Jordan. When Jesus was to go to Jerusalem, knowing that death awaited him there, God's voice resounded again, on the Mount of Transfiguration. But now there isn't a word or a sound from the heights of heaven.

Why not? Why must Jesus die in such solitude with this desperate question on his lips? Why doesn't he die saying the words of the next psalm?

> *Though I go through a valley of deep darkness,*
> *I fear no evil.*

Because, Mark would probably say, because Jesus died as so many of the righteous died before him, forsaken by God. That's how children of God die to the present day. It cries out to heaven.

But it does cry out *to heaven*. In his godforsakenness Jesus continues to call on God. He doesn't detect God's presence anywhere, yet he believes that God can hear his complaint.

'Eloi, Eloi, lama sabachthani?'

'Do you hear that?' exclaim some of the bystanders. 'He is calling Elijah.'

They deliberately misunderstand him. Elijah is the spokesman of people in need, the patron of hopeless cases.

Someone ran up, drenched a sponge with wine and vinegar, put it on a reed and gave it to him to drink. 'Let us see if Elijah will come to take him down.'

They want to keep him alive. Perhaps Elijah will still come in time for a miracle.

Again the evangelist is being guided by the psalms:

> *Insults have broken my heart,*
> *and I am in despair.*
> *I looked for a sign of pity, but in vain,*
> *for comforters, but I found none.*
> *Yes, they gave me vinegar to drink in my thirst,*
> *they gave me poison for food.*

But the evangelist leaves out that poison; the man with the reed wants to prolong Jesus' life: the torture must go on.

Jesus uttered a loud cry and yielded up the spirit. And the curtain of the temple was torn in two, from top to bottom. The Roman centurion who stood facing him saw how he had yielded up the spirit and said, 'Truly, this man was the Son of God.'

In the temple the curtain protects the holy of holies, the place where

God dwells. Jesus yielded up the spirit and God's dwelling place opened up for him.

Three times in his Gospel Mark reports that something is torn, and three times it happens when he is talking of Jesus, the Son of God.

The heavens are torn above the Jordan to let through a dove and the Voice of God: 'You are my Son.'

When Jesus has replied 'I am he' to the high priest's question whether he is the Messiah, the Son of the Blessed One, the high priest tears his high-priestly garment, made of the same precious material and in the same colours as the curtain in the temple.

Now that the Son has gone to the end the way which began at the Jordan, again a sign from heaven is perceived on earth: the curtain is torn. From now on the temple will be an open sanctuary for all sons and daughters of God, a house of prayer for all peoples.

The Roman centurion is the first to enter. What was first perceived from high heaven now also echoes from human lips: Jesus is the Son of God.

Mark has disclosed the mystery of Jesus in four scenes.

First, at his baptism, there was the Voice for Jesus alone: 'You are my Son.'

Then, on the Mount of Transfiguration, there was the Voice for Jesus' initiates: 'This is my Son, listen to him.'

They had to keep quiet about this, because Jesus' messiahship can be talked about only in the light of suffering and resurrection. Only when his hour had come, standing before the Sanhedrin had Jesus himself broken the silence. 'Are you the Son of the Blessed One?' Then came the great statement: 'I am he.'

And now, finally, we hear these words from the mouth of the Roman centurion who had commanded the guard at the cross. It is this pagan who is the first to sense what has happened here and who makes the confession which since then has been sung and spoken on earth without interruption: 'Truly, this man was the Son of God.'

53

AN ENDING THAT ISN'T
AN ENDING

MARK 15.20-70; 16.1-8

There were also women looking on from afar; among whom were Mary Magdalene, Mary the mother of James the younger and of Joses, and Salome, who, when Jesus was in Galilee, followed him and served him, and also many other women who had come up with him to Jerusalem.

There were also women. We might almost forget that. A pity that Mark hasn't told us rather more about them, how in Galilee they served the man who had come to serve and how they went up with him to Jerusalem. We had lost sight of these women, but now that the men have dropped out, Mark again introduces them on stage.

However, there's still a service to perform which at that time only a man could perform. Negotiations must be held with Pilate over the release of the body of Jesus. It would be good if this man also owned a tomb.

When it was already late, and because it was the day of Preparation – the eve of the sabbath – Joseph of Arimathea appeared. He was a reputable man, a member of the council, who was also himself living in expectation of the kingdom of God. He summoned up all his courage, went to Pilate, and asked him for the body of Jesus.

It's already late; tomorrow will be the sabbath, the seventh day. Joseph must go to Pilate today.

He's a member of the Sanhedrin, the college which resolved on the execution of Jesus, but apparently not with the assent of Joseph of Arimathea.*

It surprised Pilate that Jesus was already dead, and so he summoned the centurion to ask whether he was already dead. When the centurion confirmed that, as a favour he gave the body to Joseph. Joseph bought a linen shroud, took Jesus down from the cross, wrapped him in the linen, put him in a tomb that had been hewn out of the rock, and rolled a stone over the entrance to the tomb. Mary of Magdala and Mary the mother of Jesus saw with their own eyes where he had been laid.

So there was still one man who showed courage and love for Jesus.

And when the sabbath was past...

The eighth day has dawned, the day of God. We human beings count the days up to seven and then begin again. The eighth day doesn't appear on our calendar. This day isn't in time; this day is in eternity, it's the day which transcends the ordinary course of time. It was on the eighth day that the Eternal One made a covenant with Abraham. On the eighth day Aaron was consecrated priest. David was the eighth son of his father; he was the youngest and initially wasn't included in the count, but he was to be Israel's king. A new-born child of the male sex was circumcised in Israel on the eighth day. This day enters our lives as a reality of a higher order than everyday reality. On the eighth day, ordinary life becomes a life with God.

And when the sabbath was past, Mary Magdalene and Mary the mother of James and Salome bought spices in order to anoint him. Early in the morning on the first day of the week they went to the tomb, when the sun was rising.

In the evening the sun seems to die blood-red in the west and to sink into the tomb of night. But time and again it rises again and nourishes our dream that one day, after an eternal night, a new day will dawn with unprecedented splendour.

When Jesus died, darkness covered the whole earth; it was a black day. But now, on this Easter morning, the sun rises for the women.

And they said to one another, 'Who will roll away the stone at the entrance of the tomb for us?'

Strong men required. But there aren't any, the women are alone.

No, they aren't.

When they looked, they saw that the stone had been rolled away. And entering the tomb they saw a young man sitting on the right, clothed in a white garment; and they were alarmed.

Who is this young man? The evangelist Matthew will soon make him into an angel, but Mark says only that he's a young man. A young man with good news, as he's sitting on the right: in the Bible that's always the good side. A young man with heavenly news, as his garment is white.

The women were greatly afraid. But the young man said: 'Do not be afraid. Do you seek Jesus of Nazareth, who was crucified? He is risen, he is not here! See the place where they had laid him. Go and tell his disciples and Peter: he is going before you into Galilee. There you will see him, as he has told you.'

The tomb is empty, death has been unable to hold this man. With this image the evangelist bears witness to his faith that God has received the crucified Jesus into his glory. How does he arrive at that faith? It's a faith which has been communicated to him by other people; Jesus too has gone before him in it. But he experiences that faith as more than a gift from other human beings; it's a gift from God: the young man in the tomb is wearing a garment of heavenly white. 'He is risen!'

Jesus' disciples mustn't seek their Lord in the tomb. Where, then? In Galilee. In other words, where they live and work. In Galilee they followed and served Jesus, and the young man in white thinks that they must go on doing that. 'He is going before you. Go and tell his disciples and Peter.'

Why is Peter mentioned separately? Probably to emphasize that God is a God of forgiveness. The Eternal One has not only had pity on his Son, but in him on the world which denied him. The empty tomb depicts Israel's faith that death doesn't have the last word and *in* the empty tomb it is proclaimed that guilt doesn't have the last word either. Disciples who fell must also rise again and become disciples once again: 'He is going before you, in Galilee you shall see him.'

How will they see him? Unlike the evangelists who write after him, Mark tells us nothing of appearances of Jesus after his death. How will they see him?

They will see him by *following* him. Jesus is raised, he dwells above the clouds of heaven, he isn't here. But he doesn't just dwell with his heavenly Father, he dwells just as much in the story about him that is going the rounds in Galilee. The story of someone who is *alive.*

The women went out and fled from the tomb, for trembling and astonishment had come upon them. And they said nothing to anyone, for they were afraid.

And those are the last words of Mark's story. It's a strange ending.* Why does the evangelist end so suddenly with the fleeing women who continue to keep silent?

It's such a sad ending. Now the women also do what the men have done. With them, too, the seed seems to have fallen on rocky ground. They're afraid, and their faith, too, falls short. And all our hope was pinned on the women! Now they're the ones who've been told. How can the gospel of God continue to be told, if not by the women? Like the men, they've followed Jesus and served him, on the long way from Galilee to Jerusalem. They've heard him speaking his words in the synagogues and in people's houses, a new teaching with authority. From his hands they received the bread and the fish that he shared with Jews and pagans. They saw his concern for the sick, his love of children. They know that he ordered demons to be silent and stilled the storm; they know the parables that he told and the parables that he did, sharing meals with the least of people. They also know of the hatred that he provoked, of his denial by his friends, his fear in the garden, his silence before his judges, his crucifixion and his burial. But only the women have learned from the young man in white that nothing could separate the Son of man from the love of God, and that that's also true for his followers.

How is it all to go on, Mark? If even the women now drop out, there's no one left to pass on what happened. Why does the evangelist stop his story here?

Apparently to make us, his readers, ask *this* question. And then to suggest to us that the women aren't the only ones to have received this report from on high. We have too. Mark wants us, sitting and reading this story, now to follow Jesus, and into Galilee. That's why he has made us share in Jesus' life, death and resurrection.

Mark has made sure that we can't just shut his book and go on with the order of the day.

He began with a beginning that wasn't a beginning. He ends with an ending that isn't an ending. The story of Jesus doesn't stop with the empty tomb. We mustn't shut the book, but open it again at the beginning. We must go back to Galilee. The Son of man is going before us in true humanity. We must follow him on this way. And the empty tomb should tell us that this way is no dead end. It's the way to life.

Over the course of a year the Torah is read in the synagogue. On the day that the end of the Torah is read, they begin at the beginning again. Hardly have the faithful heard that Moses died with the promised land before his eyes than the reader takes them back to page one: *In the beginning*.

Mark wants his readers to make a similar move. Hardly have they heard that Jesus died with the promised land before his eyes than the narrator takes them back to page one of his story: *The beginning of the gospel of Jesus Messiah.*

That's how Mark's story must be read. From front to back and from back to front.

MATTHEW'S STORY

54

BOOK OF THE ORIGIN OF JESUS CHRIST

MATTHEW 1.1-2

Book of the origin of Jesus Christ, the son of David, the son of Abraham.

This is how Matthew wants to begin his Gospel, not in any other way: *Book of the genesis, book of the origin of Jesus Christ, the son of David, the son of Abraham.* Jesus didn't just drop out of thin air. He's a son of the patriarch Abraham, to whom God promised that in his seed all peoples of the world would be blessed.* He's a son of king David, to whom God promised that he would bless his seed, that his kingdom would last for ever and that his throne would never be shaken.* Matthew believes that God has fulfilled his promises in Jesus, son of Abraham and son of David, a child of Israel and a royal child. Matthew is convinced that everything that the Eternal One had begun in these long chains of generations finds its fulfilment, its crown, in Jesus of Nazareth. So Jesus doesn't stand by himself; he stands in a long tradition, and anyone who wants to understand this tradition should begin at the beginning, with the book of the beginning: the book of Genesis.

Matthew has the text in front of him, the Hebrew original and the Greek translation. *These are the generations of heaven and earth,* he reads in the Hebrew. The Greek has *This is the book of the genesis of heaven and earth.* And later on, Matthew knows, these words occur again, but then with an important variation: *This is the book of the genesis, the book of the generations of humankind.**

The evangelist wants the beginning of his Gospel to match these words. The book of Genesis told of the origin of heaven and earth, and on earth of the origin of humankind, and in the midst of humankind of the origin of Israel. Matthew will now tell of Jesus: of his origin in the house of Israel, and in Israel in the house of David. And anyone who wants to know what

Jesus generated in his turn, what this son of Abraham and David brought forth, should read the book that Matthew is now beginning to write.

But surely the story of Jesus has already been written down? Why does Matthew want to compose a new Gospel after Mark?

We don't know, but Matthew has a collection of words of Jesus otherwise unknown to us: sayings, addresses, prayers, parables. These are precious words which he apparently doesn't want to get lost.

And perhaps he also saw an artistic challenge here: just as a Te Deum or a Madonna with Child can lead a composer or a painter to produce his own Te Deum or Madonna with Child, so Mark's work could have inspired Matthew also to set down in writing *his* story of Jesus.

Thus there are four documents on Matthew's desk, alongside the white sheet of paper on which he has just written these loaded opening words: his Hebrew Bible, a Greek translation of it, the Gospel of Mark, and a collection of sayings of Jesus. Moreover Matthew has a number of stories and legends in his head which Mark didn't yet know, or which he knew but didn't include. He wants to rescue these too from oblivion.

Who was Matthew? We have to guess. Just like the Gospel of Mark, the Gospel of Matthew is really a community book in which it has proved possible to distinguish different layers from different times. So several 'Matthews' are speaking, and even more strongly than the Gospel of Mark, the Gospel of Matthew shows traces both of its Jewish background and of alienation from that background.

The Gospel must have been completed around ten years after Mark's, i.e. around the year 80, perhaps in Antioch, in Syria. The ways of the synagogue and the church increasingly diverged, until a break had become unavoidable, a fact that made 'an early Matthew' sad, but not the final redactor. The 'early Matthew' seems to be making a last attempt to win his fellow countrymen over to Jesus, for what are the Torah and the Prophets about, if not about what is embodied in the man from Nazareth? Indefatigably quoting from the scriptures, he demonstrates that Jesus is a son of Abraham, a son of David, a second Moses, a second Elijah, of whom the Torah and the Prophets dreamed. The 'last Matthew', by contrast, knows that the gulf can no longer be bridged and has anti-Jewish tendencies. So as not to make this narrative needlessly complicated, in the stories which follow, as a rule I shall continue to speak of one Matthew.

Half-way through his Gospel the narrator speaks in passing of a scribe who has become a disciple of Jesus. Has he portrayed himself here, just as in old paintings painters depicted themselves in a corner of the stable in Bethlehem, or under the cross? *Every scribe who has become a disciple of the kingdom of heaven is like a householder who brings out from his store things new and old.** Be that as it may, this is what Matthew devotedly does: from his store he brings out things new and old.

Book of the origin of Jesus Christ, the son of David, the son of Abraham.
   Abraham fathered Isaac,
   Isaac fathered Jacob,
   Jacob fathered Judah and his brothers.
   This is no ordinary genealogy. In an ordinary genealogy, attention is directed towards the past, to the fathers of the sons, the grandfathers, the great-grandfathers, and so on. Here attention is directed towards the future, to the son of the father, to his son, and so on: see what this new generation brings, who now appears in the history of God with his people.

   It began with Abraham. '*Abraham, I shall make you a great people, I shall bless you, and in you all generations of the earth shall be blessed.*'

   Abraham fathered Isaac. A great deal had been asked of Abraham's faith; he had had to wait a long time for Isaac's coming, but finally he was born, the child brought by laughter. But just one son was a precarious possession. Would God make him into a great people?

   Isaac fathered Jacob. Later Jacob's name would be Israel, because he fought so bravely with God and men.

   Jacob fathered Judah and his brothers, the twelve sons of Israel. Not yet a great people, that's true, but it's beginning to look like one.

   Judah fathered Perez and Zerach by Tamar.
   Matthew is a householder who is also fond of bringing old things out of his store. Here he reminds us of the figure of Tamar, the woman who went to extremes to become a mother in Israel.* She's the first of the five women whom Matthew includes in his list of generations. With all these women the fathering takes place in a special way. In Matthew's view, God's history with Israel is no ordinary history which is handed on from generation to generation as if it were an heirloom. It's a special history. Moreover the list of generations in which Jesus will see the light isn't so much a genealogical family tree as a theological family tree.

55

THREE TIMES FOURTEEN GENERATIONS

MATTHEW 1.3-17

Perez fathered Hezron,
Hezron fathered Aram,
Aram fathered Aminadab,
Aminadab fathered Nahshon,
Nahshon fathered Salmon.

One fathers another. Seeing the monotony of these fatherings, one might be inclined to give up reading them, like the preacher who for the sake of convenience summarized them like this: 'And then they fathered one another until verse 16'. But you mustn't do that, for if you do, you'll miss many *things new and old* which Matthew digs out of his store for us. Like:

Salmon fathered Boaz by Rahab.

One generation appears from another. Here Rahab deserves an honourable mention, the woman who practised on the city wall of Jerusalem the profession which is still practised on our walls today. A foreigner, she lives on the periphery of society, but she has a place in God's heart, this brave woman, who concealed those who were spying out the promised land. Her name had to be included among the ancestors of the man who ate with prostitutes and toll collectors.

Boaz fathered Obed by Ruth.

Ruth, too, has a special place among Jesus' ancestors, the Moabite woman who went with her mother-in-law to Bethlehem and began to pluck ears of corn behind Boaz's reapers. Ruth, too, is a foreigner, and thus she's the second woman to indicate that the blood of the Messiah isn't free from foreign taints. Boaz took her under his wing.

Boaz fathered Obed by Ruth,
Obed fathered Isai (Jesse),
Isai fathered David, the king.

What Israel is in the midst of the peoples, the house of David is in the midst of Israel. It's in the house of David that the Messiah will appear.

David, the king. Matthew trumpets it out. King by the grace of God, shepherd, poet, statesman, liberator of Israel. Is it a wonder that in popular belief the hoped-for coming of the Messiah is attached to the house of David? For the narrator Jesus will have to come from the house of David. And where else will he see the light of day than in the city where David is born, in Bethlehem? So Matthew, in the firm belief that Jesus of Nazareth is the Messiah, David's son, long-expected, has him born in Bethlehem.

David fathered Solomon by her of Uriah.

She was the wife of another man, and David knew that, but David desired her and had this other man put out of the way. This is a black page in David's life, a blot on Israel's escutcheon, but it couldn't break the bond between God and Israel. For Israel's God the last word isn't one of guilt, as Jesus too never wearied of proclaiming, and so the evangelist could give even this shameful history a place in the origin of the Messiah.

We've landed in a dark period of Israel's existence. Matthew first counted ten rising generations – from Abraham to David, the king; after David he counts fourteen generations of mostly weaker brethren on the decline, until finally we get to one Jeconiah in the Babylonian exile. The Israelites are far from home, far from the land promised to Abraham, far from Jerusalem, the city of peace which David founded. Will there still be life after the exile?

Yes, with this God there will be. He does not abandon what his hand has begun. From the origin of the twelve tribes up to and including their dispersion over the earth, he will be their God. He remains faithful, despite the unfaithfulness of the people, here personified in failing rulers. Israel rises again:

After the Babylonian exile:
Jeconiah fathered Shealtiel,
Shealtiel fathered Zerubbabel.
and so on up to ten generations:
Eleazar fathered Matthan,
Matthan fathered Jacob,
Jacob fathered Joseph, the husband of Mary,
who gave birth to Jesus, who is called Christ.

What's happening here? A centuries-long chain of generations is suddenly broken. With the origin of Jesus who is called Christ, something special seems to be happening. Wasn't he fathered by Joseph? If not, by whom?

Matthew will certainly tell us. But first of all he sums things up:

So all the generations are:
from Abraham to David fourteen generations,
from David to the Babylonian exile fourteen generations,
and from the Babylonian exile to the Christ fourteen generations.

The evangelist has had to do a bit of cheating to arrive at this nice three-some of three times fourteen generations, but he does so without any pangs of conscience. He isn't writing a scholarly genealogical treatise; he's a theologian and he's preaching. He simply wants to say that on earth we aren't left to our fate; he believes that we live from somewhere and that we live towards somewhere. There's a system behind this world, a purpose, an order. And he feels that this three times fourteen, this six times seven generations, gives an appropriate signal for the time of seven times seven that follows, the time of consummation which now dawns with the coming of the Messiah.*

Mary is by now the fifth woman to appear in this genealogy. From ancient times the figure five has stood as a symbol for Israel, for it's Israel's calling to proclaim the One God to all four corners of the earth.* One plus four is five. Mary is the fifth woman. Here she stands for the people Israel. She's a woman of Israel. She will give birth to the Messiah.

But who is the father? How did the origin of Jesus come about?

56

THE ORIGIN OF JESUS

MATTHEW 1.18-25

The origin of Jesus Messiah happened in this way. When his mother Mary had been betrothed to Joseph, before they had had intercourse she proved to be pregnant by the Holy Spirit.

A new version of an old motif. In the stories of Genesis, Israel's barren matriarchs could become pregnant and bear a son only through the grace of God. Thus these stories of Israel depicted a belief that salvation comes completely from the other side and that the Eternal One can turn death into life. Later this motif returns: whenever Israel's history is at a turning point and through the grace of God a new chapter is dawning, we're told of a barren woman nevertheless again brings a child into the world. This child will be the one who fulfils a key role in the transitional period which is now beginning. *Samson* is born from a barren woman; it is the time of *the judges*, the men who fought for Israel's freedom. *Samuel* is born from a barren woman, and he will anoint the first of Israel's *kings*. Matthew can't avoid it: now that the time of the Messiah is dawning, it too must be preceded by a miraculous birth; only in this way can he portray how people experienced Jesus as a gift from heaven.

What kind of miraculous birth will the narrator opt for? He isn't just familiar with the theme of the barren mothers from his own tradition. The Hellenistic culture of those days knows a related motif: it was often told how emperors, kings and other heroic figures had been born of a virgin, had been fathered by a deity. The evangelist opts for this possibility: in his Gospel Jesus will be born of a virgin, and God, not Joseph, will be the father. This wasn't so strange a thought for Jewish ears. Isn't Israel in the scriptures called God's Son, God's dear child, the fruit of his desire? And isn't Israel's king also called God's Son? When a king ascends his throne in Israel, the words of God from the old royal psalm ring out: *'You are my son, today I have begotten you.'**

Just as *in the beginning* the Spirit of God hovered over the waters, so now, at this new beginning, the Spirit of God will overshadow lady Israel. The Eternal One will be the father of Jesus. Jesus, the son of Abraham, the son of David, will also be Son of God. Wasn't he the telling image of his Father?

It would have been nice if the angel had also let Joseph know this. He was distraught when he learned that Mary, his betrothed wife, was pregnant. Must he take his revenge and publicly accuse her of adultery?

Joseph, her husband, was a just man and unwilling to put her to shame. Therefore he resolved to let her go secretly.

He's a just man, a *tsaddiq*, a man after God's heart. Of course Mary's infidelity is a slap in his face, but he doesn't strike back; he doesn't put her in the pillory. He prefers not to say a word. Mary and he will quietly separate.

No they won't. Heaven forbid that they should separate, and heaven indeed forbids it, for immediately an angel comes flying in to spell out the situation and to ensure that Joseph assumes the role of father. This child must be born in the house of David.

Look, the angel of the Lord appeared.

In the overture and the finale of the Gospel of Matthew the messengers of God fly to and fro. When Jesus can't yet speak and when Jesus can no longer speak, angels provide words from on high; in the stories in between, Jesus does this himself. In Israel's stories, angels are the lines of communication between heaven and earth. Angels exist for the people for whom these lines of communication exist.

Look, the angel of the Lord appeared to Joseph in a dream.

God gives things to his loved ones in sleep. Quite often the Eternal One wills to reveal himself in dreams, and like his namesake from days long past, this Joseph, too, is a master dreamer. Is that why Matthew has given Joseph this name, or does Joseph dream so much because he has this name? Be this as it may, the angel's first concern is that Jesus should be born in the house of David, and that's why the dreamer is also addressed as son of David.

'Joseph, son of David, do not fear to take to yourself Mary your wife, for what is fathered in her is of the holy Spirit.'

The child may not be born *in secret*; he isn't a bastard but a royal child. Joseph shall take Mary openly to him, and the child shall see the light of day *openly* in the house of David, the king. Joseph does what is asked of him. He's a just man.

The angel's second concern is that Joseph shall pronounce the child's name over him, since that's how Israel's narrative tradition has it: the wife brings forth a male child and the husband proclaims his name over him.

'Do not fear to take to yourself Mary, your wife. She shall bear a son, and you shall call his name Jesus, God saves. For he shall save his people from their sins.'

Jesus, Jehoshua, Joshua. He will be the namesake of the man who was the first of the people of God to enter the promised land. He will be a liberator who saves his people from all the misery into which sin brings them: slavery, fear and death.

In short, this is the messianic dream. Has Jesus saved his people from these things? Surely the consequences of sin haven't been destroyed by his coming? Slavery, fear and death still rule. Why has Matthew nevertheless proclaimed Jesus Messiah? Many people couldn't follow him here, and many people still can't follow him, even today.

*'Do not fear, Joseph. All this has taken place to fulfil the word which the Lord spoke through the prophet when he said, "Look, the virgin shall conceive and bear a son and they shall call his name Immanuel, which means God - with-us."'**

This old prophetic saying of Isaiah is about a young woman – the Greek translation says a virgin – who shall give birth to a son who shall bear the name Immanuel, God-with-us, a tangible sign of God in our midst. The prophet spoke these words centuries ago to a king in distress, Ahaz. He apparently had Ahaz's wife in view. As 'Immanuel', their child, the little Hezekiah who was to be born would be a sign to Ahaz that Israel's God does not wish to reign by power and force but in the way of a defenceless child.

This old saying of Isaiah's is running through Matthew's head. It wasn't meant as a prediction, but for Matthew the saying takes on a deep significance: God not only speaks, but also does what he says. Matthew sees in Jesus the fulfilment of God's promise to Israel: in his eyes, everything that Israel's history is about has taken form in the royal child Jesus.

Many people have endorsed Matthew's faith: 'God has looked upon us,' they say. 'Jesus is Immanuel, God's child in our midst.'

Joseph rose from sleep and did as the angel had commanded him. And he took his wife. And he did not have intercourse with her until she had borne a son. And he called his name Jesus.

God has had mercy on Joseph, as a father has mercy on his child. Now Joseph has mercy as a father on the child and the child's mother. He does what he has to do, three times, carefully and respectfully: and he took her, and he did not have intercourse with her, and he called his name. At the end of his Gospel Matthew will tell of another righteous man. He too will be called Joseph, and he too will do what he has to do, carefully and respectfully, three times. In the overture it is Joseph of Bethlehem who takes a defenceless child into his protection; in the finale it is Joseph of Arimathea who cares for a defenceless dead body.

'And he called his name Jesus.'

In the biblical sense life doesn't begin when the first breath is drawn; life begins when your name is called out. The name expresses your being, your calling; it's the name by which you are called. You truly live only when you receive the name by which you can be called in this life.

And in the biblical sense life doesn't end with the last breath. For the story goes that your name is written in the palm of God's hand.

57

WE HAVE SEEN HIS STAR

MATTHEW 2.1-12

Jesus is born in Bethlehem. However, he won't be called Jesus of Bethlehem but Jesus of Nazareth. How does that come about?

According to the evangelist Luke it comes about through the emperor. In Luke's story, Joseph and Mary live in Nazareth, but on the orders of the emperor Augustus the whole empire has to be registered, and so they return to Bethlehem, where Jesus is born in a stable. Later they return home.

According to Matthew, it comes about through the king. In Matthew's story the holy family lives in Bethlehem, but because the king seeks to kill the child they have to leave their home and escape, first to Egypt and later to Nazareth.

Now when Jesus was born in Bethlehem of Judaea in the days of Herod the king, look, magi from the East came to Jerusalem. 'Where is born the king of the Jews? For we have seen his star rise and we have come to worship him.'

Here an age-old dream of Israel's is fulfilled: the peoples of the world travel to Jerusalem, the heart of this world. In dark nights the astronomers have diligently scanned the firmament, by means of a complicated system of numbers, formulae and constellations, in search of signs from which the fate of humankind can be read.

And hardly have they seen this star rise above Israel than they abandon their horoscopes, leave their land, their kinsmen, their father's house, like father Abraham in days long past, and proceed to Jerusalem. The star goes before them. Is it the star that the prophet Balaam promised when he was taught by an ass and an angel how he had to prophesy to Israel?

> *A star proceeds from Jacob,*
> *a royal sceptre rises in Israel.* *

There they go, the peoples, up to Jerusalem, there to worship in harmony the God of heaven and earth. Isaiah also foresaw this:

> *Peoples shall go up to your light,*
> *kings to the brightness of your rising.*
> *See, they come to you with a multitude of camels,*
> *from Midian and Ephah and Saba,*
> *bringing gold and frankincense.**

It is this vision of Isaiah's that's depicted here by Matthew. And centuries later popular piety inspired the making of Christmas cribs in which Matthew's magi have become kings, three of them, sitting on camels, bringing with them gold and frankincense.

It's an ancient dream:

> *Arabia's desert ranger*
> *to him shall bow the knee;*
> *the Ethiopian stranger*
> *his glory come to see.*
> *With offerings of devotion,*
> *ships from the isles shall meet,*
> *to pour the wealth of ocean*
> *in tribute at his feet.**

Jesus is barely born, when Matthew has the kings of the peoples standing at the gates of Jerusalem full of longing.

'Where is born the king of the Jews?'

When king Herod heard that, he was troubled, and all Jerusalem with him.

Herod is alarmed. He knows infallibly that this royal child is an enormous threat to him; he prefers to play the king in this life himself. The magi want to kneel before this royal child, they want to give power over their lives into his hands. Herod can't bear to think of it; he doesn't want to let this power out of his hands. He won't abdicate, nor does he want anyone to kneel to another king than him. He's troubled, and all Jerusalem shares in his dismay.

Herod gathered all the chief priests and scribes of the people.

Men with power gather more than once in Matthew's Gospel, and when they do they're never filled with holy thoughts.

Herod gathered all the chief priests and scribes of the people and enquired of them where the Messiah would be born. 'In Bethlehem, in Judah,' they said, 'for thus it is written by the prophet:

  And you, Bethlehem, land of Judah,
  you are by no means least among the rulers of Judah,
  for from you shall come a ruler
  who will govern my people Israel.'*

The Messiah, David's Son, can of course only see the light of day in the city of David, in Bethlehem. That's how the prophet translates the popular belief of his day.

Then Herod summoned the magi secretly and questioned them closely about the time when the star had appeared. He sent them to Bethlehem and said, 'Go and enquire diligently about the child, and when you have found him, bring me news, that I too may come to worship him.'

The hypocrite! He doesn't want to worship at all; he wants to be worshipped. Heaven forbid that the magi are so unsuspecting that they go back home via Jerusalem.

But why didn't they travel straight to Bethlehem? Now they've woken that sleeping dog, Herod. Though that's the fault of the star, since it's led them to Jerusalem. But why this diversion?

Because it isn't an astrological star. Just as Jesus' family tree isn't a genealogical family tree but a theological family tree, and just as Mary isn't a biological virgin but a theological virgin, so the star of the stargazers isn't an astrological star but a theological star. And the last thing that this star wants to do is to pass by Jerusalem, since Israel is and remains called to point the way to God for the peoples of the world.

But Jerusalem shows no interest. The least that they could have done there was to look at the sky and see if indeed a star had risen from Jacob. They know their prophets, they know where the Messiah will see the light of day, but they continue to sit there and don't lift a finger. Who must now show the kings the way? If the earth takes no notice, only heaven can inform them.

And see, the star which they had seen rising went before them until it came to rest over the place where the child was. When they saw the star, they rejoiced with exceedingly great joy. They entered the house and saw the child with Mary, his mother, and they prostrated themselves and worshipped him. They opened their treasures and offered him gifts, gold, frankincense and myrrh.

Matthew tells the story in fragrances and colours. They give gold, which in all times and places is the symbol of money and power, of renown and prestige. And they give frankincense, a symbol of dedication and prayer.

> *Let my prayer rise*
> *before your face as frankincense,*
> *and the lifting up of my hands*
> *be as an evening sacrifice.**

Gold and frankincense, they're *the* gifts for the Messiah, aren't they, Isaiah?

Matthew adds a third gift, myrrh, the fragrant oil with which the dead are anointed. For from the start it's already clear that with Herod and all Jerusalem as enemies, the way of this royal child can only be a way of suffering.

In Christmas cribs the third king, the one who offers the myrrh, is usually a black king. Perhaps that's because he knows better than the white kings what suffering is. *Nobody knows the trouble he's seen, nobody knows but Jesus.**

So the magi from the East gave the child of God the golden treasure of their lives, the frankincense of their prayers and the myrrh of their dying. Their gifts express great wisdom. That's why they've also been called the wise men from the East.

Heaven forbid, we thought a moment ago, that the magi should return home unsuspecting via Jerusalem.

Heaven has indeed forbidden them. The angels exerted pressure to see that Jesus didn't disappear from the scene prematurely. First it was Joseph who, with good intentions, wanted to let Mary go secretly. An angel was needed to prevent that. Now it's Herod who secretly, with evil intentions, asks the magi to return to him. Again heaven must intervene.

Warned in a dream not to return to Herod, they departed to their country by another way.

58

THE MASSACRE OF THE CHILDREN

MATTHEW 2.13-23

The magi departed, avoiding Jerusalem, and returned to their land by another way. The encounter with Jesus had changed them.

Herod hasn't changed. He's just as afraid, and wants to kill the child. He senses that all is up with his kingdom if the God of the Torah and the Prophets has his say, and so he's exactly like the Egyptian Pharaoh who once had all the newborn Jewish boy children thrown into the Nile. At that time Moses avoided the massacre by the skin of his teeth.

What will Herod do when he's told that the magi have disappeared? It's high time for heaven to send down another angel and for Joseph to begin to dream again.

When the magi had departed, see, an angel of the Lord appeared to Joseph in a dream, 'Arise, take the child and his mother and flee to Egypt and remain there until I tell you. For Herod will seek the child to kill him.'

Then Joseph arose, took the child and his mother by night, and departed to Egypt. He remained there until Herod's death. This was to fulfil what the Lord had spoken by the prophet: 'Out of Egypt have I called my Son.'

Israel has a love-hate relationship with Egypt. Once it was a place of refuge for Jacob and his sons when famine reigned in Canaan, but it became a hell for their descendants when a Pharaoh came and enslaved the people. At that time God freed the apple of his eye from this misery: *'Out of Egypt I have called my Son.'*

Those are words of the prophet Hosea, and they match the words from God which Moses spoke to the tyrannical Pharaoh: *'Israel is my firstborn Son, therefore I say to you, "Let my Son go!"'** So Moses, a child who escaped death, delivered his people, and so he went on to the promised land, through the wilderness for forty years.

Why does Matthew recall that old story?

Because he wants to depict Jesus for us as a second Moses who delivers his people. So he makes his story of Jesus match the story of Moses. Jesus, too, will escape death as a child. He will go the same way as the people of Israel once went, out of Egypt, straight through the wilderness. He will be tempted there forty days by the devil, as Israel was once there for forty years. And on a mountain he will hand on to people the words which he himself received from God: signposts to the promised land.

Then Herod, who saw that he had been mocked by the wise men, burst into a furious rage.

He's a king who can't bear being mocked. Such a king makes victims, but thank God Jesus is no longer there: he's safe and sound in Egypt. Jesus will be put to death later. *'King of the Jews!,'* they'll cry. He'll let himself be mocked.

Herod gave orders to kill all the male children of two years old and under in Bethlehem and in the region round about, according to the time which he had ascertained from the magi.

The murder of children is a story from Egypt and it's a story from Bethlehem. It's a story of all times. Time and again tyrants will not yield, and time and again innocent children become their victims. Fear rules the rulers, and tyrants who feel threatened strike out. So it goes on through world history. The tyrants remain, along with their henchmen; only the names change.

Thus was fulfilled the word of the prophet Jeremiah:
> *'A voice is heard in Ramah,*
> *weeping and loud lamentation.*
> *Rachel weeping for her children,*
> *she refused to be consoled,*
> *because they are no more.'**

It was once in Ramah, just north of Jerusalem, that the Israelites were assembled, to be deported from there to Babylon. In the lament of the mothers whose children are being killed by Herod Matthew hears the lamentation of the matriarch Rachel, who is weeping for her children. The mothers of Israel are inconsolable.

Fortunately the terrors of the Babylonian captivity came to an end. So too did Herod's reign of terror.

Now when Herod came to an end, see, the angel of the Lord appeared to Joseph in Egypt: 'Arise, take the child and his mother and go to the land of Israel, for those who sought the child's life are dead.'

Then Joseph arose, took the child and his mother, and went to the land of Israel. But when he heard that Archelaus had become king of Judaea in place of his father Herod, he was afraid to go there.

A chip off the old block, this Archelaus. Must they depart again?

Being warned in a dream, Joseph departed to the region of Galilee. When he arrived there, he dwelt in the town of Nazareth, that what was spoken by the prophets might be fulfilled: 'He shall be called a Nazarene.'

That's not precisely what it says in scripture; probably Matthew here has the *sense* of these prophetic words in mind. When the prophets dream of a king after God's heart, they never dream of a great and mighty ruler. They dream of a king who serves, a prince of peace, without pomp and splendour. 'A Nazarene', so to speak: a simple man from the inconspicuous hill village of Nazareth in remote Galilee.

It's also possible that here Matthew is making a word-play on the word Nazirite, a holy man of God who reminds us of Samson, the Nazirite dedicated to God who delivered Israel from its enemies.* *Jesus the Nazarene* shall be his name.

With these words Matthew ends his story of the origin of Jesus. We now know Jesus by name and surname. That completes his origin. Matthew has reached the end of his overture. The real story can begin.

59

THE BAPTISM IN THE JORDAN

MATTHEW 3.1-17

The narrators of the Gospel of Matthew draw on different sources. First of all there are the books of the Torah and the Prophets; they've already quoted from them a great deal, because they can only see Jesus as the Messiah who in life and death has depicted what the Torah and the Prophets are about. In the language of the narrators, Jesus has fulfilled the Torah and the Prophets.

Then there's the collection *Words of Jesus*, to which they've given a prominent place in their Gospel. And they have the Gospel of Mark, on which they will draw abundantly. However, they don't want just to take over his words; where changes and additions can serve preaching, they won't be afraid to introduce them boldly into the text.

For example, in their eyes more can be made of the story of the temptation in the wilderness than Mark has done. They also have some hesitations about the story with which Mark opens, the baptism in the Jordan. That Jesus underwent the baptism of repentance for the forgiveness of sins doesn't fit the picture that they've formed of the Son of God.

Where do these differences between the first two evangelists come from? Is the Matthew circle more inclined than Mark's community to emphasize Jesus' exalted nature? Is it because the Gospel of Matthew was written years after that of Mark and the need to put Jesus on a pedestal had meanwhile increased?

Be this as it may, the Matthew circle also wants to write its own story of the baptism.

In those days John the Baptist appeared, and he preached in the wilderness of Judaea: 'Repent, for the kingdom of heaven is at hand.'

The time of the Messiah has dawned, the end of the world is near, and judgment is at the door. This conviction has driven John into the wilderness, away from a world that is doomed to destruction. It's there that by penance and penitence he wants to prepare for the coming of the kingdom of God. It's there that he calls on the people who've followed him to repent. Pharisees and Sadducees also come to him. You can hardly say that the prophet of repentance receives them with open arms:

'*You brood of vipers! Who warned you to flee from the wrath to come? Bear fruit that befits repentance. And do not imagine that you can say to yourselves, "We have Abraham as our father"; for I tell you, God is able from these stones to raise up children to Abraham.*'

Don't suppppose that baptism is a magic ritual by which you can safeguard yourself against God's anger. Something will have to change inside, and people know trees by their fruits. Each individual is personally responsible; one can never appeal to one's father. To use the language of the rabbis: 'Fathers cannot save their children. Abraham cannot save Ishmael nor Isaac Esau.' You can never claim that you belong to the people of God. Only the fruits on your tree count. God can create a new people for himself even out of stones.

John the Baptist doesn't pull any punches; this is a fire and brimstone sermon, an indictment. Was John really so fierce in his teaching, or are we listening here to the Matthew who in his day was entangled in a fierce conflict with the Pharisees and the Sadducees?

The evangelist believes that the time of the Messiah has dawned; the judge is coming to judge. '*Even now the axe is laid to the root of the trees; every tree therefore that does not bear good fruit is cut down and thrown into the fire. I baptize you with water, for repentance, but he who is coming after me is mightier than I, whose sandals I am not worthy to carry. He will baptize you with the Holy Spirit and with fire. His fan is in his hand, and he will clear his threshing floor and gather the wheat into barns, but the chaff he will burn with unquenchable fire.*'

Then Jesus appeared.

He came from Galilee to the Jordan to be baptized by John. But surely that's impossible? Jesus is the messianic king, the great judge of the world, the man with the flail who will separate the chaff from the wheat. Must *he* be baptized?

John forcefully sought to prevent him: 'I need to be baptized by you, and do you come to me?'

John wants to have nothing to do with a baptism. A Messiah who humiliates himself and descends into the water to be baptized by him, an insignificant servant, surely Jesus is above that?

No, he isn't. He too will put off his old self in order to become a new self, and from now on he'll devote himself to that. He too will have to learn to say 'Not my will but yours be done'. That's righteousness in Jesus' eyes, that's what he has to do; that's the way he wants to go. And John must *let* him go: that's *his* way of fulfilling righteousness.

'Let me go, John. In this way it is fitting for us, you and me, to fulfil all righteousness.'

Then John let him go.

The first word that Matthew has Jesus speak is the word righteousness. Jesus will be a righteous man, a *tsaddiq*. That's what he learned at home from his father Joseph and from his mother and from his Father in the heavens. He will be a different king from king Herod. The kingdom of the Messiah will be a kingdom of righteousness. The way of righteousness that he will go is a way through the water of baptism and death, through the wilderness of temptations. It's the way to life.

And heaven senses that it must happen like this and not in any other way: *immediately after Jesus was baptized he went up from the water. And look, the heavens opened and he saw the Spirit of God as a dove coming upon him. And look, a voice resounded from heaven, 'This is my Son, my beloved, with whom I am well pleased.'**

That's the first line of the first song about the humble servant of the Lord whom the prophet Isaiah saw centuries ago in the spirit. Apparently Jesus found his calling in these words. In the figure of this lowly man he will be the future for Israel and for the world. *'I have put my spirit upon him, he will reveal justice to the nations.'* That's the second line of that song.

So at his baptism Jesus' work had a beginning that was to end with the cross.

60

THE TEMPTATION IN THE WILDERNESS

MATTHEW 4.1-11

'This is my Son, my beloved, with whom I am well pleased.'

Then Jesus was led by the Spirit into the wilderness to be tempted by the devil.

It's as if history is repeating itself. Israel, too, is called God's Son, when the Eternal One called the people out of Egypt. For forty years the Israelites travelled through the wilderness on the way to the promised land. Many temptations came their way.

How will Jesus the Son behave, now that he's going the way to life? Many temptations will also come his way in the wilderness. Will he cope with them?

And after he had fasted forty days and forty nights, he was hungry. And the tempter came. 'Are you really God's Son? Tell these stones to become loaves of bread.'

If it was first John the Baptist who, with good intentions, wanted to deter Jesus from going the way of righteousness, now it's the devil who, with evil intentions, wants to keep Jesus off that way. Jesus has had himself baptized, and heaven has put itself behind him. 'This is my Son.' It's an abomination to the devil. 'Are you God's Son? Then tell these stones to become bread.'

After forty days and nights – after a long time, that means in the Bible – Jesus gets hungry. The round flat stones in the wilderness irresistibly remind him of loaves, and after a while he can think of nothing but loaves. 'So make loaves out of these stones,' says the devil.

Jesus is seeking God's presence, and hoping to experience it by fasting. And the devil is seeking Jesus in order to get him away from fasting and away from God. The devil, too, has his gospel. He's the champion of the absolute independence of human beings, and as a true artist he conjures up dreams which are so seductive that even the greatest spirits can come under their spell. Who doesn't want a realm which promises us satisfaction and the fulfilment of our desires without our having to do anything?

'Then make loaves out of these stones.' The devil wants him to give up the hunger of his heart for the hunger of his stomach. In that way he will alienate himself from God. But Jesus has recognized the voice in his innermost depths as an alien voice. It wasn't the same as the voice which he had just heard from heaven; it wasn't the voice of the Eternal One, who always fed his people in the wilderness with manna. It wasn't a word that had come forth from the mouth of God.

Jesus answered and said: 'It is written: Man shall not live by bread alone, but by every word that proceeds from the mouth of God.'*

A saying from Israel's time in the wilderness, a saying from the treasury of his people, a saying that gives power in temptations.

'I too can quote scripture,' thought the devil, and he took Jesus with him to the holy city and put him on the edge of the temple roof. *'If you are the Son of God, throw yourself down. For it is written: He shall give his angels charge of you, and, On their hands they will bear you up, lest you strike your foot upon a stone.'**

They're standing on the pinnacle of the temple. Jewish popular belief has it that in the end-time miracles will take place there. At his coming the Messiah will show himself to the people on the roof of the temple and announce salvation.

It's precisely at this place that the devil wants to bring Jesus down. Either as a human being he will smash into smithereens on the temple court, or as Messiah he will come to grief because he misused God to his own greater glory.

'It is also written: You shall not tempt the Lord your God.'*

Again Jesus withstands him with a word of wisdom that Israel acquired in the wilderness.

Once again the picture shifts. Jesus is standing on a high mountain, a very high mountain: all the kingdoms of the earth are lying at his feet. Is he dreaming? *'All this I will give you, if you will bow down and worship me.'*

The classic temptation for anyone who wants to be king. Only recently such a dream reduced half Europe to ashes. The dream isn't strange to anyone: to live *like* God, not *for* God. Jesus of Nazareth, too, was tempted by the thought, until he unmasked the allure as a diabolical temptation. He sensed that when the devil gives – even if he's giving all the kingdoms – he's simply taking. For he takes God away. And what does it benefit a person to win the world if he damages his soul?

'Go away, Satan. For it is written: You shall worship the Lord your God, and him only shall you serve.'*

For the third time Jesus has withstood the devil, drawing on his people's source of strength, again with a word from the time when Israel went through the wilderness.

Then the devil let him go, and look, angels came and served him.

We've just also been told that about John the Baptist, he let him go. John couldn't prevent Jesus from taking the first steps on the way of righteousness, and the devil couldn't prevent him from pursuing his way. He let him go.

It doesn't say that the devil left him in peace. The devil never does that. They will certainly meet again, these two. But now there's joy in heaven, and Jesus feasts on the bread which the angels have flown in.

For forty days and forty nights Moses fasted on the mountain in the wilderness. Then he wrote down the words which he had received from God, the Holy Torah.* For forty days and forty nights Elijah fasted in the wilderness, in an ardent desire to encounter God on the mountain where the Eternal One had also appeared to Moses.* For forty days and forty nights Jesus fasted in the wilderness to come to himself and to his God. He's withstood the three temptations from the devil with a threefold appeal to the words of scripture. He's coped with a task which every human being has to cope with in this life. He's been able to restrain his fantasies of greatness and his longing for self-satisfaction and power, and to use them for his life's work. Now it's now time for him to go. His way is beginning.

61

THE SERMON ON THE MOUNT

MATTHEW 4.12-5.3

Jesus should have been going. But just as he was about to go, news reached him that John the Baptist had been arrested. His brother in the kingdom who had taken the way of righteousness before him must now pay the price. There's a good chance that Jesus may expect the same fate. What's to be done?

He withdrew. Since a light dawned for the magi in the East there have been constant been withdrawals in this story: the magi withdrew and returned to their land by another way; Joseph withdrew with the child and his mother, twice, first to Egypt and later to Nazareth. Now Jesus too must withdraw. He won't escape suffering, but he doesn't seek it.

He withdrew to Galilee. He went to live in Capernaum. There he began to preach, and there too he chose his first disicples.

Matthew is now really settling into his story. The overture has been written; he's told of Jesus' baptism and of the temptation in the wilderness. Now the time has come for him to draw on the anthology of sayings of Jesus lying on his desk. And because he doesn't want just to limit himself to Jesus' words, immediately afterwards he will also tell of his actions.

Before we steep ourselves in the *content* of Jesus' words and actions, let's first look at the *form* into which the evangelist casts all this and see how careful his composition is.

In one major part of his Gospel Matthew wants to tell us about Jesus' sayings and healings, and he frames that part by writing the same sentence at the beginning and at the end.*

> *And Jesus went through all Galilee,*
> teaching *in their synagogues,*
> preaching *the gospel of the kingdom,*
> healing *every disease and every infirmity.*

It's a triptych: teaching, preaching, healing. Matthew gathers what Jesus *taught* the people into three chapters, and he tells of his *healings* in the next two chapters.

But mustn't the central panel, the *preaching of the gospel of the kingdom*, be developed further?

Matthew already has developed it further. For the preaching of the gospel of the kingdom consists of what Jesus teaches and what he does, namely heal. At the centre of the triptych we have what is given form in the side panels: the gospel of the kingdom is preached in word and deed.

First in word.

Jesus, seeing the crowds, climbed up a mountain.

No better place for Jesus to deliver his 'Sermon on the Mount'. As a second Moses he, too, will unfold the holy teaching from a mountain, proclaim what he has read in the Torah. For Matthew these are not words from flatland, two-dimensional words, but thoughts from the high mountain of the Spirit, words from God himself. Listen to the awesome way with which he introduces this holy event:

Jesus, seeing the crowds, climbed up a mountain, and he sat down, and his disciples came to him. And he opened his mouth, and he taught them, saying:

> *Blessed are the poor in spirit,*
> *for theirs is the kingdom of heaven.*
> *Blessed are those who mourn,*
> *for they shall be comforted.*
> *Blessed are the meek,*
> *for they shall inherit the earth.*
> *Blessed are those who hunger and thirst for righteousness,*
> *for they shall be filled.*
>
> *Blessed are the merciful,*
> *for they shall receive mercy,*
> *Blessed are the pure in heart,*
> *for they shall see God.*
> *Blessed are the peacemakers,*
> *for they shall be called sons of God.*
> *Blessed are those who are persecuted because they are righteous,*
> *for theirs is the kingdom of heaven.*

And here, too, before we look at the content, let's look at the form in which Matthew has modelled these eight* beatitudes.

Again he frames the whole with two identical sentences: *for theirs is the kingdom of heaven.* He puts the first and the last sayings in the present, and those in between in the future. Is the kingdom part of present-day life? Yes, but it's also the music of the future. Is the kingdom something in the future? Yes, but make no mistake, it's especially part of present-day life.

'Kingdom of heaven' doesn't mean 'heaven' though. To avoid the holy name of God, the evangelist prefers not to speak of 'the kingdom of God'. The passive forms 'they shall be comforted', 'be filled', and 'receive mercy' are also paraphases to avoid mentioning the name of the Eternal One. It is God who will comfort, fill and have mercy.

At the end of the first four beatitudes Matthew again lets us hear the word *righteousness,* which is so loaded in his preaching. We also hear the same word at the end.

62

THE BEATITUDES

MATTHEW 5.3-10

Blessed are the poor in spirit,
for theirs is the kingdom of heaven.

What good fortune for the poor in spirit! They can call themselves happy. Just like Jesus, they are no longer filled with the desire for self-preservation, for money and property. They needn't hide their fear with possessions, material and non-material: they've let go of their fear. They expect everything from God. They're inwardly free, and as a result they're open and receptive to the kingdom of God.

How blessed are the poor in spirit. They have a share in a hidden happiness that resists and overcomes all unhappiness: 'You can't see it, but it's the true, the only true happiness.'*

Blessed are those who mourn,
for they shall be comforted.

Blessed are those who don't obsessively evade their sadness. Happy are those who accept that we live in an imperfect world and that depression and suffering are part of this life. Happy are those who aren't ashamed of their grief and don't cut themselves off from the grief of others. Blessed and loved are those who have a thin skin. Happy are those who suffer over the injustice in the world and who nevertheless do what their hand finds to do.

Happy are the sorrowful, for only they can be comforted. God himself will wipe the tears from their eyes. So they can already live as those who've been comforted. And comfort others.

Blessed are the meek,
for they shall inherit the earth.

God finds his dwelling on earth among the meek, among those who seek to break through the vicious circle of evil with love. Happy are those who are so strong through their inner strength that they can refuse to respond to violence with violence.

They shall inherit the earth, as the psalmist already dreamed:

> *Be still before the Lord and wait patiently for him;*
> *do not fret over the man who forges evil plans.*
> *Yet a little while, and the wicked will be no more,*
> *but the meek shall inherit the land,*
> *and delight in great peace.* *

'To inherit the land' is a common phrase in Israel. Originally it meant that small-scale tenants would one day be able to call their own the land that they cultivated in the sweat of their brow. Gradually the saying took on a broader significance and expressed the dream of a world in which the first shall be last and the last first. Like the dream which the sick Levi told to his father Rabbi Jehoshua: 'I saw a world gone mad, in which the beggars ruled and the kings served.' 'My son,' said his father, 'you have seen the real world.'

Blessed are those who hunger and thirst for righteousness,
for they shall be filled.

Blessed are those who are never reconciled to the injustice in the world. They stand up for the poor, for those without rights, for oppressed people. Happy are those who continue to hanker after the ultimate righteousness; they shall be filled at the great banquet that God has prepared for all his children.

Blessed are the merciful,
for they shall receive mercy.

'Whoever has mercy on others surely belongs among the descendants of Abraham. Whoever does not have mercy on them is surely not one of the descendants of Abraham.' That's the teaching of the Talmud. Anyone who doesn't have mercy on 'people' generally, who doesn't have mercy on all the children of Adam, but only on fellow-countrymen and women, or only on those who observe the same faith, is unmerciful. Anyone who drives away rather than protects the weak, the errant and those who have gone astray is unmerciful. Blessed are those who aren't like that. Happy are those who lovingly share the suffering of others. God will have mercy on them.

Blessed are the pure in heart,
for they shall see God.

When do we see God? When there's nothing between us and God. When our hearts have been purged of deceit and aggressiveness and avarice, of all those unrighteousnesses which block our view of God. Then we see God. Then we see God everywhere. The ineffable even speaks through the least of all.

   Before you go to the temple you must purify your body, to remind you that you must be pure in heart. Then you may 'approach God'. Then you may 'see God'.

> *Who shall ascend the hill of the Lord?*
> *Who may stand in his holy place?*
> *He who has clean hands and a pure heart.**

Blessed are the peacemakers,
for they shall be called sons of God.

Those who make peace, those who create *shalom*, make something of God visible on earth. Israel is called into the world of nations to bring peace there as 'son of God'. And in Israel, the king in particular is also called 'son of God', called to go before his people in this.

   Blessed are those who understand this calling. 'All those who are led by the Spirit of God are sons of God.'* Happy are those who with St Francis pray that they may become peacemakers.

> *Lord, make us instruments of your peace,*
> *where there is hatred, let us bring love,*
> *where there is injury, pardon,*
> *where there is discord, let us bring harmony,*
> *where there is error, truth,*

where there is doubt, faith,
where there is despair, hope,
where there is darkness, let us bring light,
and where there is sadness, joy.

Blessed are those who are persecuted because they are righteous,
for theirs is the kingdom of heaven.

Jesus went the way of righteousness. In so doing he provoked the hatred of others and was persecuted. For his disciples, too, going this way can become a way of suffering. But the way ends up in the kingdom of God.

Eight beatitudes: together they depict the characteristics of the people of God. That people is the salt in the world, *'You are the salt of the earth.'*
    Salt prevents decay. Salt gives taste. You only need a little bit of it. A handful of righteous people could have saved Sodom from destruction, but there wasn't enough salt.
    'If the salt has lost its power, with what can you salt things? It is no longer good for anything except to be thrown out and trodden under foot by men.'
    You're the salt of the earth: you've been taught that eight times. But what if the salt itself has gone off? Then it can only be thrown away. And the world is without salt.

'You are the light of the world. A city on a hill cannot be hidden. You do not light a lamp to put it under a bushel; you put it on a lampstand so that it gives light to all that are in the house.'
    The light isn't there for itself, it's there to shine. It's there to penetrate the darkness so that all in the house are illuminated by it.
    Let your light so shine before people that they see your good works and glorify your heavenly Father.

63

JESUS AND THE TORAH

MATTHEW 5.17-30

Doesn't the teaching which Jesus unfolds on the mountain diverge from the teaching which Moses brought down with him from the mountain? There are scribes in Israel who see it as an attack on the tradition, but Jesus disputes that: *'Do not think that I have come to abolish the Torah and the Prophets; I have come to fulfil them.'*

Matthew gives these words a prominent place in his Gospel, and probably does so for two reasons: he wants to rid his fellow-Jews of the fear that by following Jesus they must give up their tradition, and he wants to impress on Jesus' followers from the Gentiles that Jesus can't be seen apart from the Jewish tradition in which he stood. Jesus hasn't come to abolish the old but to show it in its fullness.

The Torah is holy for him, every dot and every comma in it. *'Truly I say to you, till heaven and earth pass away, not an iota, not a dot, will pass away from the Torah until all is accomplished. Whoever relaxes one of the least of these commandments and teaches men so, shall be called least in the kingdom of heaven. But whoever does them and teaches them shall be called great in the kingdom of heaven. For I tell you, unless your righteousness exceeds that of the scribes and Pharisees, you will never enter the kingdom of heaven.'*

Matthew has collected for his readers six examples of this abundant righteousness, and six times he makes them begin with the same sentence: *'You have heard that it has been said from of old... but I say to you...'* This isn't followed by statements in which Jesus opposes the commandments of the Torah, but by powerful, provocative words by which he wants to deepen and sharpen these commandments. 'Jesus is not content with Sinai,' said Martin Buber, speaking about the mountain on which Moses received the Torah; 'he wants to penetrate the cloud above the mountain from which the voice resounds; he wants to penetrate the primal purpose of God.'

'You have heard it said from of old: you shall not kill. Whoever kills shall be liable to judgment.'

'But I say to you, even though someone bears malice against his brother in his heart, let him be dragged before the judgment. Anyone who insults his brother by calling him a fool shall be punished by the tribunal, and anyone who makes his brother out to be godless shall fall victim to the fire of hell.'

To revile anyone is also deadly. Every murder begins with hatred in the heart.

'So if you are bringing your offering to the altar and remember that you have something against your brother, leave your offering before the altar, first go and be reconciled with your brother, and then return to make your offering.'

How will you celebrate your reconciliation with God if you don't make an effort to be reconciled with your brother? And don't wait until he comes to you.

'You have heard it said: you shall not commit adultery.'

'But I say to you, if a man looks covetously at a woman, he has already committed adultery with her in his heart. If your right eye threatens to bring you down, pluck it out. And if your right hand threatens to bring you down, cut it off. It's better for you to lose one of your members than to go to hell with your body intact.'

The best way to attack evil is radically, before your eyes and hands have followed the lure of what you desire.

'You have also heard it said from of old: you shall not break an oath, but fulfil your oaths to the Lord.'

'But I say to you that you mustn't swear at all. Not by God; not by heaven, for that is God's throne; nor by the earth, for that is his footstool; far less by Jerusalem, the city of our King. Don't use God to enhance your own credibility. And don't swear by your head, since you can't make one hair of it white or black. Let your yes be yes and your no no. Anything more than this comes from the evil one.'

The teaching that Jesus unfolds on the mountain aims high and can dishearten someone in the lowland: one always falls short. But his words can also be heard as so many warnings against self-satisfaction. Hatred, covetousness, taking God's name in vain, none of these is strange to anyone. Therefore be as gentle with others as you want God to be gentle with you.

These may be impossibly high demands, but falling short of them isn't as bad as not having made any attempt at all.

64

LOVE YOUR ENEMY

MATTHEW 5.33-48

'*You have heard it said: an eye for an eye and a tooth for a tooth.*'

That is indeed written in the Torah,* and it was a great step forward in the administration of justice, for this regulation aimed at putting a limit to vengeance: a punishment may fit the crime, but it must stop there. You may repay injustice that has been done to you, but only in the same coin: an eye for an eye, no more. So this is a measure which protects the perpetrator.

'*You have heard it said: an eye for an eye and a tooth for a tooth. But I say to you, do not strike back when someone treats you unjustly.*'

Why don't you make sure that the evil stops with you? After all, the Torah also teaches you that you must love your neighbour as yourself.* This teaching isn't about the neighbour who loves us back; it's about the neighbour who hoodwinks us and threatens and mocks and strikes us.

But who is capable of such love? Who measures up to the person of Isaiah's dreams?

> *I gave my back*
> *to those who struck me,*
> *I gave my cheek to those*
> *who plucked out my beard,*
> *I did not cover my face*
> *from shameful spitting.*

If someone strikes you on one cheek, offer the other one. Don't let your behaviour be determined by your opponent's behaviour; break through the spiral of violence. Try to see your neighbours not so much in the light of their actions and disposition as in the light of their suffering. Why don't you pay more attention to their need than to the way in which they express it? Love your neighbours; they're like you. They too are in search of love and a place in the sun.

If someone wants to sue the shirt off your back, offer your coat too. Don't stand on your rights. If a Roman soldier asks you to go a mile with him, then go two. You know that he's allowed to ask you to carry his baggage for a mile. If you added another, wouldn't that change both of you?

'You have heard it said: you shall love your neighbour and hate your enemy.'

There isn't a contrast here between Jews and Christians, in which the Jews are said to have taught hatred of their enemies and the Christians love of their neighbours. Jesus and Matthew are taking up a position on a question which was topical in the Judaism of those days. There was apparently an interpretation of the Torah going the rounds which sought to limit love of neighbour to one's own circle: Jesus and Matthew are opposed to that.

It becomes quite another matter when outsiders, for example Christians, declare that what they feel to be the reprehensible view of some Jews is *the* Jewish view. Ironically enough, the fronts then seem to be reversed: we see Christians beginning to hate their enemies. In so doing, they in turn have limited love of neighbour to their own circle.

'I say to you, love your enemies. Pray for those who persecute you.'

No, it isn't that you can immediately cherish warm feelings for your enemy; that sort of thing doesn't happen to order. But you mustn't write your enemy off; you must never tire of looking for ways of seeing enemies as brothers and sisters. They too are children of God. Seek to win them over, dare to be loving, and be royal in that, as God is royal when he makes his sun rise on the wicked and the good and makes the rain fall on the just and the unjust. If God is so good and gentle with you, shouldn't you be good and gentle with another child of God? Surely this other person doesn't need to earn your goodness and gentleness first? Surely that's not how God deals with you? So love your enemy. There's no merit in loving only those who also love you. Even the toll-collectors do that. If you greet only your friends, what's so special about that? Don't the pagans also do it? *Love your enemies, that you may be sons of your Father who is in heaven.*

'You therefore must be perfect, as your heavenly Father is perfect.'

Those who live by the undivided goodness of their heavenly Father will radiate the same undivided goodness to others out of sheer gratitude and joy.

With this seventh saying the evangelist sums up what Jesus preached six-fold. Matthew knew what he was doing when he made Jesus pronounce these words on a high mountain. Who can rise to such heights?

65

RIGHTEOUSNESS IN SECRET

MATTHEW 6.1-6, 16-18

Matthew impresses on us that righteousness must be done in this world. But it must be done with the right attitude.

'*Beware of doing righteousness with an eye to others, in order to be seen by them, for then you will have no reward from your Father who is in heaven. So when you give alms... and when you pray... and when you fast...*'

Jesus is talking about the classic three virtues with which a person can do righteousness. One's relationshp to one's neighbour can take shape in works of mercy; one's relationship to God in prayer; and one's relationship to one's own body and soul in fasting.

But wait a minute! Before we know it, piety becomes a show of piety. Then we become the kind of Pharisee who, afraid of losing the appreciation and esteem of others, is constantly engaged in winning this appreciation and esteem. Then piety has become theatre. Look at me being generous, look at me being pious, look at me cutting into my own flesh! Admiring looks from others are our lot, but we mustn't expect also to win admiring looks from God. We've already had our reward. We mustn't expect to be paid twice for the same work.

The question is one of righteousness and of the person to whom righteousness is done. The question isn't about the benefactors. May they remain invisible. Their reward is the joy that the others have been given their due.

'*When you give alms, do not sound a trumpet before you, as the hypocrites do in the synagogues and in the streets, that they may be praised by men. Truly, I say to you, they have their reward. But when you give alms, do not let your left hand know what your right hand is doing, so that your good deed may remain secret. And your Father who sees in secret will reward you openly.*'

You're doing it for God. So don't just sit there satisfied with looking at your own open hands. It's better to give in such a way that you hardly pause over it, and then quickly forget it again. Let your good gifts slip from your hands almost playfully, and derive your joy from the fact that it is given you to give.

'And when you pray, do not pray like the hypocrites. They love to stand and pray in the synagogues and on the street corners, so as to be conspicuous. Truly I say to you, they have their reward. But when you pray, go into your room and shut the door and pray to your Father who is in secret, and your Father who sees in secret will reward you.'

Prayers have their fixed times, so it can happen that the hour for prayer strikes when you're on your way somewhere. But to go out into the street specially and look for a cross-roads has nothing to do with serving God, however religious it may appear. Go into your room and pray in secret. There's no one to see you. God sees you.

'And when you fast, do not put on a sad face, like the hypocrites, for they disfigure their faces, that their fasting may be seen by people. Truly I say to you, they already have their reward. But when you fast, anoint your head and wash your face, so that no one can see that you are fasting, but only your Father who is in secret. And your Father who sees in secret will reward you.'

What is fasting? It's an art which almost everyone has forgotten. Fasting is total or partial abstention from eating and drinking in order to still earthly longings and to make room for God. For people in our day, fasting can mean refraining for a while from watching television, reading newspapers, going out, or other diversions which can keep a person from the 'kingdom of God'. Be this as it may, fasting is an act of self-discipline, of devotion or repentance. In biblical times people demonstrated that they were fasting by pouring ashes over their heads.

If you fast, don't do it like the hypocrites. They may seem to be sitting in sackcloth and ashes, but it's only outward show; they don't put anything of themselves into it. They've only made themselves unsightly in order to attract people's attention. Don't think that for them fasting is a way of approaching God in order to have a better sense of priorities, to be clear once again that human beings don't live by bread alone. These hypocrites want to earn their place as children of God, rather than showing what children of God are like. If you want to fast, do so with a free and joyful heart. Anoint your head and wash your face as if you were going to a party. After all, you are.

The ritual of fasting, which has been practised down the centuries in almost all the religions of the world, has fallen into disuse in our Western world. Does that mean that we're losing a valuable form of expressing belief?

'In itself, fasting is worthless,' wrote Han Fortmann. 'It's a neutral technique which can be valuable or not, depending on the spirit in which it is undertaken. With love and prayer it makes us strong and light-footed. Without these, it contributes directly to subtle and hidden sins which are already unmasked by Jesus.' Fortmann expresses the hope and the expectation that fasting will be rediscovered as a fine and powerful expression of human solidarity, and perhaps also again as an expression of religious hunger. But he adds that it's pastorally prudent not to compel people to do anything that doesn't make sense to them.

66

OUR FATHER

MATTHEW 6.7-15

The fragment of the Gospel that we've just read is carefully composed and has a clear structure. But the narrator disrupted the symmetry by putting the text of the Our Father in the passage about prayer. This broke up the balanced structure. However, in so doing he ensured that the Our Father came to stand at the centre of the triptych of almsgiving, prayer and fasting, and thus at the centre of the Sermon on the Mount.

'*When you pray, do not heap up empty phrases as the Gentiles do; for they think that they will be heard for their many words. Do not be like them, for your Father knows what you need before you ask him. Pray then like this: Our Father...*'

The gods of the pagans have many names, and they rule different domains. How can one know which is the right name in a particular case and whether one is properly connected? The best thing to do is to name all the names that one knows; that's the best chance of getting a hearing.

Those who see God as Father don't need to pray like this. The Father in heaven has made them, has willed them; it does him good to see them, and they may come as they are, joyful or at the end of their tether, grateful or embittered. They may just drop in; after all, aren't they part of the family? And God already knows what they need before they've said anything. But God likes to hear it. 'Tell me,' he says. And they tell him.

Jesus addresses God as 'Father', an image of God which wasn't unknown in Israel but wasn't really common. *Abba.* Just like 'Mamma', it's one of the first words a child says. There were people to whom that *Abba* sounded irreverent – it was far too familiar a form of address to use when talking to God. Perhaps they also thought that the image of God was too personal.

Gandhi said wise words about this: 'God is an impersonal God for those who do not need a personal image of God. He assumes a face for those who long for a personal encounter.'*

Pray then like this: Our Father...

Jesus probably wasn't giving his followers the fixed text of a prayer. We may turn the Our Father into such a text; there's nothing against that, but the prayer which is offered us here is meant more as a model, as an exercise for all our praying. When you pray, do so in this spirit.

Matthew begins with three petitions in which the person who prays concentrates on the essentials, on God's cause: that his name may be hallowed, that his kingdom may come, that his will may be done. After that he turns to God with the great human questions: the questions of bread, of guilt, and of redemption. These are three petitions for bodily and spiritual preservation.

Our Father, who is in heaven

I call you Father because I am your child. I call you Father because I believe that you love me and because I put all my trust in you. Much in your creation is obscure to me; there are bitter riddles of which I can make no sense. However, for me the signs of your loving presence are stronger than the signs of your hiddenness which cries out to heaven. So I continue to call you Father. At the same time I feel small and insignificant compared with your majesty. You are indeed a Father, but a Father in hiding, a Father who is in heaven. I also sense that you aren't just *my* Father, but also the Father of my brothers and sisters on earth. Whenever I call you *our* Father, I try to remind myself of that.

Hallowed be your name

'I shall be there,' you've said. With these words you've given us your name, revealed to us who you are. You're our partner. We pray that despite our mistakes you will keep your promise to us. And we pray that we may uphold your name and give honour to you alone. Just as you're the God of people, we want to be people of God.

Your kingdom come

Don't let us stand in the way of the coming of your kingdom of peace and righteousness. Let the dreams of your prophets be fulfilled. Where Jesus appeared, your kingdom already broke through; those whose backs were bent stood up straight and went on their way reborn. Direct us, too. Strengthen our trust that your kingdom is coming, and make us its useful servants.

Your will be done, as in heaven, so on earth

Don't let our will obscure yours. Grant that your heavenly Torah may show us the right way on earth, the way of love. Let us complete what you've begun.

Give us today our daily bread

We ask no riches from you, no abundance, but bread for today. The earth is yours and all that grows on it. Give your food to all of us. Make us open and carefree, living day by day.

Forgive us our debts, as we also forgive our debtors

We ask something from you which we ourselves find difficult: to forgive. Looking back in anger comes easily to us, trapped as we are in our fear and our pride. Forgive us for not loving you heart and soul. Bring home to us how dependent we ourselves are on forgiveness and make us as generous as you are in our dreams.

And do not lead us into temptation, but deliver us from evil

Lead us so that we don't go astray. And when we're put to the test, give us the strength to withstand the testing. Like your Son, we too are tempted to satisfy our hunger for life with bread, with the esteem of others and power over them. Teach us how disastrous these longings are. Deliver us from evil. Grant that evil doesn't hold us prisoner.

Amen

So it is. So be it. Truly, I want to make it true in my life.

The first Christian community added a doxology here. Probably it's an answer from the community to the prayer which was spoken only by the celebrant.

For yours is the kingdom and the power and the glory, for ever.

67

DON'T BE ANXIOUS

MATTHEW 6.19-34

'*Do not gather treasure on earth, where moth and rust devour and where thieves break in to steal, but gather your treasure in heaven, where moth and rust do not devour and where no thieves break in and steal. For where your treasure is, there will your heart be also.*'

The man on the mountain doesn't ask us to dissociate ourselves from money and property. He asks what our heart is set on. We mustn't sell our souls for earthly treasures. Jesus knows from his own experience that a life of love and mercy makes a person rich. We gather treasures in heaven by sitting loose to them on earth. That's how we serve God and our neighbour; they rejoice in our goodness. The only ones who are sorry are the moths and the thieves.

'*The eye is the lamp of the body. If your eye is good, your whole body will be full of light. But if your eye is not sound, your whole body will be dark. And if the light in you is darkness, how dark is the darkness!*'
    A good eye lets in a world of light. If the eye isn't sound, then a person comes to sit in darkness. And so do those around him.

Those who have an evil eye hanker after wealth,
those who have a friendly eye share their bread with the poor.*

The eye is the mirror of the soul. Sometimes we see something of God glinting in it. Sometimes we see only money glinting in it, with 'in God we trust' on it.

'*No one can serve two masters. For either he will devote himself to the one and neglect the other, or he will cling to the one and despise the other. You cannot serve both God and Mammon.*'

The Lord is my shepherd, I lack nothing. Or is the bank your shepherd? Make sure that you don't make your possessions idols. Try to possess as if you had no possessions.* Don't think that as a servant of two masters you can serve the God of the Torah and the God of money.

'Therefore I say to you: Do not be anxious about your life, what you must eat or what you must drink, nor about your body, what you should put on. Is not your life more than food, and your body more than clothing? Look at the birds of the air; they neither sow nor reap nor gather into barns, yet your heavenly Father feeds them. Are you not far above them? And which of you by being anxious can add one cubit to his span of life? And why are you so anxious about clothing? Consider the lilies of the field, how they grow; they do not toil or spin. Yet I tell you, even Solomon in all his glory was not clothed like one of these. If God so clothes the grass of the field, which today is alive and tomorrow is thrown into the oven, will he not much more clothe you, who have so little faith?'

Jesus had many cares, but he was carefree. The cares didn't have *him*; anxiety had given place to trust in God. When anxiety again threatened to get the upper hand, he retreated into solitude. He sought and found comfort in the birds of the air and the lilies of the field. The birds gather their food, meanwhile singing the most beautiful songs; the flowers stand there, quietly being beautiful. How much more does God care for the children of humankind?

'Therefore do not be anxious, saying "What shall we eat?" or "What shall we drink?" or "What shall we wear?" For the Gentiles seek all these things, and your heavenly Father knows that you need them all. But seek first God's kingdom and God's righteousness, and all these things will be given to you. Therefore do not be anxious about tomorrow, for tomorrow will be anxious for itself. Every day has troubles enough of its own.'

Life passes by those who let themselves be paralysed by cares. That's a shame. Why so anxious? God cares.

And don't think that all is up when you die. If you trust that this life isn't the only one, then you needn't obsessively try to get whatever you can out of it, living greedily, irritably, fearfully, as if it's almost closing time.

Let the dream of God's kingdom and his righteousness stand at the heart of your life. Above all seek this treasure.

68

WHAT YOU WOULDN'T WANT DONE TO YOU

MATTHEW 7.1-12

Arranging and composing his material carefully, Matthew wants to give a place in his Gospel to some more sayings, fragments of Jesus' teaching.

'Judge not, so that you are not judged. For with the judgment you pronounce you will be judged. The measure you give will be the measure you get. Why do you see the speck that is in your brother's eye, but do not notice the log that is in your own eye? How can you say to your brother, "Let me take the speck out of your eye," when there is a log in your own eye? You hypocrite, first take the log out of your own eye, and then you will see clearly to take the speck out of your brother's eye.'

Don't judge. Is that possible? Surely a choice must always be made between good and evil, between clean and unclean? Doesn't Jesus argue for that? Yes, but he argues that first you should look into your own soul. Have you, for example, ever asked why you react so fiercely to someone else's failings? Do you remember your own mistakes, which you had suppressed so nicely just now? Could it also be that you abhor in the other what you don't want to recognize in yourself? Has the other person's splinter anything to do with your log?

First remove the log from your own eye; only then can you pass judgment on someone else's splinter. No, it doesn't say that; you may never judge anything. It says that only then do you see clearly enough to help the other person with his splinter.

'Do not give what is holy to the dogs, do not cast your pearls before swine, lest they trample them with their feet and turn and savage you.'

The gospel of God isn't always welcome everywhere. There are closed hearts and bolted doors. You must learn to accept that.

Faith is a hidden treasure which has to be found, and therefore people must seek it. Soon, when Jesus sends out his disciples, he will say: '*And whatever town or village you enter, find out who is worthy in it, and stay there until you depart. As you enter the house, give it the greeting of peace. If the house is worthy, your peace will come over it. If not, then let your peace return to you. And if someone will not receive you or listen to your words, leave that house or town and shake the dust from your feet.*'*

Meanwhile it seems that Jesus didn't observe his own command. What did he do, if not give what is holy to the dogs, his pearls to the swine? He gave the holy to the sacrilegious. They trampled him and finally savaged him. He entrusted the most precious thing that he had to a world which understood as much about it as a pig understands about a pearl.

'*Pray, and it will be given you; seek, and you will find; knock, and it will be opened to you. For everyone who prays receives, and whoever seeks finds, and to whoever knocks it will be opened. Which of you, if his son asks him for bread, will give him a stone? Or if he asks for a fish, will give him a serpent? If you then, though you are evil, know how to give good gifts to your children, how much more will your Father in heaven give good things to those who ask him?*'

Pray and it will be given you. It doesn't say that you will receive all that you ask for. Praying is far more than asking. Praying is being all ears so as to be able to hear God in the silence. Praying is emptying oneself, thanking, singing, lamenting, wondering; praying is despairing, hoping, longing, seeking, knocking. Those who devote themselves to it find God.

Jesus spoke from experience. He had learned to pray from his father and mother and from the prophets, and these in turn had learned it from their fathers and mothers and from the prophets. Thus says the Lord:

> *You will call upon me, and I shall hear you,*
> *you will seek me, and I shall let myself be found by you.**

Never say:

> *The Lord has forsaken me, my Lord has forgotten me.*
> *Can a woman forget her sucking child,*
> *know no love for the child of her womb?*
> *Even if she should forget her child, I will not forget you.**

Pray without ceasing to the God who doesn't give stones for bread. Don't be shy, talk to the Eternal One as if you were talking to your father or your mother. Just say everything that a child can share with its father and mother.

> I walked, I walked alone,
> I walked and I talked to the Lord.
> He spoke and I listened, and He listened and I spoke,
> and I walked and I talked to the Lord.*

There are people with a poor God, because they expect little or nothing of him. Those who expect little also receive little. Those who expect much receive much. Pray. Seek. Knock.

In conclusion Matthew has also added another summary saying of Jesus:
'Whatever you want men to do to you, also do that to them; for this is what the Torah and the Prophets want.'
The Golden Rule: what you wouldn't want done to you, don't do to another.
But we don't need the Torah and the Prophets for that. Surely everyone knows that?
That's so. But perhaps we need the Torah and the Prophets to keep it in mind.

69

PEOPLE OF THE WAY

MATTHEW 7.13-29

'Enter by the narrow gate; for the gate is wide and the way is easy that leads to destruction, and those who enter by it are many. Narrow is the gate and hard the way that leads to life, and those who find it are few.'

Life is more than just taking breath and thoughtlessly going along with the crowd. Life is choosing and looking carefully where you're going. Israel's first psalm already tells us that there are two ways:

> *Blessed is the man who does not walk*
> *in the counsel of the wicked,*
> *and who does not set foot on the way of sinners,*
> *but whose fervent delight is*
> *in the Torah of God,*
> *and who lives with this Torah,*
> *day and night.*

The Torah, in which Moses says to the people: *'I set before you life and death, the blessing and the curse. So choose life, that you may live.'**

Many people just take breath and go along with the crowd, on the broad way, the way of least resistance. There's no need to look for it; this way is quite obvious, it's a crowded way and you're never alone. Better to choose another way, the way of the Torah, the way to life. It has to be looked for. First you have to go through a little gate. Beyond that is a narrow path, and you can really only go along it in single file. If you look carefully, you can see the Psalmist and Moses and Jesus ahead of you on this way.

'Beware of false prophets who come to you in sheep's clothing. Inwardly they are ravenous wolves. You will know them by their fruits. You do not gather

grapes from thorns or figs from thistles. So every good tree brings forth good fruit, and a bad tree evil fruit. A good tree cannot bring forth bad fruit nor a bad tree good fruit. Every tree that does not bring forth good fruit is cut down and thrown into the fire. So you will know them by their fruits.'

The Sunday-school Jesus is meek and mild; Matthew's Jesus is sometimes hard and strict. The evangelist loves dramatic tension, probably afraid that subtleties don't work.

Who points out the way to life for us? So many guides are available, and they keep telling us to follow them. But what is truth and what is deceit? Who is from God and who isn't? You can't look anyone in the heart. It's impossible to see from the outside whether a tree is sick or healthy. You see it from the fruits, at harvest time.

'Not everyone who says to me "Lord! Lord!" will enter the kingdom of heaven, but whoever does the will of my heavenly Father. On that day many will say to me, "Lord! Lord!, did we not prophesy in your name and cast out demons in your name and do mighty works in your name?" Then I shall say to them openly, "I never knew you, depart from me, you workers of lawlessness."'

There's plenty of God-talk on earth, pious words, but much of it is empty talk which hasn't any cash value in heaven. However attractive the exposition of holy scripture, however indefatigable the fight for peace and justice, it's more for self-glorification than for the glory of God. When the harvest time comes it proves to be chaff, not wheat.

Matthew has almost come to the end of the Sermon on the Mount. He's saved just one more word of Jesus for the end, a little parable.

'Everyone who hears my words and does them is to be compared with a wise man who built his house on a rock. The rain fell and the floods rose, and the winds blew and beat against that house, but it did not fall, because it was grounded upon the rock.

Everyone who hears these words of mine and does not do them is to be compared with a foolish man who built his house on sand. The rain fell and the floods rose, and the winds blew and beat against that house, and it fell; and great was its fall.'

When Moses had come down the mountain and the people had heard the holy word of God, they replied, 'All that the Lord has spoken we will do.'*

The holy word of Jesus must not only be heard but done. If you live by a rock-hard certainty and do what you've heard, nothing and no one will shake you.

'And it happened that when Jesus had finished these words, the crowds were astonished at his teaching, for he taught them as one with authority, and not like the scribes.'

'And it happened that when Jesus had finished these words...' We meet that sentence five times in Matthew, always at the end of a collection of sayings of Jesus.* Matthew has divided Jesus' preaching into five 'discourses'. He sees Jesus as a second Moses, and just as Moses' teaching has been collected in the five books of the Torah, so Matthew has unfolded the teaching of Jesus in fives. The Torah and the Gospel belong together; they fit together; not a jot or a tittle of the Torah is lost in the Gospel.

They learn this: that people should live in love and peace with one another if they experience something of the mystery of God. Or conversely, that people should experience something of the mystery of God if they live in love and peace with one another.

> *Blessed is the man*
> *who does not stand in the way of sinners,*
> *who lives with the Torah,*
> *day and night.* *

The followers of Jesus will be called *people of the way*.

70

THE CENTURION OF CAPERNAUM

MATTHEW 8.5-13

Jesus preached the kingdom and its righteousness in word and deed, teaching and healing. Matthew has now told us carefully in his first and most important discourse how Jesus taught. Now it is time for Jesus to come down from the mountain to add actions to words, and to heal. He's a master teacher and a master healer.

When Jesus had come down from the mountain, look, a leper came to him.

Thus the mountain of the kingdom lies close to the place where the lepers live. Those who've been banished from the human world will be the first to experience personally that the kingdom of God breaks through all limits.

A leper came to him, a lost sheep from the house of Israel. Jesus will heal this sick man, and then demonstrate his power over sickness, demons and death in nine other stories. Matthew will tell us about ten miracles, and again in so doing he makes the figure of Jesus match that of Moses, the prophet who by God's grace also performed ten miraculous signs.

We won't be looking at these stories here: Matthew has taken them from Mark. However, Matthew gives a place of honour in his Gospel to a story that Mark apparently didn't yet know: immediately after the healing of the Jewish leper he tells of the healing of the servant of the centurion of Capernaum, a lost sheep from the Gentiles. The salvation which is first given to Israel must enter the world. This frontier, too, must be broken through.

He was the garrison commander of Capernaum, a centurion, commander of one hundred men. When Jesus enters the city he addresses him. *'Sir, my servant is lying at home, paralysed, in great pain.'*

'Shall I come to heal him?'

Jesus is a Jew, and Jews weren't expected to enter the houses of pagans.

The centurion understands that. And he understands more than that.

'*Sir, I am not worthy that you should come under my roof, but only speak a word and my servant shall be healed. For I too am a man under authority, and I have soldiers under me, and I say to one "Go" and he goes, and to another "Come" and he comes, and to my servant "Do this!" and he does it.*'

The centurion understands all this. 'I am subordinate to the emperor of Rome, and I have subordinates in my turn. I say to one of them "Go", and he goes, and to another "Come", and he comes. In me they obey the emperor of Rome, who has given me power. He speaks through my mouth. What I mean is: why should you come under my roof? That isn't necessary. Just speak a word in the name of the God who has empowered you, and my servant shall be healed. What else can the demons do but go if you give them the order?'

When Jesus heard this he was amazed, and said to those who were following him, 'Truly I say to you, I have not found such great faith in anyone in Israel. Many shall come from east and west and shall recline with Abraham, Isaac and Jacob in the kingdom of heaven.'

Israel's old dream: at the end of time God holds a feast on his holy mountain for all his people. Abraham is there, along with Isaac and Jacob. The Jews come from far and near, from the Dispersion to Jerusalem, all the scattered tribes of Israel. The *goyim* also stream in, the Gentiles, united with Israel and with Israel's God at the heavenly banquet, where all walls between individuals, races and peoples fall away. The coming of the magi from the east to the city of David was already a foretaste of the fulfilment of this dream.

'*But the sons of the kingdom shall be cast into the outermost darkness. There shall be weeping and gnashing of teeth.*'

By the sons of the kingdom Matthew means the Jews with whom the Christian community of his day was entangled in a vigorous and sordid fight. They have no perception of the trust in God that can be found among pagans. Is greater faith conceivable than that of the Roman centurion? Those who can't see that light shining are in a darkness which in Matthew's judgment will finally be permanent.

'Go,' said Jesus to the centurion of Capernaum.

And he went.

He went to a servant who had been healed.

71

THE MISSION DISCOURSE

MATTHEW 9.35-10.42

And Jesus went through all the towns and villages, teaching in their synagogues, preaching the gospel of the kingdom, healing every disease and infirmity.

Matthew has already let us hear these words earlier, when he began to tell of Jesus, who preached the gospel of the kingdom, teaching and healing. Matthew then described to us how Jesus, seeing the crowds, called his disciples to him on the mountain.

Now that the evangelist has told us about the teaching and the healings, he concludes this part of his book with the words with which he began. He gives it a frame. And again he comes to talk about the crowds.

Jesus, seeing the crowds, was moved with compassion for them, because they were harassed and helpless, like sheep without a shepherd. Then he said to his disciples, 'The harvest is plentiful, but the labourers are few; pray therefore the Lord of the harvest to send out labourers into his harvest.'

First the disciples were taken *out from the crowds*, up the mountain, to sit at Jesus' feet and to listen carefully to his teaching. Whoever has ears to hear, let him hear... After that they followed him through the towns and villages of Galilee, where Jesus illustrated the story by healing. Whoever has eyes to see... And now that he's proclaimed the gospel of the kingdom to his disciples in words and deeds, they have to go *to the crowds* to bear witness there. Or rather, they must tell what they have heard and seen. For the people are weary and exhausted, sheep without a shepherd. Jesus hopes that his disciples will have compassion on them. The fields are white for the harvest. 'Pray the Lord of the harvest to send out labourers into his harvest.'

And Jesus called his twelve disciples to him and gave them power over unclean spirits, to cast them out, and to heal every sickness and ailment. 'Go out and preach, saying, "The kingdom of heaven is at hand." Heal the sick, raise the dead, cleanse lepers, cast out demons.'

What Jesus saw as his calling is also the task that he sees imposed on his disciples. Jesus and the twelve are together the Messiah. Moreover we mustn't make Jesus' miracles into signs that only he could perform. If we do, we miss our calling. You can expect miracles of a good disciple of Jesus.

He sends out twelve disciples: the kingdom is near and everyone must hear and see it, all twelve tribes of Israel, all Jacob's children. Could these twelve restore the unity of former times? The evangelist dreams of this.

'Go nowhere among the Gentiles, and enter no town of the Samaritans, but go rather to the lost sheep of the house of Israel.'

First Israel must be won for the kingdom. For if Israel isn't salt, with what shall the world of the Gentiles be salted? If Israel itself isn't a powerful light, with what shall the towns of the Samaritans then be illuminated?

Matthew doesn't just include in his mission discourse texts from the very beginning of the preaching of the kingdom; he also makes Jesus speak encouraging words to the persecuted disciples of his days. So for example they're called on to remain steadfast when they're flogged in the synagogues. It's clear that the evangelist is then no longer speaking about the Israel that was called to be one by the twelve disciples, but about the Israel that meanwhile has become hopelessly divided.

We've already met in Mark many of the sayings which Matthew uses in this second discourse of Jesus. Matthew adds just one saying from another source. It's an anthology of an anthology.

'Look, I send you as sheep among wolves.'

One day, at the end of time, the prophet Isaiah* foresaw that wolf and sheep would live in peace with each other. This peace is still a long way off and for the moment Jesus' servants are as vulnerable and defenceless as their Lord.

'So be wise as serpents and innocent as doves.'

Snakes have no eyelids and are always on guard; nothing escapes them. Be as watchful as the snakes, but at the same time as receptive and open as a dove.

'Do not be afraid of those who kill the body but cannot kill the soul. Rather fear Him who can destroy both body and soul in hell.'

The death of the body isn't the end, for God will have mercy on the soul. No human being can also kill the soul; the soul is God's. The only thing to be afraid of is how God judges the soul.

'Do not be afraid. Are not two sparrows sold for a penny? And not one of them will fall to the ground without your heavenly Father.'

Popular piety turns this into *without your heavenly Father's will*, which is a pity, because that suggests that God wishes the death of such a sparrow. And of people. But what is said is that no sparrow falls to earth without God knowing about it. If God has compassion over that sparrow worth a halfpenny, how much more will he have compassion on a precious human being! *'Even the hairs on your head are all numbered.'* But you really needn't count them all yourselves. Don't be afraid.

'Do not think that I have come to bring peace on earth. I have not come to bring peace, but the sword. For I have come to set a man against his father, and a daughter against her mother; and a man's foes will be those of his household. Whoever loves father or mother more than me is not worthy of me, and whoever loves son or daughter more than me is not worthy of me.'

Life is dangerous, and people try to seek protection with others. In a group people feel safe, and on the broad way they don't have to be alone.

Jesus wants to deprive us of this protection of our own making. The kingdom calls for people who dare to break with their doctrines of salvation and who are prepared to put their trust in God. Israel's faith began when a Voice called Abraham to break with his family and his country and to go to a land which God would show him. In order to go through the narrow gate which gives access to the way to life, it may be necessary to break with your parents or your child or the members of your household. The sword cuts.

With these words Jesus sent out his disciples.

And it happened, when Jesus had finished instructing his twelve disciples, he went on from there to teach and preach.

With the words with which he concludes the Sermon on the Mount, Matthew now concludes this second discourse of Jesus as well. The evangelist is about to begin a new chapter.

72

JOHN AND JESUS

MATTHEW 11.2-19

Jesus went through Galilee, teaching and healing. And all this time John the Baptist has been in prison. He's lost sight of Jesus, and heard of his words and deeds only from a distance. And with the chill dampness of his dungeon, doubt creeps over him. All that Jesus is saying and doing is so different from what he'd imagined. Is Jesus the Messiah?

John was a prophet of repentance, a voice calling in the wilderness, convinced that the end of the world was at hand. 'You brood of vipers! Who warned you to flee from the wrath to come? Even now the axe is laid to the root of the trees; every tree that doesn't bear good fruit will be cut down and thrown into the fire. The one who is coming after me is stronger than I, I am only the herald. His fan is in his hand, and he will thoroughly clear his threshing floor and gather the wheat into barns, but the chaff he will burn with unquenchable fire.'*

But is Jesus, who came after him, stronger? He never swings an axe at the roots of the trees and he seems to like chaff better than wheat. He calls people to repentance and dedication, but he's also full of compassion for the weak and those of little faith. And yet the Romans are still in the land! Is he the Messiah?

'Are you he that should come, or have we to look for another?'

It's John the Baptist's disciples who come to ask Jesus this desperate question.

Jesus answered, 'Go and tell John what you hear and see: the blind receive their sight and the lame walk, lepers are cleansed and the deaf hear, the dead are raised up and the poor receive the gospel.'

Those are six prophetic sayings. Six times Jesus quotes Isaiah, the prophet who above all others dreamed of the messianic age.

Why not seven? Why does Jesus leave out something else that Isaiah dreamed of: *the prisons open for the captives?* Of course John particularly longed for the fulfilment of this prophecy. Instead, he hears another message, a beatitude specially for him: *'Blessed is he who is not offended in me.'*

'Tell him that above all,' says Jesus. For Jesus will be a stumbling block for John unless John begins to sense that although the messianic time has dawned, its realization will have to be waited for a long time, and for John perhaps too long. For John the Baptist, too, the way to the kingdom will be a way of suffering.

While Jesus' disciples were making arrangements to depart, Jesus said to the crowds: 'Once you went into the wilderness by the Jordan. What did you go to see? A reed shaking in all the winds? Did you go to see a man in fine clothing? You won't find such people there, you'll find them in the summer palace of Herod Antipas, a bit further on. So why did you go? To see a prophet? I should think so! More than a prophet! He's the prophet of whom all other prophets dreamed, from Moses onwards: the messenger sent by God to prepare the way of the kingdom. He's the Elijah who is said to return at the end of times. That's who he is. Truly I say to you that among those born of women there is no one greater than John the Baptist. But the least in the kingdom of God is greater than he.'

John was great in his preaching of the one who was to come, but he was small in the understanding of the Messiah whose way he had prepared. 'Are you or aren't you the Messiah?' John has something about him of Moses, who brought his people to the edge of the promised land but couldn't enter it himself.

Jesus and John are kindred spirits, and the same fire for the kingdom and its righteousness consumes their hearts. But we hear a world of difference in the tone of their preaching. However, it doesn't make much difference to the people; the people of this generation don't listen to either of them.

'To what shall I liken this generation? It is like children playing in the market place and calling out to other children: "We have played the flute for you but you have not danced. We have sung laments, but you have not wept."'

John the Baptist had come to the market place, where people were, and they had rushed to hear him and see him. An ascetic. He didn't eat and he didn't drink. 'Prepare the way of the Lord, repent, the Messiah is coming, and he won't accept you as you are, he won't meet you. So bewail your old life, do away with it, bury it, submerge it in the purifying water and then arise – to a new life.'

Some listened to his call, but many turned away. They didn't join in. *'He has an evil spirit.'*

Jesus came into the market place, where people were, and they rushed to hear and see him. He ate and drank, broke the bread and shared the wine. 'Let's eat and drink and celebrate life, we're safe with God for time and eternity. And go into the streets and alleys and invite everyone to the banquet of the faith.'

Some listened to his call, but again many turned away: 'He's a *glutton, a drunkard, a friend of toll collectors and sinners.'* They didn't join in.

Neither the lament nor the festal song find a response in the human market place where people are. Most of them don't want to get involved.

73

PARABLES

What does a human being know of God? How do we speak about God?

To speak about God and about the kingdom of God is to circle round a mystery, with images, stories and parables. Matthew has brought seven together in Jesus' third 'discourse', the 'parable discourse'.

'*A sower went out to sow...*'

That's the first parable. We already know it from Mark.

The second parable is also about a sower:

'*The kingdom of heaven is like a man who sowed good seed in his field; but while people were sleeping, his enemy came and sowed weeds among the wheat, and went away. When the crop came up and bore grain, the weeds appeared also. And the servant of the landowner came and said to him, "Sir, did you not sow good seed in your field? So where did these weeds come from?"*

"*An enemy has done this,*" *he said.*

The servants asked, "Do you want us to go and pull them up?"

"*No,*" *he said, "lest in pulling up the weeds you pull up the wheat with them. Let both grow together until the harvest. At harvest time I will tell the reapers, 'Gather the weeds first and bind them in bundles to be burned, but gather the wheat into my barn.'"*'

When they got home the disciples asked, 'Can you explain this parable to us?'

'*The sower of the good seed is the Son of man,' said Jesus, 'and the field is the world. The good seed is the children of the kingdom; the weeds are the children of the evil one. The enemy who sowed the weeds is the devil; the harvest is the end of the world, and the reapers are the angels. Just as the weeds will be pulled up and burnt with fire, so will it be at the end of time. The Son of man will send his angels, and they will gather out of his kingdom all that is bad and all those who practise unrighteousness and evil and throw them into the fiery furnace. There will be weeping and gnashing of teeth. Then the righteous will shine like the sun in the kingdom of their Father. Whoever has ears to hear, let him hear.'*

Matthew and his people have a problem: the end of the ages hasn't yet come, the hour of the harvest is still awaited. And those around keep asking how it's possible to continue to see Jesus as the Messiah then. At the coming of the Messiah surely the field of the world will be purged of the weeds? But there's little to be seen of that, the weeds are rank!

'Patience; patience!' Matthew tells himself and the others. The kingdom doesn't come with a wave of the wand, it has to grow. Weeds and wheat are entangled to begin with. Once the wheat has ripened and grown strong it will easily be distinguishable from the weeds.

Where do the weeds come from? That's a bitter riddle. The enemy sowed them while people were asleep.

So weren't people watchful enough? Have they only themselves to blame? Is it the fault of human beings that the weeds grow and flourish? That may well be. But is it also the fault of human beings that the weeds are there in the first place? Or do we have to say that the weeds came into the world independently of human beings? When the human being opened his eyes for the first time they were already there; he didn't create them himself.

So there's an element of mystery in this parable. Weeds grow in the field through human neglect; they were asleep during the sowing and so have made this earth a wilderness. But people didn't sow the weeds themselves in the darkness of the night. Who then is this dark figure who sowed the weeds? It's the devil. We're inclined to think that this helps the narrator in keeping God out of the picture as a possible origin of evil.

Be this as it may, there's no simple explanation for the weeds. And we have to be careful in fighting them, because we can make mistakes. What looks like magnanimity can turn into arrogance; tolerance can stem from spiritual laziness; and often what is called love is really possessiveness. Conversely, someone who seems to be harsh and indifferent can unexpectedly show signs of magnanimity. Everything runs into everything else, and the one is entangled in the other. Who will stand up as judge? Don't judge.

Yes, but surely there's a difference between good and evil, between clean and unclean, between money honestly earned and money that stinks?

That's true, but in the kingdom we may not write off our neighbours; they must be able to come to maturity. To believe is always to change. With God, in a manner of speaking, weeds can become wheat. Conversion is always possible. Those who are firmly tied to their past never have a future.

'Let them both grow together to the harvest,' says Matthew. He'd been a witness to how Jesus, God's precious wheat in the field of the world, was pulled up by servants of God, firmly convinced that it was a weed. Here, if anywhere, it becomes clear that when human beings attempt it, the work of purging isn't in good hands...

Matthew has begun the parable discourse with two parables: an old parable of Jesus about a sower who went out to sow, and another parable about the wheat and the weeds. The evangelist attributes both parables to Jesus, but he's also signed them himself: *'Therefore every scribe who has become a disciple is like a householder who brings out of his treasure things new and old.'*

74

THE KINGDOM IS LIKE...

MATTHEW 13.31-52

Jesus told them another parable: 'The kingdom of heaven is like a grain of mustard seed which someone sowed in his field. It is the smallest of all seeds, but when it has grown, it is greater than all the garden shrubs. It becomes a tree, and the birds of the air come and nest in its branches.'

The seed that you sow is pitifully small. You might just as well not sow it. But those who believe have high expectations. They trust that they don't sow in vain. The God who can make a tree grow out of a mustard seed will make the kingdom blossom out of the dedication and faithfulness of his followers, a safe refuge for many.*

He told yet another parable: 'The kingdom of heaven is like leaven which a woman put in three measures of meal, till it was all leavened.'

For those who dedicate themselves to the kingdom of God, it's good to know what a housewife knows when she puts a tiny bit of yeast into a large container of meal. It disappears. There's nothing to be seen. But the next morning, wonder of wonders, it's permeated the whole dough. Three measures of meal. As much as Sarah prepared when God came to visit, accompanied by two angels.* It's the quantity for a banquet, enough for a wedding!

'The kingdom of God is like a treasure hidden in a field. Someone found it and covered it up. Then in his joy he went and sold all that he had and bought that field.

Likewise, the kingdom of God is like a merchant in search of fine pearls. When he found a precious pearl, he went, sold all that he had, and bought that pearl.'

In fairy tales the seeking and finding of a treasure always signifies the seeking and finding of a calling, a destiny. So too in this parable. Jesus is speaking from experience. He has found the love of God and finally parted with everything to devote himself to it completely. He knows that he is loved and safe in time and eternity. 'You are my child, I love you!' This word of love came flying down from the heights like a dove. The devil also came to haunt him, but Jesus no longer allowed himself to be ruled by desire. He dreamed only of the kingdom of God and his righteousness, and he taught his followers to seek their happiness there. 'Don't dream of treasures which do not bring you happiness. Why do you seek salvation where you won't find it? The treasure is straight in front of you, in the field of everyday life.'

The poor day labourer sold what he had; he parted with everything which up to that moment had given content to his life. So did the well-to-do merchant. They did that with all their heart. Now that they've found this treasure, this precious pearl, the one through a chance find, the other after diligent seeking, the old has lost its splendour for them.

'Likewise, the kingdom of heaven is like a dragnet thrown into the sea. Everything gets into it. When it is full, fishermen pull it ashore. They sit down to sort the good into boxes and throw away the bad. So it will be at the end of time. The angels will go out and separate the evil from the righteous, and throw them into the fiery furnace. There will be weeping and gnashing of teeth.'

Everything is in the dragnet of the kingdom, good and bad. One day God's holy angels will come to separate the good from the bad.

Using a well-tried recipe, Matthew has again heated his pen in the fire of hell. Convinced that the end of time is near, he wants to save as many souls as possible at the last moment, and he thinks that only threats may perhaps still help.

75

KEYS AND A FISH

MATTHEW 16.13-20; 17.24-27

And it happened that when Jesus had finished these parables, he went away from there.

Jesus' third discourse, the parable discourse, is at an end, and Matthew continues his Gospel with a number of stories which, with two exceptions, he takes from Mark. After that he will make Jesus give his fourth discourse.

In this chapter I shall tell the two stories which he adds from a source of his own. There's a story about keys and a story about a fish.

'Who do people say that I am?,' Jesus asked his disciples.

They gave an answer.

'And who do you say that I am?'

'You're the Messiah,' confessed Simon Peter, 'you're the Son of the living God.'

Jesus answered: 'Blessed are you, Simon, for flesh and blood has not revealed this to you, but my Father who is in heaven. And I tell you, you are Peter, a Rock-man, and on this rock, this petra, *I will build my community, and the powers of death shall not overwhelm it.'*

These words are as well known as the interpretation of them is disputed. The text itself isn't very complicated, but it's become complicated, because this saying of Jesus has been misunderstood, and because an imposing structure has subsequently been built on that misunderstanding, a church empire.

Jesus expected the imminent end of the world age. For that reason alone we can't assume that he occupied himself with the establishment of a community, a church organization, let alone that the primacy of the bishop of Rome is on the messianic agenda here. In the Gospel stories Peter is also more than an individual of flesh and blood; he always represents the disciples. What is said to him is said to them all.

So what does Matthew mean by these words?

This: the structure of the community is founded as firmly as a rock on the confession that Jesus is the Messiah, which is spoken by Peter in the name of all. This structure cannot be upset by any power in the world. It forms the entrance to the kingdom of God.

'I will give you the keys of the kingdom of heaven. Whatever you bind on earth shall be bound in heaven, and whatever you loose on earth shall be loosed in heaven.'

It must be emphasized once again that the kingdom of heaven never means the next world. As a believing Jew, Matthew is avoiding the holy name of God. He prefers to speak of the kingdom of heaven rather than of the kingdom of God. Thus Peter isn't receiving any appointment as heavenly porter; he's receiving the keys of the messianic community. It is for 'the twelve' to express what is binding in the messianic teaching and the messianic life and what is not. That this calling is not only given personally to Peter but *in* him to all disciples is – perhaps unnecessarily – confirmed by the discourse which Matthew will let us hear soon.*

And then the remarkable story of the fish. It's set in Capernaum, where the collectors of the temple tax come to test Jesus' loyalty with a question to Peter.

When they came to Capernaum, the collectors of the temple tax went up to Peter and said, 'Does your teacher pay the half-shekel tax?'

'Certainly,' said Peter.

When he came home, Peter wanted to give an account of this, but Jesus anticipated him: 'Simon, from whom do kings of the earth take tolls and taxes? From their sons or from others?'

'From others.'

Jesus said, 'So the sons are free.'

It was clearly a question in those days whether they should continue to make their annual contribution to the temple or whether they might think themselves relieved of this duty.

The sons of the king are exempt from paying taxes. So too the Son of God doesn't need to pay tax to the house of God. Nor do the disciples, the brothers of the Son.

'But I will do it,' says Jesus, 'for the sake of peace.'

The freedom of the disciples doesn't represent a revolution in which the old order is destroyed in order to establish a new order.

'So that we give no offence, go to the sea and cast a hook. You must take the first fish that comes up. Open its mouth, and you will find a silver coin. Take that and give it to them, for me and for yourself.'

With good reason Jesus has just addressed Peter with the name which he bore when he was still a fishermen. For a moment Simon must resume his old calling and pay the temple tax with his catch. And to illustrate once again how they will never lack anything, despite their poverty, the evangelist weaves into his story the well-known fairy tale about the coin in the fish.

It's one piece of silver. Let it now be the exact contribution that these two have to pay! It's the last fish that Peter caught; now he becomes for ever a fisher of men.

76

THE COMMUNITY DISCOURSE

MATTHEW 18.1-20

'Who is the greatest in the kingdom of heaven?,' the disciples came to ask.

Typically, this is a question which doesn't belong in the kingdom. How can Jesus make his followers understand this once and for all?

He called a child to him, put it in the midst of them, and said, 'Truly I say to you, unless you turn and become like children, you will certainly never enter the kingdom of heaven. Whoever humbles himself like this child, he is the greatest in the kingdom of heaven.'

People have to change. They mustn't *remain* children, they must *become* like children. Those who don't think too highly of themselves can be open and receptive to their heavenly Father, as full of trust as a child. That seems simple, but it isn't. Only through conversion will an adult be able to become what a child is by nature.

'Whoever receives one such child in my name receives me; but anyone who brings down one of these little ones who believe in me, it would be better for him to have a great millstone fastened around his neck and to be drowned in the depths of the sea.

Woe to the world in which one person brings another down! Of course it is inevitable that this will happen, but woe to the person through whom it happens. And if your hand or your foot threatens to bring you down, cut it off. If your eye threatens to bring you down, pluck it out. It is better for you to enter life maimed or lame than with two hands and feet and eyes to end up in hell fire.

See that you do not despise one of these little ones. For I tell you that in heaven their angels always see the face of my Father who is in heaven.'

Children and those who are as vulnerable as children, the poor, the widows, the sick, the inconspicuous, in short all those who disparage themselves, are the little ones whom one may not threaten. Their heavenly angels do not lose sight of them for a moment, nor should you. Before

God the least are of the greatest importance; let that also be the case for you.

'What do you think? If a man has a hundred sheep and one of them has gone astray, will he not leave the ninety-nine on the hills and go in search of the one that went astray? And if he finds it, truly, I say to you, he rejoices over that one sheep more than over the ninety-nine that did not go astray. Likewise it is not the will of my Father who is in heaven that one of these little ones should perish.'

The loss of a child can never be made good in a family by the children who are still there. 'Don't let one of God's little ones be lost. If just one has strayed, go in search of it. If you do that, you're a child of my heavenly Father.'

Matthew makes Jesus begin his fourth discourse, the so-called community discourse, with this story. In the discourse the evangelist has brought together wisdom of Jesus and wisdom of the first Christian community in an anthology.

How to deal with quarrels, for example. For even in the first community things were human, all too human, and after all, there will be many things in the dragnet of the kingdom. What is one to do with the neighbour who has gone wrong?

Matthew insists that this mustn't be proclaimed from the rooftops, nor should a whispering campaign begin. 'Go and speak to him, just the two of you. Talk with him, not about him. Then he can make good his mistake without loss of face and quietly return to the fold.'

'If he listens to you, you have won him over. But if he does not listen, make a new attempt. Take one or two others with you who can act as witnesses. If he refuses to listen to the community, then let him be to you as a Gentile and a toll collector.'

It may be doubted whether Matthew's simple recipe worked in all cases, but the careful approach for which he argues is in any case praiseworthy. The way in which he speaks here of Gentiles and tax collectors is less friendly.

'Truly I say to you, whatever you bind on earth shall be bound in heaven, and whatever you loose on earth shall be loosed in heaven.'

The words which were recently spoken to Peter as representative of the disciples are now said by Jesus to them all. What can and what cannot be in teaching and in life is determined by the community of believers.

'Again, truly I say to you, if two of you agree on earth about anything they ask, it will be done for them by my Father in heaven. For where two or three are gathered in my name, there am I in their midst.'

Here Matthew is playing on an old rabbinic saying: 'If two men are sitting together and the words of the Torah are their words, then the Eternal One is in their midst.'

For the evangelist, Jesus is Immanuel, God with us. Matthew is saying in other words: 'If two or three people of one mind study the scriptures in the spirit of Jesus Messiah, then Jesus is in their midst, and thus the Eternal One himself.'

77

FORGIVING

MATTHEW 18.21-35

Matthew wants to make Jesus conclude his community discourse with words about forgiveness. For a characteristic of the messianic community should be its unlimited ability for forgiveness.

Unlimited? The disciples ask about that through Peter. Must a disciple of Jesus really forgive *seven times*, in other words, always?

Jesus said to him, 'I say to you, not seven times, but seventy times seven.'

Once Lamech preached vengeance, seventy-seven fold.* Moses tried to limit this unbridled retribution: an eye for an eye and no more.* Jesus preaches unlimited forgiveness.

But isn't that asking too much? At a given moment surely the measure is full? Really this is a saying which an ordinary person would prefer to forget.

Jesus knows that, so he told a parable which is unforgettable to ordinary people.

The kingdom of heaven is like a king who wanted to settle accounts with his slaves. When he began the reckoning, one was brought to him who owed him ten thousand talents.

An enormous sum, too much for a servant ever to pay back in one servant's lifetime.

Because he could not pay, the king ordered that he must be sold, with his wife and children and all that he had, so that payment could be made.

The slave fell on his knees, imploring him, 'Lord, have patience with me and I will repay you everything.'

In his perplexity he doesn't know what else to say. However, he doesn't dispute the amount he owes: indeed he owes the king *everything*. He can only appeal to the patience of his lord.

The king was moved and let the slave go; he released him and forgave him the debt.

And you would have thought that someone who has been forgiven much would have become grateful and gentle.

Hardly had the slave gone out when he met one of his fellow slaves who owed him one hundred pennies.

A trifle. These hundred pennies are to the ten thousand talents what a splinter is to a log.

He seized him, took him by the throat and said, 'Pay me all that you owe me!'

His fellow-slave fell down and besought him, 'Have patience with me, and I will pay you.' But he refused, and put him in prison till he had paid the debt.

The other slaves saw what had happened and very sorrowfully reported it to their lord. He summoned the man and said, 'You wicked slave! I forgave you all that debt because you begged me. Should you not have had mercy on your fellow slave, as I had mercy on you?' And in anger his lord delivered him to the gaolers until he should pay all his debt.

Royal mercy initially removed the anger. However, a strange blindness has seized the slave: grace isn't received and experienced as a precious gift, but is met with gracelessness. Now only anger is left. The slave ends up in hell. He's forfeited his life.

So also my heavenly Father will do to every one of you, if you do not forgive your neighbour from the heart.

Matthew is a hard teacher.

78

THE WORKERS AT THE ELEVENTH HOUR

MATTHEW 19.27-30; 20.1-16

And it happened that when Jesus had finished these sayings, he went away from Galilee, crossed the Jordan, and entered the region of Judaea.

Jesus is approaching Jerusalem. He is approaching death. In the meantime there is Peter with a question to which he very much wants to have an answer. '*We have given up everything and followed you. What reward then may we expect?*'

Yes, the disciples may expect some reward there. Except in the story of Job, in which the Satan expects a person to serve God *for nothing*, there is no one in the Bible who thinks like this. Not even Jesus. To serve God is rewarding. It's rewarding on earth, for it's a blessing to be able to work in the vineyard and be fruitful. And it's rewarding in heaven, for discipleship has eternal value.

But look out, Peter. For it's said that the lord of the vineyard of the world is free to deal in his own way with his own. Righteousness is his top priority, but you mustn't be surprised when his goodness surpasses this. Matthew doesn't derive this thought from the previous parable but from the next one.

For the kingdom of heaven is like a householder who went out early in the morning to hire workers for his vineyard. He agreed with them for a shilling a day and the men went to work. He went out around the third hour (nine o'clock) and saw other workers standing in the market place. 'You go into the vineyard, too, and whatever is right I will give you.' About the sixth and the ninth hour he did the same. When he went out again about the eleventh hour, he found yet others standing at the employment booth. 'Why have you been standing here without work all day?'

'*Because no one has hired us.*'

'You go out to the vineyard too.'

Evening came, and the lord of the vineyard said to his steward, 'Call the workers and pay them their wages.'

The hour of reckoning has come. The Torah prescribes that now the wages must be paid. *The wages of a day labourer shall not remain with you over night until the morning.** The day labourer urgently needs the shilling to buy bread, olives and a melon, food for this evening and for tomorrow. That's how he lives from one day to the next. So give him his daily bread today.

'Call the workers and pay them their wages, beginning with the last, up to the first.'

When those hired about the eleventh hour came, each of them received a shilling. Those who were hired first thought they should receive more, but each of them also received a shilling. They grumbled to the householder: 'These last worked only one hour, and you have made them equal to us who have had a long heavy day in the heat.'

He replied, 'Friend, I am doing you no wrong. Did we not agree for a shilling? Take what belongs to you and go. I choose to give to these last what I give to you. Am I not allowed to do what I choose with what belongs to me? Is your eye evil because I am good?'

The master of the house paid the last first. He wanted the first to see that; he didn't want them already to have gone home with their shilling.

Is this shilling the wage which the workers of the eleventh hour earn? No, they don't get wages for their work. The lord of the vineyard gets rid of accountants with pay slips; the morality of the *quid pro quo* is transcended here. What counts is not when you came, but the fact that you've come. For Matthew's community, this means that they mustn't make any distinction between the people of the first hour who may perhaps have known Jesus, and those who came later. Each shares in the grace of God. And those who cannot rejoice about that with the lord of the vineyard are rebuked. 'Friend, why are you so cross?'

In Matthew's Gospel, Jesus three times addresses someone as friend, and three times we hear a mixture of sadness and bewilderment in his voice. For all three times this friend doesn't want to join in the feast of God's freely-given love; three times this friend doesn't want to be a friend.

'Friend, I do you no wrong. Are you cross because I am good?'

'Friend, how did you get in here without a wedding garment?'*

And to Judas in the garden of Gethsemane. 'Friend, why are you here?'*

Three questions, and to all three questions the friend gives no answer.

'Master, we've given up everything, may we expect a reward for that?' asked Peter. Jesus answered with the parable about the workers at the eleventh hour.

That's now long past. The storyteller is dead, workers in the vineyard have killed him. Their eye was evil because he was good. He had called them his friends; they became his enemies.

But the story lives on. It has found new performers, and new workers have come into the vineyard. Now they're the workers of the first hour, so they must look out. Petty-mindedness wasn't just a characteristic of the workers of the first hour at that time; it's always lurking. Now they too must make sure that they're not so self-satisfied that they despise what is great with God. Their eye mustn't be filled with jealousy; they mustn't want to prescribe to him how generous he can be.

Peter may expect a reward, in due course. It's to be hoped that our friend can find something to enjoy when the Lord again 'makes a mistake' on pay day.

79

SAYING AND DOING

MATTHEW 21.23-32

Jesus has entered Jerusalem; he's walked into the temple area, overturned the tables of the money-changers, cursed the fig tree, and given a new teaching. Can he do that? Has someone authorized him to do it? If so, who can it be? We've already met that question in Mark.

The high priest and elders of the people came to him. 'By what authority do you do all this? And who has given you this authority?'

Jesus said, 'I shall also ask you a question. If you tell me the answer, then I will tell you by what authority I do all this. The baptism of John, where was it from? Was it from heaven or from men?'

Is what John the Baptist has set in motion a human affair? In that case it wasn't from heaven. And if it was from heaven, then it wasn't a human affair. There's no third possibility.

They put their heads together: 'If we say "From heaven" he will say to us, "Why then did you not believe him?" But if we say, "From men," we are afraid of the multitude; for all hold John to be a prophet.'

They answered Jesus, 'We do not know.'

Jesus said, 'Neither will I tell you by what authority I do these things.'

It's clear what the leaders of the people are thinking about Jesus. So their question wasn't a real question, and the answer couldn't be a real answer.

What Jesus thought about *them*, about *their* leadership, the exercise of *their* authority, is now told to us, in another three parables. We already know one parable, that about the wicked tenants, from Mark. Another, about the royal wedding feast, I shall keep for the next chapter. The first parable of the three is about a father with two sons.

Israel is called *the Son of God* in the scriptures. But the people of God is inwardly divided and is quarrelling in the temple area. There are those who want to go the way of John the Baptist and Jesus, the way of the kingdom and its righteousness. However, the people of God can't stand behind this as one: the Father has two sons who go different ways.

A father had two sons. 'My child,' he said to the first, 'go and work in the vineyard today.'

' Yes, sir,' said the son.

It's polite to say 'sir' to your father. Honour your father and mother. A well-behaved young man.

But he did not go.

The father turned to the second son and asked the same of him. 'I will not go,' he replied. But later he changed his mind and went.

'Which of these two,' asked Jesus, 'do you think did the will of the father?'

'The last,' they said.

Jesus said to them: 'Truly, I say to you, the toll collectors and the prostitutes are going into the kingdom of God before you. For John showed you the way of righteousness and you did not believe him. The toll collectors and the prostitutes believed him. And you saw it, but you did not repent, and persisted in your unbelief.

You can make mistakes over people. Some look pious; you hear them say 'Lord, lord,' but they don't lend a hand in the Lord's vineyard. And there are people who seem to heed neither God nor commandments, but suddenly turn up in the vineyard after all.

Jesus simply wants to say that lip service to the holy faith isn't the same as living by it. Saying is one thing, doing's another. Believing is quite different from exclaiming 'Lord, lord' and leaving it at that. Believing involves repenting and going the way of righteousness.

It isn't easy to go this way. It can even cost you your life, as the story of John has shown and as the story of Jesus will show. So we can well understand those who exclaim 'I won't'. Those who say yes quickly probably haven't heard the question properly. A person's yes is different when it's been preceded by a no. Such people have grown in knowledge of God and of themselves.

80

THE ROYAL WEDDING FEAST

MATTHEW 22.1-14

That's roughly how it must have been, after Jesus' death, in the springtime of the church, when on the first day of the week the believers came together to hold a meal. At a given moment the conversations would fall silent, because someone was going to tell a story, a story about Jesus. For example, about how Jesus had meals with them and how at a given moment the conversations fell silent because he was going to tell a story. For example, about a meal.

Jesus said much *with* meals and said much *at* meals. There's something intimate about being gathered round a table. You show solidarity and celebrate fellowship. If you want to know the nature of a community, look carefully at its eating customs: who eats with whom. Jesus had meals with those who were excluded from other people's tables: the unclean, strangers, prostitutes and toll collectors. That was a parable in itself, but sometimes, to make things quite clear, he added a parable.

'The kingdom,' Jesus would then say, 'is rather like us here and now. Children of one Father, God's guests. It's rather like a wedding feast, a celebration of love. When you think of the kingdom of God, just think of a king who's arranged a wedding feast for his son. Servants are sent out right and left to deliver the invitations. "Come, for all things have been prepared."'

'That's nice,' said the people round the table.

'Yes, it's nice,' said Jesus. 'But what wasn't so nice was that the people didn't come. The king sent his servants out again: "Our master has prepared a meal, his oxen and fatted calves are slaughtered. All is ready, come to the feast."'

But one said, "I've bought a field, and I need to go to see it, please excuse me." Another said, "I've bought five span of oxen and I must go and try them out, please excuse me." A third said, "I've just got married, you'll understand, please excuse me."'*

240

'Do you understand that?', I asked the children at the school in my old village. 'The tables are laid, the food is hot, the wine is cool, but the house is empty. Why don't the guests come?'

A small boy put up his hand. 'They're afraid they'll have to ask him back.'

That must be it. The king wants a celebration of love, but people prefer to keep him at a distance. They respond with thin excuses and finally even with hatred and violence: *they seized his servants and maltreated and killed them.*

Later Matthew collected the stories about Jesus and sometimes turned them into new stories, for the people at table with him. These were people who knew that Jesus' prophetic words had become reality: John and Jesus, those servants of the king who took round the invitations, had been maltreated and killed. But then Matthew has to bring the conclusion of this old parable up to date.

The king became angry, and he sent out his army; he destroyed those murderers and burned their city.

For the sight of burning Jerusalem had deeply shocked Matthew, and he can only see the fall of the holy city as a disaster that the people has brought upon itself by paying no heed to the King's call.

That's risky theology. And when non-Jews got hold of it, this theology led to disastrous events. A pity, because the evangelist never meant that with his threatening language.

Then the king sent out his servants for the third time. 'Go to the crossroads and invite all whom you meet there to the wedding.' The servants went to the crossroads and gathered all whom they found there, both bad and good. So the wedding hall was filled with guests reclining at table.

Strange guests, in the palace. Not the rich and the complacent; they've stayed at home with their wives, their oxen and their fields. No, they're the poor people without obligations elsewhere, just off the street. For them the table is laid; they're welcome in God's new world.

The bad are as welcome as the good, but they must be clothed with the *cloak of righteousness.** You may come as you are, in your ordinary clothes, but as soon as the king appears he wants to see you in party dress.

The evangelist lives in the expectation that the King will come soon. No precious time must be lost, and no precious person must be lost. So

Matthew puts pressure on his fellow-guests. Suppose that the king appears and you don't arrive in a wedding garment? What will he say?

'Friend,' he will say, 'how did you get in here without a wedding garment?' And to his servants he will say, 'Bind him hand and foot, and throw him into the outermost darkness; there will be weeping and gnashing of teeth.'

All have been called, but only those who wear party dress will be chosen.

That's roughly how it must have been.

81

WOE TO YOU, HYPOCRITES

MATTHEW 23.1-15

The conflict with 'the Pharisees and scribes' escalates. 'Woe to you,' exclaims Jesus in a kind of indictment. 'Woe to you,' seven times. He calls them *hypocrites, fools, blind, brood of vipers.*

Are these words for someone who preaches love of enemy? Wasn't it unnecessarily provocative, making his death inevitable?

No, in this form these aren't sayings of Jesus. We certainly hear an echo of his preaching in them, but the words must be those of Matthew. Of the many Jewish movements which were active before the destruction of Jerusalem, in Matthew's day only two are left: the Pharisaic trend and the Jesus movement. Their clash is vigorous; both groups are firmly convinced that they're being loyal to the Jewish tradition, and a break seems inevitable.

Matthew is writing when the conflict is still in full swing. He does so in the style of his time, crude and blunt, with torrents of abuse, in a language which we already know from the Old Testament prophets, who could also castigate the people with their 'Woe to you'. This fierce accusation isn't anti-Jewish, since here we have an internal dispute between Jews: Jewish Christians are being persecuted by Jews. But when later, for many centuries, the roles were reversed and Christians persecuted Jews, these texts were clearly lying around, torn from their historical context, to batter Jewish ears with.

It's notable that Matthew inserts Jesus' indictment of the Pharisees and scribes into a discourse which Jesus addresses to the crowd and to his disciples. Here the evangelist apparently isn't so concerned to condemn a particular group as to warn against Pharisaism as a pernicious spiritual attitude which also threatens the Jesus movement. Matthew – and here he has Jews faithful to the Law on his side* – can only see the destruction of Jerusalem as God's judgment on an unfaithful people. So his main concern is that his readers don't take this disastrous way: 'Look where it all ends up. We too are threatened with the perversion of our faith and our religion. The Eternal One didn't spare Jerusalem and the temple when they went wrong; so too a messianic community which goes wrong loses its right to exist before God.'

That's how the evangelist admonishes his readers. He does so in an indirect way, by means of an outburst against the Pharisees, as the prophet Nathan admonished the adulterous David. Had Nathan accused David directly of his misdeed, David would probably have protested indignantly. Instead, Nathan tells him a parable about the wickedness of someone else. 'How mean of that man,' says David. 'Yes,' says the prophet, 'that's you.'

Rather than pointing an accusing finger at the Pharisees, Jesus' followers could point that finger at themselves.

Jesus spoke to the crowds and to his disciples: 'The scribes and the Pharisees sit on Moses' seat, so practise and observe whatever they tell you.'

You can't accuse Jesus of disloyalty to the Torah; the books of Moses are holy to him. Moreover he asks his disciples to listen carefully to those who sit in Moses' seat and to do what they say.

'But do not do what they do, for they preach, but do not practise. They bundle heavy burdens, hard to bear, and lay them on people's shoulders, but they themselves will not lift a finger to move them.'

There are hundreds of commandments and prohibitions, and an ordinary person collapses under them. Why do the Pharisees have so little compassion for those for whom this burden is too heavy?

'They do all their deeds to be seen by men. For they make their phylacteries broad and the tassels on their coats long. They love to sit in the places of honour at feasts and the best seats in the synagogue. They enjoy being greeted in the market place, and being addressed as "Rabbi".

But you are never to let yourselves be called rabbi, for you have one teacher, and you are all brothers. And call no man your father on earth, for you have one Father, who is in heaven. Do not be called leaders either, for you have one leader, the Messiah. The greatest among you shall be your servant. Whoever exalts himself will be humbled by God, and whoever humbles himself will be exalted by God.

Woe to you, scribes and Pharisees, you hypocrites. For you shut the kingdom of heaven against people. You neither enter yourselves, nor allow access to those who want to go in.'

Matthew began his Gospel with beatitudes, and he ends it with words of woe: the poor in spirit are blessed, and a sevenfold woe rings out over those who exalt themselves. Woe to the leaders who mislead the people. Instead of going before the people to the kingdom of God, they block their way.

'Woe to you, scribes and Pharisees, you hypocrites; for you travel over sea and land to make a single proselyte, and when he becomes one, you make him twice as much a child of hell as you are yourselves.'

Woe to you! You've shown the convert a monstrous faith, so God gets a hypocrite instead of a royal child. And then to think that such a new-comer is usually just as fanatic!

82

WOE TO YOU AGAIN

MATTHEW 23.16-39

'Woe to you, blind guides, who claim that swearing by the temple means nothing, but that swearing by the gold of the temple is binding. You blind fools! For which is more important, the gold or the temple that has made the gold holy? Whoever swears by the temple swears by it and by him who dwells in it. And whoever swears by heaven, swears by the throne of God and by him who sits upon it.'

When is an oath valid and when isn't it? That's an urgent question for the Pharisees. On the one hand they don't want an oath to lose its force, and on the other they're looking for ways to declare invalid an oath which has been lightly spoken. 'I swear it by the temple' is quickly said, and they think that it isn't an oath to which anyone can hold you. But if you've sworn 'by the gold of the temple', then you must keep your oath.

'As if the gold makes the temple holy,' says Jesus scornfully. 'The temple is holy because God lives there. Swearing by the temple is swearing by God. And swearing by heaven is swearing by God's throne and by the Eternal One who sits on it.'

Here Jesus proves to be more radical than the Pharisees. 'You mustn't swear at all. Let your yes be yes and your no no.'*

'Woe to you, scribes and Pharisees, you hypocrites. For you tithe mint and dill and cummin, but have neglected the weightier matters of the law, justice, mercy and faith; these you ought to have done, without neglecting the others. You blind guides! You strain out a gnat and swallow a camel!'

That's what Moses taught, that you must return a tenth of the harvest to the good Giver. The earth is God's, and on this earth people are called to give form to justice, mercy and faithfulness. In order to impress that upon themselves they must constantly give away part of God's gifts. This gift is destined for the temple and for the poor.

The Pharisees not only give tithes of grain and grape, but of their own accord add tithes of garden herbs. According to Jesus there's nothing against that, but you mustn't lose sight of what it's really all about: justice, mercy and faithfulness. The Pharisees are obsessed with not swallowing any unclean gnat (*kamla* in Aramaic), but they calmly swallow down an unclean camel (*gamla*).

'Woe to you, scribes and Pharisees, you hypocrites!. For you cleanse the outside of the cup and the plate, but inside you are full of extortion and rapacity. You blind Pharisees! First cleanse the inside of the cup and the plate, then the outside will also be clean.'

There's no point in thinking about outward cleanliness if you constantly leave all kind of dirt inside. If you cleanse yourself of unrighteousness within, you'll automatically be clean outside.

'Woe to you, scribes and Pharisees, you hypocrites! For you are like whitewashed tombs, which outwardly appear beautiful, but within they are full of dead men's bones and all kinds of filth. So you outwardly appear righteous to people, but within you are full of hypocrisy and iniquity.

Woe to you, scribes and Pharisees, you hypocrites! For you build the tombs of the prophets and decorate the monuments of the righteous, and you say, "If we had lived in the days of our fathers, we would not have been guilty with them in shedding the blood of the prophets." Thus you witness against yourselves that you are sons of those who murdered the prophets. Fill up then the measure of your fathers!'

The sons of the fathers again are on the point of making themselves guilty of the blood of a prophet. They decorate the tombs of former prophets and at the same time harden their hearts to the man of God in their midst. Soon yet more scribes will arise to erect a monument to him and to revile his brutal murderers. But they won't be the slightest bit better than previous generations.

'Serpents, brood of vipers, how do you think you will escape the judgment of hell? Therefore, look, I send you prophets, wise men and scribes. Some of them you will kill, and crucify, and others you will scourge in your synagogues and persecute from town to town. So there will come upon you all the righteous blood shed on earth, from the righteous Abel to the blood of Zechariah the son of Barachiah, whom you murdered between the temple and the altar.'

The first book of the Bible tells of the murder of Abel,* and the last book of the murder of one Zechariah.* From a to z blood has flowed, from the bitter beginning to the bitter end. Matthew's fervent desire is for things to be different in the messianic community.

A vain hope. All through church history people have been cast out and put to death, and the next generation erects handsome monuments to the prophets who were crucified as heretics by their forefathers.

'O Jerusalem, Jerusalem, killing the prophets and stoning those whom God sends to you! How often would I have gathered your children together, as a hen gathers her chickens under her wings, and you would not.'

Just as the great prophets Isaiah and Jeremiah chastized the Jerusalem that they loved, so too does Jesus. He remains bound up with his people and his city, even when he sees disaster approaching.

Jesus has tried to unite the children of the Father as brothers and sisters, but they've turned away. Jesus' love, his freedom, his joy, all have been misunderstood. Now he will be silenced. And then? Then God will remove his protective hands from the city and from the temple.

'Behold, your house is forsaken and desolate. For I tell you, you will not see me again until you say, "Blessed is he who comes in the name of the Lord."' *

Is God now leaving the house of Israel to its fate, Matthew, and will that be for ever? Is that 'and you would not' the last word?

No, for the Matthew who is speaking here there is still hope. One day the Messiah will return. Then he will be greeted with the same words with which he was once welcomed on his entry into the city.

83

THE DISCOURSE ABOUT THE
LAST THINGS

MATTHEW 24.1-51

Jesus left the temple. Once and for all. He also left the city. What has to be done has been done, and what has to be said has been said. In a little while he will also leave life.

But something else has to be said. He still has to speak about the last things. For the kingdom, which has shone out, sometimes, just now, where he appeared, will one day come in full splendour at the end of the ages. One day the messianic age will dawn, when the first things have passed away. That's what the Jews believe, and that's what the followers of Jesus believe. The former speak about the coming of the Messiah and the latter about the return of Jesus, but with these images they also share the same fantasy of faith, the same expectation that one day the Son of man will descend from on high to establish his kingdom of peace and justice on earth. Israel knows where that will happen, on the Mount of Olives. When it will happen, no mortal knows. Or does Jesus?

When Jesus was sitting on the Mount of Olives, the disciples came to him, and while they were alone with him, they asked: 'Tell us, when will this happen? What will be the sign of your coming and of the consummation of the world age?'

So something more has to be said. These will be Jesus' last words, his fifth discourse: the discourse about the last things. Just as Israel collected all that it had heard from God in the five books of the Torah, so the evangelist has collected all that he has heard Jesus say from God in five discourses.

Matthew borrows the beginning of this fifth discourse from Mark.* We shall now pass over those words and take up the thread again where Jesus is answering the disciples' question whether he knows when they can expect the end of the ages,

Jesus said, 'Of that day and hour no one knows, not even the angels of heaven, nor the Son. Only the Father knows it.'

Jesus isn't God. Only God knows when the end of the ages is coming. Noah didn't know when the flood was coming either. He knew that it was coming, though, and he kept on hammering.

'As it was in the days of Noah, so shall be the coming of the Son of man. For as people behaved in those days before the flood – they were eating and drinking, marrying and giving in marriage, until the day when Noah entered the ark, and they had no idea until the flood came and swept them all away – so will it be at the coming of the Son of man. Then two men will be in the field; one shall be taken and the other left. Two women shall be grinding at the mill; one will be taken and the other left.'

The men are cutting the wheat, the women are grinding the flour, they marry and are given in marriage. That's how things go, and that's good. But it isn't good if life stops at that. Life is above all a matter of having one's eyes intently fixed on a goal which transcends everyday cares. 'Seek first the kingdom of God and his righteousness, and all the rest will be given to you.'*

Matthew sees the fact that the one is taken up into God's glory while the other is left behind as the extreme consequence of the choice that people have made during their lifetimes. There are men and women who didn't listen to Jesus' invitation. Just like the people in Noah's time, they preferred to live a life of 'after us the deluge'. There are also those who follow him on his way. These are often the poor, the sorrowful, people on the fault-lines of life, to whom the world brings suffering, and who look for a kingdom of peace and righteousness. In the midst of life they hunger and thirst for another life. They never give up hope. They're the ones who are said to be blessed, now and in the future.

'So be watchful, for you do not know on what day your Lord is coming. But know this, that if the householder had known in what part of the night the thief was coming, he would have watched and would not have let his house be broken into. Therefore you also must be ready; for the Son of man is coming at an hour you do not expect.'

Thieves don't announce their coming; they turn up unexpectedly. Make sure that you aren't surprised, either by the thief or by the Son of man. Don't be like the theatre public that laughed when the clown appeared on the stage to say that the theatre was on fire, and laughed even harder when he appeared a second time, to say that the fire was spreading all round them. When the theatre collapsed there was no more laughter.*

'Who then is the faithful and wise servant, whom his master has set over his household, to provide them with food and drink in time? Blessed is that servant whom his master finds doing this work when he comes. Truly, I say to you, he will set him over all his possessions. But if that servant is so wicked as to say to himself, "My master is not coming now, he is coming later," and begins to beat his fellow-servants and eats and drinks with the drunkards, the master of that servant will come on a day when he does not expect him and at an hour that he does not know, and will punish him and put him with the hypocrites. There will be weeping and gnashing of teeth.'

If the Messiah delays, people may begin to live as if this world is their world, and as if they have the say in this world. They aren't guided by the promises and commandments of the Lord. Don't join them, in God's name. Show yourself to be a trustworthy servant, someone who does what needs to be done. Be watchful!

84

THE WISE AND THE FOOLISH VIRGINS

MATTHEW 25.1-13

Jesus is speaking with his followers about the last things. *'Be watchful, for you do not know the day or the hour.'*

Matthew also knows a story about that, and it has to be included in Jesus' discourse on the last things: the parable of the wise and the foolish virgins. You often see these bridesmaids depicted in paintings, sculptures and tapestries, always warnings to be as watchful as the wise virgins. They lived in tense expectation of the coming of the bridegroom. He will come quickly; the evening of the world is near. How will he find them then?

These are questions about the last things, about the evening of life. Our forefathers were more preoccupied with them than we are. Luther was even preoccupied with them every evening. Then he would pray:

> Lord, remain with us for it is evening
> and the night will come.
> Remain with us in the evening of the day,
> in the evening of life,
> in the evening of the world.

What will it be like, in the evening of the world?

Ten virgins went out with their lamps to meet the bridegroom.

They're ten bridesmaids who will soon accompany the bridegroom in a festal procession to the bride's house.

Five of them were foolish, five were wise. The foolish ones took their lamps along, but did not have sufficient oil; the wise ones took their lamps along with oil in their jars.

The bridegroom was delayed, the virgins nodded off and all fell asleep. At midnight there was a cry, 'The bridegroom! Go to meet him.' All the virgins

got up and made their lamps ready. And the foolish ones said to the wise ones,
'Give us some of your oil, for our lamps are going out.'

But the wise ones replied: 'No, for then there will not be enough for us and
for you; go to the dealers and buy some for yourselves.'

It isn't very kind of these wise girls not to share their oil. The gospel
teaches otherwise.

Yes, but this isn't a story from everyday life, in which we're called to
share. This is a story about the end of time, when the former things are
past. It takes place at midnight, the hour when God freed his people from
Egypt.* It's the hour of liberation.

The oil in this story can't be transferred. This oil stands for what people
have made of themselves in the course of their lives, their personal
achievements, the good deeds that they've done. So the oil is theirs and
theirs alone. There's a personal responsibility, an 'ultimate' seriousness,
which no one can transfer to anyone else. It's a shame that these foolish
virgins haven't prepared more carefully for the coming of the bridegroom.
For Matthew it's even a crying shame.

And while they were on their way to buy oil, the bridegroom came. The
virgins who were ready went in with him to the marriage feast. And the door
was shut. Afterwards the others also came.

Still without oil, we may assume, because this oil can't be bought
anywhere.

They said, 'Lord, lord, open up to us.'
But he replied, 'Truly I say, I do not know who you are.'
So be watchful, for you do not know either the day or the hour.

There's no more attractive example of a watchful person than Blumhardt*,
the servant of God who believed so literally in Jesus' return and so
passionately longed for it that he had a horse and carriage standing ready
to go out to meet the Messiah immediately.

> *His coach stood ready all his whole life long*
> *with horses, reins, and robe, in case the time*
> *should be fulfilled in which the angels' song*
> *would ring out gloriously, then he would climb*
> *into his seat – tall hat and Sunday best –*
> *sitting up straight, he would go trotting forth*
> *to meet his Lord, who'd surely come at last –*
> *and now for good – as King of all the earth.*

O God, what have you done with such a heart,
so full of homesickness and such great dreams?
He now lies still and waiting in the ground.
What will you do with all of us who wait
in this dark age, longing for your return,
*calling to you with pleading, doubtful sound?**

85

THE PARABLE OF THE TALENTS

MATTHEW 25.14-30

For those who are close, a person's last words are often precious. They're cherished. 'Did he say anything more before he went?'

Jesus indeed said something more before he went. He told a parable. About a master who went abroad and said something more before he went.

The master called his servants and entrusted his possessions to them. To one he gave five talents, to another two, to a third one, to each according to his ability. Then he went away.

So things are shared out unequally in this world: one gets more than another. But before the Lord that doesn't count; for the Lord, the only important thing is for all to take care of what has been entrusted to them.

The servant who had received the five talents went at once and traded with them; and he made five talents more. So also the one who had the two talents made two talents more. But the servant who had received the one talent went away, dug a hole in the ground, and hid his master's money.

The third servant can't think of anything better to do than to keep his talent safe by burying it. Why does he do that? Is he paralysed by his anger that others are more talented than he is? Is he afraid that he will lose that one talent and be punished for it? Is it a lack of trust?

Before Jesus died, he put his treasures in the hands of his servants. One day he will come again. Then the books will be opened, and the hour of reckoning will come.

After a long time the master of those servants came and settled accounts with them. The one who had received the five talents came to him with another five talents: 'Master, you entrusted me with five talents; look, I have made five talents more.'

'Well done, you good and faithful servant, you have been faithful over a little, I will set you over much. Enter into your master's feast.'

The one who had received the two talents also came forward: 'Master, you entrusted me with two talents; look, I have made two talents more.'

'Well done, good and faithful servant, you have been faithful over a little, I will set you over much. Enter into your master's feast.'

Then came the one who had received the one talent. 'Master, I know you. I know that you are a hard man, reaping where you have not sown and gathering where you have not scattered. I was afraid and went away and hid your talent in the ground. Look, here it is back again.'

The third servant had no confidence: we already suspected that. And he was also malicious. In his eyes his master's a hard-hearted master, concerned only for his own interests. He's a master who will punish him if he makes a mistake, and if he does things well, then his master grabs everything. Instead of living freely and daring to do something with his one talent, the third servant plays safe. Nothing ventured, nothing gained: his talent goes underground. Really he's burying himself with it, burying himself alive. He doesn't want to lose anything and in so doing loses everything.

Jesus wants to impress on his followers once again before his departure that life mustn't be lived like that. 'You're destined for the light. Do you want to end up in eternal darkness? In that case you must go on like this.' And Matthew wouldn't be Matthew if he didn't add force to this plea for a watchful and active life with some more weeping and gnashing of teeth.

'You wicked and slothful servant! You knew that I reap where I have not sowed, and gather where I have not scattered. You should have invested my money in the bank – at my coming I should have received back my property with interest. Take the talent from this man and give it to him who has the ten talents. For to everyone who has, more will be given and he will know abundance. But from him who has nothing, even what he has shall be taken away from him. As for this useless servant, cast him into the outermost darkness. There shall be weeping and gnashing of teeth.'

You can bury the love of God, the treasure of Jesus, and thus do nothing with it. Then your life is poor and you end up poor. You can also put it to work. Then the blessings pile up, and your cup overflows.

86

THE SHEEP AND THE GOATS

MATTHEW 25.31-46

Matthew wants to give us one more word from Jesus. One last word, and with that word he will end Jesus' discourse about the last things. It's a word about the judgment at the end of time.

When the Son of man comes in his glory, and all the angels with him, then he will sit on his glorious throne. Before him will be gathered all the nations, and he will separate them one from another as a shepherd separates the sheep from the goats. He will place the sheep on his right hand, the goats on his left hand.

The judge sits on his throne to judge. How does Matthew arrive at that picture? People have already been reflecting on this for centuries. Does it make any difference what you did in your life and what you didn't do? Surely it isn't such a strange thought that a responsible person will one day be called to account, that he will then be asked what he did with his talents? Of course we don't know; it's fantasy. But if it's good, this fantasy about the end time puts the present day in a healthy tension.

Then the king will say to those on his right hand, 'Come, you blessed of my Father, inherit the kingdom prepared for you from the foundation of the world. For I was hungry and you gave me food, I was thirsty and you gave me drink. I was a stranger and you gave me lodging, I was naked and you gave me clothes, I was sick and you visited me, I was in prison and you came to me.'

Then the righteous will answer him, 'Lord, when did we see you hungry and give you food, or thirsty and give you drink? When did we see you a stranger and give you lodging, or naked and clothe you? When did we see you sick or in prison and visit you?'

And the king will answer them, 'Truly, I say to you, as you did it to one of the least of these my brothers, you did it to me.'

Jesus is king in this story, but he's a king who identifies with the least of people. And he asks his subjects whether they've followed him here and whether they were helpers for those who had no helpers. Blessed are those who loved righteousness. And inevitably there's another side to this coin; woe to those who kept so damnably distant from their fellow human beings in need.

The king will say to those on his left hand, 'Out of my sight, you accursed ones, into the eternal fire that is prepared for the devil and his angels. For I was hungry and you gave me no food, I was thirsty and you gave me no drink. I was a stranger and you gave me no lodging; I was naked and you gave me no clothes, and I was in prison but you did not visit me.'

Then they too will answer him and say, 'Lord, when did we see you hungry or thirsty or a stranger or naked or sick or in prison and did not minister to you?'

The king will answer them, 'Truly, I say to you, everything that you did not do to one of these least, you did not do to me.'

These will go away into eternal punishment, but the righteous into eternal life.

Jesus came. He came as a king, a king who serves.

Jesus will come, as a king in glory.

If he delays, don't think that he isn't coming. Until he comes as a king in glory he comes to you in the least of people.

And it happened when Jesus had finished all these words...

Everything has now been said. Jesus spoke his first words on the bank of the Jordan. 'Thus it is seemly for us to fulfil all righteousness.' Then he spoke the Sermon on the Mount, the mission discourse, the parable discourse, the community discourse and his discourse about the last things.

And it happened when Jesus had finished all these words, that he said to his disciples, 'You know that after two days the Passover is coming, and the Son of man will be delivered up to be crucified.'

Everything has been said. All that Jesus can still teach his disciples is that he will be faithful to the death.

87

THIRTY PIECES OF SILVER

MATTHEW 27.1-57

Matthew tells of Jesus' last hours, and in so doing keeps closely to Mark's account of the passion. Only once does he diverge from it, and it's to this passage that we shall be paying attention.

Matthew here has an account of Judas' repentance, a fact about which Mark is silent.

Judas, who had betrayed him, repented and brought back the thirty pieces of silver to the chief priests and elders. 'I have sinned in betraying innocent blood.'

In the Torah, thirty pieces of silver is the compensation that must be paid for killing a servant.* It's also the scant wage paid by bad masters to a good shepherd.* For Jesus, the good shepherd, the servant of God, the chief priests had offered the same number of silver pieces. A pittance by comparison with the generous gift of the woman with the alabaster jar.

The traitor's reward is burning in Judas's hands. He goes with it to the temple and repents of his sins: 'I have betrayed innocent blood.'

Broken, he goes before God's presence: *A broken and contrite heart you will not despise, O God.**

But the chief priests do what God does not: they despise this broken and contrite heart. Whereas God's loving-kindness must be proclaimed and celebrated above all in the temple.

'What is that to us? See to it yourself.'

It isn't their problem. And for Judas the problem is too great. He's done something that can't be undone. With an impotent gesture he throws the wretched silver pieces into the temple. There's no more that he can do. He could only go to the house of God, but there wasn't a priest there to have pity on him.

Judas went out and hanged himself.

In solitude he commits suicide. Judas didn't have faith that the God of

Israel takes no pleasure in the death of the sinner but wants him to be converted and live.*

Meanwhile the priests are so sensitive about the silver pieces that they don't put them in the chest of offerings dedicated to God. However, they do have a charitable cause. People often cover up injustice with charity. The priests decide to buy a piece of land and turn it into a burial place for strangers: an unclean place for unclean people, bought with blood money.

Therefore that land is called the Field of Blood, to the present day.

88

PILATE'S WIFE

MATTHEW 27.11-26

Jesus is taken before Pilate. 'Are you the king of the Jews?'

'You say it.'

What a strange people this is! What a strange man and what a strange answer! Why is he so dangerous in the eyes of the leaders of the people? The governor tries to discover this, but Jesus is silent. Pilate truly isn't a man with many scruples when it comes to condemning someone to death, but to have this Jesus crucified is going too far for him. He thinks up a device to make the people plead for Jesus's release. If he lets them choose between a pardon for the notorious Barabbas and a pardon for Jesus, beyond doubt their choice will fall on the latter. *'Whom do you want me to release to you, Barabbas or Jesus?'*

At that moment a servant comes forward with a note from Mrs Pilate. She's had a dream.

That night the angels who make people dream appeared again, just as in the springtime of the life of the man who now stands before Pilate's judgment seat. 'Get away,' the angel then warned Joseph in his dream.

A note from Mrs Pilate. The session is adjourned for a moment, the servants around the throne stand there grinning. Women!

Yes, women. As in Mark, in Matthew it's the women who understand who Jesus is, while the men conspire against him. If first there was a Jewish woman who anointed Jesus, now it's a pagan woman who senses what's going on here and tries to avert disaster: 'Pontius, last night I dreamed of this man. He's a just man.'

Pilate raises his eyes to heaven. Why doesn't she leave politics to the professionals?

'You must keep out of this, Pontius, this man is a just man. I have suffered much over him in my dream.'

Suffered much, where have we heard those words earlier? Jesus spoke them to his friends when he had resolved no longer to turn aside but to go to Jerusalem. 'I know that I must suffer much, but I'm going, come what may. Don't leave me on my own.'

They promised, the men. But one by one they dropped out. However, in her dream this woman is suffering with him. 'Let him go free, Pilate.'

Yes, that's precisely what I'm trying to do, don't think that I'm... Good, where were we? I shall repeat my question: *'Which of the two do you want me to release to you?'*

'Barabbas! Barabbas!'

How is this possible? Pilate was firmly convinced that the people would opt for the release of Jesus. What's happened for their mood to have changed so suddenly?

This: a rapid campaign of whispers and urgent shouts from chief priests and elders have changed the will of the people in the twinkling of an eye. 'Barabbas!' And the chief priests and elders had been able to do their devastating work because the governor had just adjourned the gathering... to read his wife's note in support of Jesus. The evil couldn't be averted; the good couldn't avert the evil either, but cynically enough even contributed to it.

'Barabbas! Barabbas!'

'What then must I do with this Jesus who is called Christ?

They all said, 'He must be crucified!'

'But what evil has he done?'

But they shouted all the more, 'He must be crucified.'

Now when Pilate saw that he was acheiving nothing, but rather that a riot was beginning, he took water and washed his hands before the crowd, 'I am innocent of his blood; see to it yourselves.'

The chief priests and elders also said that to Judas when he confessed that he had shed innocent blood. 'What is that to us? See to it yourself.' Pilate foists the blame on the leaders with the very words with which the leaders had foisted the blame on Judas.

And the whole of the people answered and said: 'His blood be on us and on our children.'

What you, governor, dissociate yourself from, we take upon ourselves. 'His blood be on us and on our children.'

If only these words had never stood in the Gospel!* Armed with this text, the church has done violence to the children of Israel from generation to generation. Whereas the church should have been the first to know what kind of blood it is that the crowd before the governor's palace has called down upon itself. It's the blood of Jesus. It's the blood which the church confesses Sunday by Sunday to have been shed for the forgiveness of sins!

Then Pilate released Barabbas. But when he had had Jesus scourged, he delivered him to be crucified.

What did Pilate say to his wife when he got home that evening? And what did she say to her husband? Did he rebuke her for bringing about the death of this just man precisely through her letter? Did she shout out to him that all the water in the world couldn't wash away the blood which clung to his hands? Or were they both silent, and did each of them have their own thoughts about that strange Jewish man who had to suffer so much and who now was dead?

89

THE BURIAL

MATTHEW 27.55-66

Matthew is approaching the end of his story. Once again he wants to use his talents to complete his Gospel with a powerful final chord. In five scenes he will tell of Jesus' burial, of his resurrection from the dead and his appearance to the disciples.

scene one: the disciples

scene two: the leaders

scene three: the resurrection

scene four: the leaders

scene five: the disciples

At the heart of these five scenes stands the heart of the Gospel: the story of the resurrection. This core of the story is framed by what happened in the Sanhedrin before and after the resurrection. This triptych is in turn framed by two passages which relate what happened to the disciples.

The third scene, the heart of the finale, consists of three scenes each of seven lines. In the central scene we hear an angel of God proclaim the resurrection. That makes us curious about the words which Matthew, who composes his work so carefully, makes this angel say at the centre of the centralmost scene, and thus at the heart of the heart of the heart. *'Come, see the place where he lay,'* the angel says there. The tomb is empty. That's the heart of the Gospel. Everything revolves around these few words, that image.

We shall follow these five scenes through, beginning with the first.

There were also many women there, looking on from afar, who had followed Jesus from Galilee, to serve him. Among them were Mary Magdalene and Mary the mother of James and Joses, and the mother of the sons of Zebedee.

The disciples have dropped out. Only the women are still around; they stand closest to the mystery of death and life. They followed Jesus to serve him and they continued to follow him, although they could do no more for him.

When it was evening, there came a rich man from Arimathea, named Joseph, who had also become a disciple of Jesus. He went to Pilate and asked for the body of Jesus. Pilate ordered it to be given to him.

A disciple of Jesus and at the same time a rich man. What a coincidence! In contrast to Mark, in the Gospel of Matthew he isn't a member of the Sanhedrin. So he must indeed be rich if he wants to have an audience with Pilate. The man's name is Joseph, Joseph of Arimathea. That's a coincidence. When Jesus was still a child, a defenceless child, there was a Joseph who looked after him, a *tsaddiq* who did three things that had to be done: *And he took his wife. And he did not have intercourse with her until she had borne a son. And he called his name Jesus.*

Now at the end, when Jesus is a defenceless corpse, another Joseph appears, also a just man, who takes care of him and does the three things that have to be done: *Joseph took the body, wrapped it in clean linen, and laid it in his new tomb, which he had hewn in the rock, and he rolled a great stone in front of the entrance. Then he departed.*

We can sense the devotion and the affection: clean linen, a new tomb, a great stone. When he has done what he has to do he goes away again. He came and he went. Only the women are still there.

Mary Magdalene and the other Mary were there, sitting opposite the tomb.

It's quiet. The whole Jesus movement has come to a standstill, first on the cross, now in the tomb. It's deadly still.

And what are the men of the Sanhedrin doing? The second scene shows us that.

The next day, that is, after the Preparation, the chief priests and the Pharisees gathered before Pilate.

As if we hadn't guessed: the men begin to gather again. They also did that right at the beginning of Matthew's Gospel: hardly had Jesus been born than they met together in dismay, Jews and pagans. And hardly has he died than the men assemble again, Jews and pagans. If his birth was threatening, remarkably his death is just as threatening.

Deceit and theft are on the agenda. Granted, this lot has put an end to the life of the deceiver from Nazareth by having him nailed to the cross, but with such a man you never know. They've silenced him, but they can still hear him say that they'll never be able to silence him, that he'll continue to speak, even after his death. Just suppose that his followers spirited away the corpse and went on misleading the people by claiming that he'd risen from the dead!

'Sir, we remember how that impostor said, while he was still alive, "After three days I will rise again." Therefore order that the tomb is made secure until the third day. Otherwise his disciples will come to and steal him away and tell the people, "He has risen from the dead". The last fraud will be worse than the first.'

For if the people begin to believe in this last fraud, then there will be no stopping the teaching of this innovator. So the stone must remain in front of the tomb.

Pilate ponders. But not for long. *'I will put a guard at your disposal.'*

A *custodia.* With some satanic satisfaction the narrator uses the Latin word. *Custodia!* You can see the Roman troops setting out. What are you going to do? Guard a dead body! By the left, quick march. Rome marches off. Society must be protected against theft. And against deceit.

So they went off, sealed the stone and made the tomb secure with a guard.

Again it's still. Jesus is crucified. Jesus is buried. There's a stone in front of his tomb. And a guard before the stone. It's deadly still.

90

THE RESURRECTION

MATTHEW 28.1-10

Late after the sabbath, at the dawn of the first day of the week,
Mary Magdalene and the other Mary came to look at the tomb.
And see, there was a great earthquake,
for an angel of the Lord descended from heaven and came;
he rolled back the stone and sat upon it.
His appearance was like lightning and his garments white as snow.
For fear of him the guards trembled and became like dead men.

An angel descends, all light. What happens now, happens from God's side. An angel descends and the earth quakes. That has to be. When God's reality touches ours, everything is shaken to its foundations; existing certainties fall away. It's shocking and the bottommost stone comes to the top. 'Take cover!' shouts the captain of the *custodia*. The earth quakes and the *custodia* quakes. They become... like dead men. The living who have to watch over a dead body become like the dead. And the dead body...? Here everything is turned upside down.

   With one finger the angel rolls the stone away from the tomb. What will he do with this stone? Will he hurl the boulder away from him with magic power? No, the angel does something far more majestic. He goes and sits on it, a smile playing over his face. The angel sits down on the stone that proclaimed that Jesus was dead, this great stone with a whole *custodia* in front of it. 'He is not dead,' this angel proclaims. The tombstone has become a pulpit.

But the angel said to the women,
'Do not be afraid. I know that you seek Jesus who was crucified.
He is not here, for he is risen as he said.
Come, see the place where he lay.
Then go immediately and tell his disciples that he is risen from the dead.

Look, he is going before you into Galilee, there you will see him.
Look, I have told you.'

With these words we've reached the heart of the heart of Matthew's finale and thus the core of his Gospel. 'He is risen!'

Matthew doesn't doubt that the Eternal One has raised his Son from the dead. To make that quite clear, in the three so-called 'passion predictions' which Mark put three times in the mouth of Jesus he has also three times changed the words 'I shall rise again' into 'I shall be raised'. For it must be clear that God is at work here. This isn't human work; this comes from heaven. Moreover at the heart of his account of the resurrection the evangelist doesn't say that Jesus went to meet his disciples. He tells what has happened from heaven and what has been made known from heaven: 'Look, I have told you.' The women and the disciples are told by an angel that Jesus has been raised. Only when they have heard it from heaven do they begin to 'see' on earth.

God has had mercy on the crucified Jesus. Jesus also trusted that God would not forsake him. The Eternal One would, to use the age-old Jewish language of faith, raise him 'on the third day'. With that faith he lived, and with that faith he went to his death, and that faith now also takes possession of his followers. Surely God hasn't abandoned what he began? God the Father has raised this his Son, they firmly believe, and they experience that faith as a gift from heaven, for flesh and blood have not revealed it to them. An angel did that.

'He is risen. Come, see the place where he lay. Then go immediately and tell his disciples that he is risen from the dead. Look, he is going before you into Galilee, there you will see him. Look, I have told you.'

What movement all of a sudden! Everything had come to a standstill, first on the cross, then in the tomb: silence, deadly silence. But now, on the third day, the angel sets everything in motion again. 'Come,' he says, and he leads the women into the empty tomb. But immediately he leads them out again with his 'Go!' Jesus isn't here.

Then where is he?

Jesus is going before them into Galilee, the region where they'd learned to follow him. There is the mountain of the Sermon on the Mount and there are the valleys and the villages and the towns where he healed the sick and raised the dead to life. There he told his parables, there he walked on the water and there he gave them bread and fish.

They have to go away from the tomb. Back to Galilee, back to every-thing of which they'd been witnesses. If they keep that before their eyes, they'll see him. Not one of his words, not one of his actions has been nullified, contradicted or lost. Jesus is alive.

And immediately they went away from the tomb with fear and great joy,
and ran to tell his disciples.
And look, Jesus met them and said, 'Hail!'
They came up, took hold of his feet and worshipped him.
Then Jesus said to them, 'Fear not,
go and tell my brothers
that they must go away to Galilee. There they will see me.'

They went, immediately, as fast as their legs could carry them, in awe and with great joy. What Jesus had lived for, what he had died for, is all going on; it has a future after all, for all his followers. Even for those who forsook him and denied him.

And look, Jesus met them.

A vision. We needn't doubt the witness of many that Jesus appeared to them after his death. For mourners in our day, too, it's a comforting experience when a loved one who is dead appears in dreams or visions. So the appearances of Jesus encouraged and strengthened the women and later also the men.

And look, Jesus met them and said, 'Hail!'. Then they came close and took hold of his feet and worshipped him. Then Jesus said to them, 'Fear not, go and tell my disciples...'

No, that's not what it says. Matthew needs only one word to conjure up a world of mercy: '*Go and tell* my brothers *that they must go to Galilee. There they will see me.*'

God has mercy on the crucified Jesus and in him on the disciples who failed as brothers. They're all included in the forgiveness.

And what are the leaders doing?

While they were going, look, some of the guard went into the city
and told the chief priests all that had taken place.
They assembled with the elders and took counsel,
and gave much money to the soldiers and said:

'Tell people, his disciples came by night
and stole him away while we were asleep.
And if this comes to the governor's ears,
we will satisfy him and keep you out of trouble.'
So they took the money and did as they were directed.
This story has been spread among the Jews to this day.

It's unavoidable, the men are gathering again. Once again *deceit and theft* are on the agenda. In the previous gathering the two things had to be prevented; in this gathering they have to be organized. While the women on the orders of the angel go to proclaim that Jesus is risen, the soldiers on the orders of the men and in return for payment proclaim that the body has been stolen.

And they took the money and did as they were directed.

You can teach a person anything. These people have learned to lie. Fortunately the disciples, the brothers, have just learned something else.

This story has been spread among the Jews to this day.

Is it hostility that resounds in these words of Matthew, or is it sadness?

91

I AM WITH YOU

MATTHEW 28.16-20

The eleven disciples went to Galilee, to the mountain to which Jesus had directed them.

Each evangelist sings his own song. In Matthew Easter, Ascension and Pentecost fall on the same day. Luke will later separate them and make three stories of them. Matthew has Jesus taking his farewell of his disciples in Galilee, Luke opts for Jerusalem. That's also very profound, but it's another story.

Matthew writes Jesus back to Galilee, to the Galilee *of the Gentiles,* for that's where the good news has to go, to the peoples. The movement of the kingdom of God, which came to a standstill on the cross and in the tomb, but which has been set in motion again from the depths of death by the angel, must now go into the wide world.

And where else in Galilee will Matthew set this last scene than on a high mountain from which you can see all the kingdoms of the earth? On just such a mountain the devil tempted Jesus. 'I will give you all power over these kingdoms if you worship me.' If Jesus kneels before the devil, all this will be his. For a moment against God and from then on as God. Jesus rejects the temptation: 'Depart from me, Satan, a person must worship God alone.'

And Jesus also taught his friends on a mountain what he understood by worshipping God, loving God and one's neighbour. He gave them words from the heights.

Now, before they take their farewell, Matthew brings Jesus and his disciples together once more on a mountain.

And when they saw him...

Now Jesus also appears to the disciples and they, too, draw strength from his appearance. It's a confirmation of the faith that had grown up in Israel that death doesn't have the last word. That faith is further reinforced by the stories about these appearances which quickly went the rounds. Jesus is alive! Jesus' followers found new words and images for an old secret.

And when they saw him they worshipped him, but some doubted.

A good monk who copied these words in a distant past thought it weird that even the disciples could have their doubts. He was quite sure that this must be a mistake on Matthew's part. On his own initiative he altered the text to *and they did not doubt.*

Fortunately Matthew knows better. Faith never comes ready made; it has its ups and downs. Belief is about unbelief, trust about fear, and there are questions which always keep recurring. But with the man on the mountain we need never be ashamed of all that.

When the women heard that Jesus had been raised from the dead they were overjoyed, but at the same time afraid. Then Jesus came to them, '*Do not be afraid,*' he said, and they worshipped him.

Now it's the men who worship him. But some doubted.

And Jesus came and said: 'To me is given all power in heaven and on earth.'

All power? The devil had once offered him this. At that time Jesus didn't give way to this temptation. Now he's standing here with pierced hands, signs of his impotence. Nevertheless, 'To me is given all power in heaven and on earth.'

Not the power that nothing bad will happen to us. It's the power to complete things. This world is coming to an end. This is a beginning which has begun for good.* What has now begun will be completed.

'*Go therefore and make disciples of all nations.*'

Do you see them, the kingdoms of the earth? From this mountain you can see them all lying there. See how people are pursued and exhausted, like sheep which have no shepherd. You have to go to them.

'*And baptize them in the name of the Father and of the Son and of the Holy Spirit.*'

Splendid words, but not words of Jesus. This is theologians' language. The triune God – Father, Son and Holy Spirit – is a later reconstruction. But at an early stage the first Christian community already knew the attractive and profound ritual of baptism and of course liked to see Jesus as its source.

'*And teach them to observe all that I have commanded you.*'

So they mustn't teach people what the soldiers are taught – to lie and to deceive. Really they needn't teach people anything more, because they've already been taught it. The only thing that people need to learn is to hang on and not to let go when the cunning devil comes along with something else. They mustn't be put off by anything or anyone.

'And look, I am with you, always, to the consummation of the world age.'

With these words Matthew ends his Gospel.

Again, how did it begin?

Book of the genesis, the origin, of Jesus Christ.

Here he called to mind the first book of the Bible, Genesis, the book of *In the beginning.* The book that tells of the origin of heaven and earth, and on earth of the origin of the nations, and in the midst of the nations of the origin of Israel. In his Gospel Matthew continued this line: he made us share in the origin of Jesus Messiah in the midst of Israel.

Now that he's come to the end, Matthew broadens the perspective again. God's salvation, as it has taken form in Jesus Messiah, fans out again: first the report is entrusted to the women, then to the men, and then the story goes from Israel to all peoples, to the ends of the earth and to the consummation of the world age, which began in the beginning.

ABOUT THE BIBLE

The Bible (from the Greek *biblia,* meaning 'books') is a library in itself, comprising a varied collection of books – sixty-six in all – written during a period of more than a thousand years (900 BC – AD 130). Most of the texts underwent a long development, and in the form in which we know them today they are the result of an age-old process of growth. The book consists of two main sections.

Christians call the first section the Old Testament; it comprises the thirty-nine sacred books of the Jewish faith, written in Hebrew. The second section is called the New Testament, and comprises the twenty-seven sacred books of Christianity, written in Greek.

The First, or Old, Testament is referred to by Jews as the 'TeNaKh', an acronym consisting of the T of Torah (Law), the N of Nebi'im (Prophets) and the K of Ketubhim (Writings), the main divisions of the book.

The *Torah* (called 'Pentateuch' in Greek) comprises the first five books of the Bible and describes, primarily in narrative form, the way to live. *Instruction, guidance,* is a better translation of the word Torah than law. Because Moses was thought to be the author, these books are also called *the books of Moses.*

In the Nebi'im, the prophetic writings, the people of God are summoned to follow the Torah. The Nebi'im are subdivided into the 'Former Prophets' (Joshua, Judges, Samuel, Kings) and the 'Latter Prophets' (Isaiah, Jeremiah, Ezekiel and the twelve minor prophets). In an unguarded moment, Christianity called the 'Former Prophets' 'the historical books', thereby wrongly giving the impression that these stories are historical and not prophetic in character. It is especially because of this that in my retelling of the Old Testament I have preferred to follow the division of the TeNaKh.

In the Ketubhim we find a more individual reflection on the Torah.

These writings offer a richly varied collection of prose and poetry (including Psalms, Job and Proverbs), as well as the Five *megilloth*, the scrolls read publicly in the synagogue during Jewish days of remembrance (Ruth, Song of Songs, Ecclesiastes, Lamentations, Esther).

The Second or 'New' Testament consists of four Gospels (Matthew, Mark, Luke and John), the Acts of the Apostles, a number of letters and the Book of Revelation. The Gospels and Acts were written some time after Jesus' death (AD 60 – 100), and bear witness to the faith of the first Christian community. They are not 'historical' texts in our sense. The letters, written by various authors, are among the oldest books of the New Testament. The Book of Revelation was written as a work of the Christian resistance, intended to offer comfort to persecuted believers in a language accessible only to the initiated.

TRANSLATOR'S ACKNOWLEDGMENT

Translating Nico ter Linden's remarkable books have presented enormous problems. In retelling the stories of the Bible he uses a special kind of Dutch, at times colloquial, at times archaic, and often reflecting the original Hebrew. This interplay of various levels of Dutch is one of the appeals of the books, but is sometimes all but impossible to reproduce in English. In addition, he makes use of Dutch hymns and children's hymns, Dutch traditional songs and other indirect allusions, which again cannot be translated directly; sometimes it is possible to introduce English equivalents to retain the effect, sometimes this cannot be done.

I wish to acknowledge here the interest and concern shown in the English translation by Nico ter Linden himself, but more particularly the painstaking work and the help of Dr Henk Aertsen, Senior Lecturer in the English Department of the Free University of Amsterdam, who has checked out the translation and has been a sure guide through the minefield of sub-meanings as well as correcting errors and misunderstandings. Without him the translation would have been much inferior, and he deserves my deepest gratitude. Any errors that remain are mine.

John Bowden

BIBLIOGRAPHY

A list of the Dutch works which I have used can be found at the back of the Dutch original of this volume. Here I list simply those works which are available in other languages:

For Mark's story I consulted:

J. D. Crossan, *Jesus*, San Francisco 1994 (especially for chapters 12 and 20)
J. D. Crossan, *Who killed Jesus?*, San Francisco 1995
E. Drewermann, *Das Markusevangelium I and II*, Olten 1988 (especially for Chapters 2, 15, 16, 17, 18, 19, 25, 27, 28, 33, 34, 46, 50)
M. Goulder, *A Tale of Two Missions*, London 1994
B. van Iersel, *Reading Mark*, Edinburgh 1989
D. Lührmann, *Das Markusevangelium*, Tübingen 1987
D. E. Nineham, *Saint Mark*, Harmondsworth 1987
D. Rhoads and D. Michie, *Mark as Story*, Philadelphia 1982
M. A. Tolbert, *Sowing the Gospel*, Minneapolis 1989 (especially for Chapter 13)
R. M. Towler, *Let the Reader Understand*, Minneapolis 1991

For Matthew's story I consulted:

D. Bonhoeffer, *The Cost of Discipleship*, London 1959 (especially for Chapter 64)
E. Drewermann, *Das Matthäusevangelium* I and II, Olten 1992, 1993 (especially for Chapters 63, 64, 65, 69)
D. E. Garland, *Reading Matthew*, London 1993 (especially for Chapters 59, 76, 81, 82)
R. H. Gundry, *Matthew*, Grand Rapids 1994
P. Lapide, *The Sermon on the Mount*, Maryknoll 1986

I am most grateful to the De Keizerskroon Foundation, which has made it possible for me to devote myself to this work full-time. A number of other foundations (most particularly the VSB Foundation) made it possible for De Keizerskroon Foundation to do this. I am also most grateful to all those who read the typescript and made critical comments (they are listed in the Dutch edition). They have saved me from many mistakes and given me many new insights.

OTHER SOURCES, SOURCES OF QUOTATIONS

Preface

p. ix   One consequence of this choice is that it is not possible to show the reader how Matthew not only takes over the Mark passages but alters them, reorders them and sometimes abbreviates them. These changes need to be noted, but unfortunately they have had to be left out of account in this retelling.

Chapter 1

D. Monshouwer, *Exodus*, Zoetermeer 1995.

p. 4   Messiah is the Hebrew, Christ the Greek word for anointed. It is a royal title in Israel: at their accession, kings in Israel were anointed with oil in the name of God.

p. 5   Exodus 23.20; Isaiah 40.3; Malachi 3.1.

Chapter 2

J. W. van Henten, *De eerste beproeving van Jezus*, Kampen 1994.

C. J. den Heyer, in *Amsterdamse cahiers* 1, Kampen 1980.

J. Tigcheler, in *Speling*, March 1981, Tilburg 1981.

p. 6   Psalm 2.

p. 7   Isaiah 42.1.

p. 7   Isaiah 64.1.

Chapter 6

E. Drewermann, *Zwischen Staub und Sternen*, Düsseldorf 1991.

E. Drewermann, *Wat ons toekomt*, Zoetermeer 1993.

E. Drewermann, *Hij legde hun de handen op*, Zoetermeer 1993.

Chapter 7

E. Drewermann, *Hij legde hun de handen op*, Zoetermeer 1993.

p. 23   Psalm 103.3.

p. 23   Daniel 7.13.

Chapter 8

p. 25   D. Bonhoeffer, *Letters and Papers from Prison*, London and New York 1971.

Chapter 9

F. Boerwinkel, *Meer dan gewone*, Baarn 1997.

H. Faber, *Cirkelen om een geheim*, Meppel 1972.

H. Fortmann, *Hoogtijd*, Bilthoven 1966.

L. Geysels, in *Schrift* 66, Heilig Landstichting 1979.

A. Herzberg, *De man in de spiegel*, Amsterdam 1980.

H. Küng, *On Being a Christian*, London and New York 1977.

p. 27   Augustine.

Chapter 10

p. 30   Deuteronomy 5.14, 15.

p. 32   The passage was probably added later. There is not such negative talk about the Pharisees even in the passion narrative. There the chief priests, scribes and elders are Jesus' deadly enemies. According to Acts 5.38 the Pharisees will not have voted for Jesus' execution in the Sanhedrin.

Chapter 11

J. van Goudever, *Phoenix Bibelpocket* 20, Hilversum 1966.

p. 33   It seems to me that a dialogue about the messiahship of Jesus between Jews and Christians can only hope to get anywhere once the term 'Messiah' has been defined. So Christians cannot enter this conversation with the statement that Jesus *is* the Messiah. In belief, one cannot be too sparing with is-statements.

p. 34   According to a report in the Talmud Jesus had five disciples. That too is a nice piece of symbolism: five is the number of Israel.

p. 34   Galatians 3.26-28.

p. 35   Isaiah 51.1, 2.

Chapter 12

J. D. Crossan, *Jesus*, San Francisco 1994.

A. A. van Ruler, *Dichterbij Marcus*, Nijkerk 1974.

J. Tigcheler, in *Speling* 4/1980, Nijmegen 1980.

p. 37   Mark 6.34.

Chapter 14

P. Farla, B. van Iersel and H. de Wit, in *Schrift* 160, Heilig Landstichting 1995.

E. Drewermann, *Hij legde hun de handen op*, Zoetermeer 1993.

p. 44   Psalm 44.23, 24.

p. 44   Psalm 107.23-30.

p. 44   Jonah 4.2.

Chapter 16

O. Jager, *Daglicht*, Kampen 1970.

Chapter 19

p. 58   Matthew 13.55.

Chapter 20

p. 61   Esther 5 and I Kings 19-21.

Chapter 21

J. van Goudoever, *Phoenix Bible Pocket* 20, Wageningen 1966.

p. 65   I Samuel 21.

p. 65   Psalm 23.

p. 65   Exodus 18.25.

p. 65   I Kings 17.

p. 65   II Kings 4.42.

p. 66   Mark 14.22.

Chapter 22

p. 68   Job 9.8; Psalm 77.20; Isaiah 43.16.

p. 68   Exodus 33.19, 22 and I Kings 19.11.

p. 69   Exodus 3.13, 14. See *The Story Goes*, I, 207.

Chapter 23

p. 70   Isaiah 29.13.

p. 70   Exodus 20.12; Leviticus 20.9.

Chapter 25

p. 74   Isaiah 35.4-6.

Chapter 28

L. Grollenberg, *Unexpected Messiah*, London 1988.

C. J. den Heyer, *Jesus Matters*, London and Philadelphia 1997.

B. van Iersel, in *Schrift* 63, Heilig Landstichting 1979.

M. de Jonge, *Jesus als Messias*, Boxtel 1990.

S. Schoon, *De weg van Jezus*, Kampen 1991.

Chapter 29

E. Schillebeeckx, *God among Us. The Gospel Proclaimed*, London and New York 1983.

p. 84   Exodus 24.15.

p. 84   Exodus 34.29, 35.

p. 84   I Kings 19.

Chapter 32

J. Tigcheler, in *Speling* 31 no.1, Nijmegen 1979.

Chapter 33

J. Tigcheler, in *Speling* 31 no.4, Nijmegen 1979.

Chapter 34

C. Aalders, *Onze Vader*, Amsterdam nd.

E. Drewermann, *Tiefenpsychologie und Exegese* II, Olten 1985.

p. 98   Mark 4.19.

Chapter 35

P. Luttikhuizen, in *Schrift* 94, Heilig Landstichting 1984.

p. 100   Acts 12.1-2.

Chapter 37

p. 104   Zechariah 14.4.

p. 104   K. A. Deurloo.

p. 105   Zechariah 9.9-10.

p. 105   Psalm 118.25.

Chapter 38

L. Geysels, in *Schrift* 66, Heilig Landstichting 1979.

p. 107   Isaiah 56.7 and Jeremiah 7.11.

p. 108   Hosea 9.16; Jeremiah 8.13 and Micah 7.1-6.

p. 108   Joel 2.22.

p. 108   Isaiah 56.7.

p. 109   Jeremiah 7.5 and Hosea 9.15.

Chapter 39

p. 111   Deuteronomy 18.20.

p. 111   Mark 1.5.

p. 111   Mark 6.20.

p. 111   Mark 4.11.

p. 112   Isaiah 5.1-7.

p. 113   Psalm 118.22, 23.

p. 113   Pascal.

Chapter 40

E. Drewermann, *Tiefenpsychologie und Exegese* II, Olten 1985.

E. L. Smelik, *Achterstallige postille*, Nijkerk 1972.

Chapter 41

T. J. M. Naastepad, in *Werkschrift mei 1992*, Amsterdam 1992.

p. 116   Deuteronomy 25.6.

p. 117   With the exception of Daniel 12.2 and Isaiah 26.19.

p. 118   H. M. Kuitert.

Chapter 42

p. 119   Deuteronomy 6.5 and Leviticus 19.18.

p. 120   Hosea 6.6.

Chapter 44

H. Berkhof, *Gegronde verwachting*, Nijkerk 1967.

J. Lambrecht, in G. van Oyen (ed.), *De tijd is rijp*, Leuven 1996.

J. Tigcheler, in *Speling* 36 no.3, Nijmegen 1984.

p. 125   Zechariah 14.4.

p. 125   Flavius Josephus.

p. 125   Deuteronomy 34. See *The Story Goes* I, 289.

p. 126   Daniel 9.27; 11.31; 12.11.

p. 127   Huub Oosterhuis.

p. 127   Daniel 7.13, 14.

Chapter 45

K. H. Miskotte, *De vreemde vrijspraak*, Amsterdam 1938.

U. Ranke-Heinemann, *Nee en amen*, Baarn 1993.

p. 130   Psalm 23.

p. 131   Psalm 41.10; II Samuel 20.9f.; Zechariah 11.12f.; II Samuel 17.23.

Chapter 46

E. Drewermann, *Leben das dem Tod entwächst*, Düsseldorf 1991.

p. 133   Psalm 41.10.

p. 133   II Samuel 15-17.

p. 133   Isaiah 53.1-7.

Chapter 47

F. Lefevre, in *Collationes* 11 no.1, Bruges 1981.

E. L. Smelik, *Ongevraagde postille*, The Hague 1954.

J. Tigcheler, in *Speling* 36 no.1/38 no.4, Nijmegen 1984/1986.

p. 135   Psalm 113.

p. 135   Psalm 118.

p. 136   Zechariah 13.7.

p. 136   Hosea 6.1, 2.

p. 137   Mark 13.33-37.

Chapter 48

L. Geysels, in *Schrift* 66, Heilig Landstichting 1979.

F. Lefevre, in *Collationes* 11 no.1, Bruges 1981.

p. 139   II Samuel 20.9.

p. 139   Mark 13.13.

Chapter 49

W. Barnard, *Lieve gemeente*, Amsterdam 1961.

L. Geysels, in *Schrift* 66, Heilig Landstichting 1979.

F. Lefevre, in *Collationes* 11 no.1, Bruges 1981.

p. 142   Psalm 38.12.

p. 142   Psalm 38.14-16 (abbreviated).

Chapter 50

p. 147 *Herzliebster Jesu,* by J. Heermann, *English Hymnal* 70.

p. 148 Isaiah 53.7.

Chapter 51

F. Lefevre, in *Collationes* 11 no.1, Bruges 1981.

p. 151 Psalm 22.17-19.

p. 151 Isaiah 53.12 in the Septuagint version.

p. 151 Psalm 22.8.

Chapter 52

L. Geysels, in *De Heraut* 110 no.10, Nijmegen 1979.

B. Hemelsoet, in *Om het levende woord serie,* nos 2 and 3, Amsterdam 1968.

p. 152 Amos 8.9.

p. 152 Psalm 22.2.

p. 152 Psalm 22.3.

p. 153 Psalm 23.4.

p. 153 Psalm 69; 21.22.

Chapter 53

B. Hemelsoet, in *Om het levende woord serie,* nos 2 and 3, Amsterdam 1968.

p. 155 Acts 5.39 indicates that the Pharisees, who made up part of the Sanhedrin, probably did not vote for Jesus' death.

p. 157 The abrupt conclusion has caused puzzlement for centuries. Unknown authors have added a 'more satisfactory' ending here in various versions. This is not by Mark and so we shall not be considering it in this book.

Chapter 54

T. C. de Kruiff, in *Schrift* 108, Heilig Landstichting 1986.

p. 163 Genesis 22.8.

p. 163 II Samuel 7.12-16.

p. 163 Genesis 2.4; 5.1.

p. 165 Matthew 13.51.

p. 165 Genesis 38 (*The Story Goes* I, 149).

Chapter 55

p. 168 It is also possible that the evangelist is playing with the numerical value of the letters in the word DaViD (in Hebrew script, the words were written only with consonants). The D is the fourth letter of the alphabet, the V the fifth: $4 + 6 + 4 = 14$.

p. 168   See also *The Story Goes*, I, 68.

Chapter 56

K. A. Deurloo and K. Bouhuys, *Dichterbij de profeten*, Amsterdam 1968.
J. de Kwaadsteniet, in *Schrift* 108, Heilig Landstichting 1986.

p. 169   Psalm 2.7.
p. 171   Isaiah 7.14.

Chapter 57

p. 173   Numbers 24.17.
p. 174   Isaiah 60.1-6.
p. 174   'Hail to the Lord's Anointed' (J. Montgomery), *English Hymnal* 45, v.4.
p. 175   Micah 5.1.
p. 176   Psalm 141.2.
p. 176   Negro spiritual.

Chapter 58

E. L. Smelik, *Ongevraagde postille*, The Hague 1954.

p. 177   Hosea 11.1 and Exodus 4.22.
p. 178   Jeremiah 31.15.
p. 179   Judges 13.5.

Chapter 59

p. 182   Isaiah 42.1.

Chapter 60

W. J. Berger, in H. M. M. Fortmann, *Als ziende de Onzienlijke* 3a, Hilversum 1965.
B. P. M. Hemelsoet, in *Amsterdamse Cahiers* 9, Kampen 1988.
A. Uleyn, *Psycho-analytisch lezen in de bijbel*, Hilversum 1985.

p. 184   Deuteronomy 8.3.
p. 184   Psalm 91.11-12.
p. 184   Deuteronomy 6.16.
p. 185   Deuteronomy 6.13.

p. 185   Exodus 34.27.

p. 185   I Kings 19.8.

Chapter 61

p. 186   Matthew 4.23 and 9.35.

p. 188   Verses 11 and 12 can be read as a more specific form of the last Beatitude, added later.

Chapter 62

J. B. Lotz, *De acht zaligsprekingen*, Boxtel 1977.

K. H. Miskotte et al., *Een nieuw volk*, Amsterdam 1941.

p. 189   Martin Buber.

p. 190   Psalm 37.7-11 (abbreviated).

p. 191   Psalm 24.3, 4.

p. 191   Romans 8.14.

Chapter 64

E. Drewermann, *Der offene Himmel*, Düsseldorf 1990.

J. van der Wiel, in *In de waagschaal*, 1968.

p. 196   Exodus 21.24. According to the rabbinic interpretation, the thought here is not literally of 'an eye for an eye' but of financial compensation.

p. 196   Leviticus 19.18.

p. 196   Isaiah 50.6.

Chapter 65

H. Fortmann, *Hoogtijd*, Bilthoven 1966.

Chapter 66

W. R. van der Zee, *Gebed met open ogen*, The Hague 1982.

p. 202   Quoted by E. Drewermann, *Das Matthäusevangelium* I, Olten 1992, 453.

Chapter 67

J. van Goudoever, in *Phoenix Bijbel Pocket* no.21, Hilversum 1966.

p. 206   Proverbs 28.22; 22.9.

p. 207   I Corinthians 7.30, 31.

Chapter 68

p. 209   Matthew 10.11-15.

p. 209   Jeremiah 29.12-14.

p. 209   Isaiah 49.14, 15.

p. 210   Guido Gezelle.

Chapter 69

J. Tigcheler, *De bergrede*, Kampen 1983.

p. 211   Deuteronomy 30.19.

p. 212   Exodus 14.7.

p. 213   In 7.27 after the Sermon on the Mount, in 11.1 after the mission discourse, in 13.13 after the parables discourse, in 19.1 after the community discourse and in 26.1 after the discourse on the last things.

p. 213   Psalm 1.1, 2.

Chapter 71

p. 217   Isaiah 11.6.

Chapter 72

p. 219   Matthew 3.7-12.

p. 219   Isaiah 35.5; 61.1.

Chapter 73

E. Drewermann, *Wat ons toekomt*, Zoetermeer 1993.

Chapter 74

p. 225   Daniel 4.10-21.

p. 225   Genesis 18.6.

Chapter 75

p. 228   Matthew 18.18.

Chapter 77

L. Geysels, in *De Heraut, February 1989*, Nijmegen 1989.

p. 233   Genesis 4.24.

p. 233   Exodus 21.2.

Chapter 78

J. W. Falkenburg, in *In de waagschaal*, 1967.

E. Flesseman-van Leer, in *Schrift* 68, Heilig Landstichting 1980.

E. Drewermann, *Wenn der Himmel die Erde berührt*, Düsseldorf 1992.

p. 236   Leviticus 19.13.

p. 236   Matthew 22.12.

p. 236   Matthew 26.50.

Chapter 79

E. W. Korff, *Eeuwigheid en tijd, tweede bundel*, Amsterdam nd.

W. Weren, in *Getuigenis*, 25 no.6, Hilversum 1981.

Chapter 80

p. 240   Luke 14.15-24.

p. 241   Isaiah 61.10.

Chapter 81

p. 243   Rabbi Johanan quoted by P. Lapide, *The Sermon on the Mount*, Maryknoll 1986.

Chapter 82

J. Tigcheler, in *Speling jaargang* 39, no.3, Nijmegen 1987.

p. 246   Matthew 5.35, 37.

p. 248   Genesis 4.8.

p. 248   Zechariah the son of Berechiah occurs in the book of Zechariah (1.1). He is identified by Matthew with the prophet Zechariah, the son of Jehoiada, in II Chronicles 24.20. In the Hebrew canon that is the last book of the Bible.

p. 248   Psalm 118.26 and Matthew 21.9.

Chapter 83

G. Boogaard, *Wonen in het Woord*, The Hague 1977.

p. 249   Mark 13.1-32.

p. 250   Matthew 6.33.

p. 251   The story comes from Søren Kierkegaard.

Chapter 84

p. 253   Exodus 11.4; 12.29.

p. 253   J. C. Blumhardt (1805-1880), pastor in Möttlingen and Bad Boll.

pp. 253f.   Poem by J. W. Schulte Nordholt, translation by Henrietta ten Harmsel, *So Much Sky*, Grand Rapids 1994

Chapter 86

E. Schillebeeckx, *God among Us. The Gospel Proclaimed*, London and New York 1983.

J. Tigcheler, in *Speling*, 34, no.4, Nijmegen 1982.

Chapter 87

p. 259   Exodus 21.32.

p. 259   Zechariah 11.12.

p. 259   Psalm 51.19.

p. 260   Ezekiel 53.11.

Chapter 88

p. 262   Probably these are the words of the last, non-Jewish, redactor of this Gospel.

Chapter 91

p. 272   M. Nijhoff.